SATAN, PRINCE OF THIS WORLD

By William Guy Carr, R.D.

Commander R.C.N. (R)

TABLE OF CONTENTS

PREFACE

When the author of this book, Commander W.J.G. Carr died on October 2, 1959, he left this book in manuscript form along with many scribbled notes, reference books, half formulated thoughts, etc. His last wish was that the book be finished and published in order that all men might know of the plot which exists to wipe out every trace of decency in the world and all civilizations as we know them now.

Such a task is manifestly beyond ordinary means. I, his oldest son, have been asked to try and edit, revise and correct the manuscript as best possible before publication. This I have done to the best of my limited ability. I have not added anything to the original draft or changed anything except where requested to do so in marginal notes in my father's own handwriting.

I found the work frustrating because it was far beyond the scope of my ability. At the same time, I found it extremely interesting and rewarding as I tried to sort out the thoughts and ideas of a man who died almost seven years ago.

At some points in the manuscript I found notes such as: "Check the accuracy of such and such a point" or "dig out more information on such and such a person". On each occasion, I deleted the point queried completely, for it was always my father's strong belief that nothing should ever be written until completely proved out in the light of existing knowledge. Since I do not have the necessary sense of values to decide what information should or should not be used in such cases, I felt safest by leaving the information out completely.

The fact that there are only thirteen chapters in this book will annoy some people and frustrate others: I think all who read it will be left in a state of restlessness. "The Unfinished Symphony" has never been completed and this book will not be completed either, except as each reader finishes it for himself in the future by personal experience as the story unfolds.

Many of you will scoff at the statements made in this book; many will toss it aside as the ravings of a madman; some will be unable to finish the book because it will arouse anxieties and fears that cannot be faced. But many others, and I hope that they will be in the majority, will find in this work the answers to some of the most perplexing of the problems that have faced men since the beginning of time and provide material for pondering possible solutions to the future.

It is up to this latter group principally, but to all men of goodwill generally, regardless of color, race or creed, that this work is respectfully dedicated in my father's name. With the dedication goes my earnest hope and prayer that each one of you will strive, each in his own way, to avert the catastrophe that is surely to come upon us if the Devil's plots are not thwarted soon.

For those of you who do read further, please try to remember that this is an uncompleted work and that if there appears to be a gap or lack of continuity at some points, it is only because this book was published from little better than a rough draft of what undoubtedly would have been a polished literary effort had Cmdr. Carr lived a few more months to finish it himself.

Please accept my apologies for my obvious lack in preparing this work completely and I hope that in spite of its shortcomings, it will be a rich source of material for your future thought. Even more, that it will be the inspiration for future good work to continue the author's efforts to: "Tell the truth and shame the Devil". If we all work together, perhaps with the help of our Creator, we shall be able to make the world just a little more like God intended that it should be.

Sincerely and fraternally yours,

W.J. Carr, Jr.

Lima, Peru

June 2, 1966

Foreword

BEING fully aware of my limitations, I am frank to admit that since I published Pawns in the Game (1955) and Red Fog Over America (1957), and because I did publish these books, I have learned a great deal more about the World Revolutionary Movement (W.R.M.) and its relationship to the existence of the continuing Luciferian conspiracy directed against God and man by those who comprise the Synagogue of Satan (S.O.S.) on this earth than I knew before I published them.

A wealth of additional information has come in from a great variety of people of all classes, colors, and creeds. They have supplied the additional evidence I include in this volume. I admit I was ignorant of most of the facts I now present to my readers when I published the other two books.

I am not in the least ashamed of the fact that my knowledge regarding the struggle being directed by Lucifer to cause human beings to defect from God, so he can enslave them for all eternity, physically, mentally and spiritually, was as limited as it was in 1955. It should teach others a great lesson. I had honestly and sincerely worked and studied since 1911, trying to find the answer to the question: "Why can't the Human Race live together in peace, and thus enjoy the bounties and blessings that God, The Creator, has provided in such abundance for our use and pleasure?" The last two books of my nine already published, prove that after forty-four years I still had a great deal to learn.

I feel I would be remiss in my duty to God and my fellow man if I did not make this additional information public. I know the enemies of God will ridicule me and point out statements published in the other two. I publish what I believe to be the truth-I never claimed inviolability. To err is human, to forgive, divine.

In fairness to myself, I wish to state that the ONLY real mistake I made was that I had been unable to tie in the supernatural relationship of the Luciferian revolt in Heaven with the World Revolutionary Movement as it is being conducted today. I blamed the international bankers; selfish international Capitalism, Nazism, and Communism as the root-causes of our evils. I knew, deep down in my heart, that wars and revolutions were planned years and years ahead, and designed to ultimately bring about the destruction of ALL existing forms of government and religion in order that a totalitarian dictatorship might

v

be imposed on what is left of the world's population after the last social cataclysm has ended; but I didn't know for certain, as I feel sure I know now, that the W.R.M. is an exact replica of the struggle Lucifer and his followers put up for control of the Universe in that part of the celestial world we know as heaven.

I called my last book Red Fog Over America because I was fully aware of the fog of propaganda put out by the Forces of Evil for the purpose of preventing the vast majority of people from finding the TRUTH. I thought I had penetrated that fog. I was mistaken! The additional evidence and information I submit to my readers in Satan, Prince of This World proves that I had groped my way only to the outer fringe of the fog of lies and deceits which are the stock-in-trade of those who comprise the Synagogue of Satan and put the Devil's (Luciferian) conspiracy into effect upon this earth.

I wish to make it clearly and emphatically known that I do not believe the Synagogue of Satan (S.O.S.) is Jewish, but, as Christ told us for a definite purpose, it is comprised of "Them who say they are Jews ... and are not ... and do lie" (Rev. 2:9 and 3:9). I hope I prove in this book that the Protocols, which contain the details of the diabolical plot Weishaupt revised and modernized between 1770 and 1776 are not those of the Learned Elders of Zion, but those of the Synagogue of Satan based on the Luciferian ideology designed to bring about a One World Government, the powers of which will be usurped by the High Priests of the Luciferian Creed who have always secretly controlled the Synagogue of Satan at the top.

This book is written for the information of the masses. In my limited way I am trying to put the mandate Christ gave us into effect. I do not intend to clutter up the pages of this book with hundreds of footnotes giving title, chapter, and verse of so-called Authorities. I find that far too many authors quote as authorities those who secretly serve the Luciferian cause. I shall ask my readers to accept what I publish as being what I believe to be the truth.

As proof of my sincerity, I mention that I have previously had published nine books and hundreds of articles of nonfiction so far, without being proven to be in serious error. I have fully and completely renounced all mercenary considerations. While studying, conducting investigations and writing my books I have never accepted financial aid, neither have I any desire to benefit financially as the result of my work. I have used the income received from my labors and writings first to provide for my family, and then to continue further study and research. When my family was able to go on their own, I turned my work and records over to the Federation of Christian Laymen to be used entirely for educational purposes.

My wife and I live on the pensions I receive for physical disabilities received during service in World Wars One and Two.

I fully realize that the Devil's agents have it unpopular to believe in the Bible; I know it isn't "The Thing" to believe in Hell or a Devil; I know I shall be ridiculed because of what I write ... BUT I KNOW THAT WHAT I WRITE IS THE TRUTH.

Nobody is going to enjoy reading the contents of this book, but those who do read will be able to see things in their true perspective; they will be able to understand what is happening in the world today and why.

What I am about to say will sound strange coming from a man with a war record such as mine, but because wars and revolutions forced upon the masses (Goyim) are the means by which the Synagogue of Satan intend to make those they plot to subjugate destroy their own forms of governments and religion so they can be enslaved under a Luciferian dictatorship, obviously the only way to prevent them carrying out this diabolical plan through to its logical conclusion is to refuse to become involved in any more wars and revolutions under any circumstances. This would require individuals to practice passive resistance to authorities who would force them into war.

I once held all conscientious objectors in contempt. I considered them cowards, traitors to their country, people who failed to appreciate the benefits citizenship gave them. But I realize now, after studying the Luciferian conspiracy from all angles what God really meant when He gave us the command "thou shalt not kill." He didn't qualify this command by saying killing on a mass scale, i.e., wars and revolutions can be justified.

Weishaupt's revised version of the Age Old Conspiracy says that wars and revolutions shall be forced on the Goyim, so that those who direct the conspiracy to usurp world domination shall "proceed towards their goal in peace." They make us fight while they sit back and cheer us on from the sidelines. Then again Weishaupt said that those who direct the conspiracy shall arrange, makers, so that not even the nations who are victorious in a war shall benefit or annex additional territory. Can any informed person deny that this policy has not been followed to the letter in World Wars One and Two? But on the other hand, Communism has been built up in size and strength until it is equal in power to the rest of the world.

It is true that in the revolutions fomented to put Communism where it stands today the masses (Goyim) were made to fight each other, but those to usurp power, like Lenin, never got involved in actual fighting except by accident. It is another strange fact that if top level agenteurs of the Synagogue of Satan got caught while engaged in subversion and/or fomenting revolutions they were never shot but invariably imprisoned only to be subsequently released so they could continue their subversive activities as I have proved in my previous books.

I now believe God intended man to protect his own life against an aggressor; to protect his wife and family and his home, but I believe extending this principle or natural law to national and international levels was undoubtedly part and parcel of the Luciferian conspiracy. Soldiers and police were in the first instance supposed to preserve law and order and protect the weak from criminal elements who refused to accept the moral code and natural laws as adopted by civilized society. This is the reason ONLY the king and/or ruler was supposed to exercise force to maintain law and order. If he abused his rights the people could set things to right as was done by the Magna Carta, but under God's law it was never intended they should destroy dynastic rule. The Protocols boast that by leading the Goyim into making this mistake they caused them to abandon their only protection against those who claim to deliver them from their old oppressions in order to lead them into the new subjection of a totalitarian dictatorship.

I realize that the Illuminati will work to shoot those statements full of holes, but the fact remains that I can no longer find authority in the Scriptures, or by reasoning, to justifying allowing ourselves to be divided into opposing camps, then armed, and made to fight and kill each other in order to solve political, social, economic, or other problems which are no nearer solution now than they ever were. It just doesn't make sense that Christians can be divided into opposing camps and made to kill each other off by the tens of millions without having the slightest personal animosity for one another.

To return the passive resistance! Ghandi was doing a great job using this principle, so he was assassinated.

What do we have in his place? A man who says he is neutral, but in reality helps the Synagogue of Satan maintain a "balance of power so that when the Goyim are thrown at each other's throats again" in World War Three, the sides will be more or less equal and therefore able to fight a more prolonged and destructive war. It would seem to me that we could become heroes defending a principle, such as passive resistance, even if doing so caused us to suffer death at the hands of those who serve the Synagogue of Satan. It seems to me that it would be better to die expressing our Faith in God than in physical combat with others who are our spiritual brothers, and people who should be our friends. In support of the above statements of opinion I quote: 2 Kings 7:4; Ps. 44:22; Matt. 10:28; Luke 12:4; Rom. 8:36; Jas. 5:6.

Chapter 1

THE DEVIL, THE WORLD AND THE FLESH

Because lies and deceits are the stock-in-trade of those who direct the World Revolutionary Movement (W.R.M.) AT THE TOP, never, since history began to be recorded, has a grant been made by governments, educational institutions, so-called charitable foundations or other sources of wealth and power to enable historians to compile an accurate, documented history of the World Revolutionary Movement (W.R.M.).

Unable to finance the help necessary to do a thoroughly satisfactory job (which would require at least ten more years of study and research) necessary to prove to the hilt the knowledge I have acquired trying to find the answer to the question, "Why is it that the Human Race cannot live in peace, and thus enjoy the blessings and bounties God has provided for our use and pleasure in such abundance?" I offer what evidence I have been able to obtain to prove that what we term W.R.M. is nothing more or less than the continuing Luciferian revolt against the RIGHT of God to exercise Supreme Authority over the Entire Universe.

Many historians, including such outstanding students as Mrs. Nesta Webster; Count De Poncin; Copin-Albancelli; (Copon P.O. Copin C.J.) Dom Paul Benoit; Ed. Em. Eckert; Arthur Preuss; Domenico Margoitta; Witchl; His Eminence the Most Rev. Cardinal Caro Rodriguez; Don Bell, of Palm Beach, Florida, and many others seem to have been unable to connect the wars, revolutions and general chaos prevailing in this world today, with the fact that the Holy Scriptures, the inspired Word of God, tell us clearly and plainly that when God decided to inhabit this earth of ours with human beings, Satan arrived in the Garden of Eden to cause our first parents to defect from God. He accomplished his purpose, despite the fact that God had walked with them and talked with them in the early paradise we call Eden, explaining to them His plan for the rule of the entire universe, and telling them how He wished them to live for a period of time on this earth to prove they honestly loved Him and earnestly desired to serve Him voluntarily for ALL eternity out of respect for His infinite perfections.

Study of the history of comparative religions proves that even the most primitive nomads and Sephardic tribes not only believed that other worlds existed before the "Supreme Being" created this world, but proves positively that what some of us call the "uncivilized" tribes (who existed by hunting, fishing, and gathering wild fruits of the earth, before human beings began to cultivate the soil and breed animals so they could be used for productive purposes), believed that at some time, in some place, before God decided to create this earth, there had been a revolution originated because one of the creatures God created challenged His right to exercise Supreme authority over the entire Universe.

Because this aspect of the origin of the W.R.M. would fill many bulky volumes, it is sufficient for our purpose to state that this basic principle of "religious" belief was shared by the aborigines. W Schmidt, author of Der Ursprung des Gottesides, has had seven volumes published. (Munster i.W 1912-1940). Volume VIII was in the press at the time this book was being written, i.e., 1958, and volumes IX to XIII are still in manuscript form. He is considered to be the greatest authority on this subject, and Fr. Schmidt distinguishes the primitive people of this world as the "Urkulturen," e.g., those who lived by gathering food, and hunting fowl, fish, and game   from the "Primarkulturen," who developed from the former into producers by becoming tillers of the soil and breeders of animals. The people we call aboriginals today are the remnants of human society which never developed beyond the Urkulturen stage.

Fr. Schmidt does not intend that the word "Urkulturen" means the civilizations with which he deals are identical with the original civilization of the human race. He uses it to mean the most ancient type of civilization our means of investigation and research can reach.

Fr. Schmidt divides what remains of the "Urkulturen," i.e., primitive civilizations, into three groups; (1) The Southern, comprising several tribes, (Aboriginals) in southeastern Australia, (2) The Central, comprising the pygmies and pygmoids in Africa and southeastern Asia, including Ceylon, the Andaman Islands and the Philippines, and (3) The Northern, or Arctic-Americans, whose representatives are also found in northern Asia and disseminated among the Esqumaux and American Indians.

All of these so-called uncivilized human beings share the fundamental belief that (1) Before this world was created other worlds existed, (2) at some time, before the Supreme Being created this world, a revolution had occurred in the celestial world (Universe), caused by the fact that some of the Creator's creatures had challenged His right to exercise Supreme authority over the entire universe, (3) that, as a result of this revolt against the absolute supremacy of the Creator (God), the Universe was divided into "Good" and "Evil" parts, (4) that the Evil Spirits tried to interfere with God's work while He was actually engaged in creating this world, (5) that ever since this world was finished these evil forces have been at work trying to prevent human beings from doing the Will of God, (6) that it was the representative of the leader of the heavenly revolt who brought death, sickness and ALL other EVILS to the Human Race because he deceived our first parents into defecting from God.[1]

Each group of descendants of the Urkulturen, who have survived without contact, until very recently, with so-called civilization, has its own particular belief regarding HOW the leader of the evil spirits, whom we term "The Devil," tried to interfere with God while in the act of creating this earth. Each group has had its own particular way of informing its children HOW and WHY the devil brought death, sickness, wars, and other tribulations to the human race. But all agree that the Devil was, and still is, the "ADVERSARY" of God, the Supreme Being who created the heavens and the earth.

According to the Algonquins of the north-central part of California, the Devil comes on the scene when the Supreme Being has almost finished the work of creation. He tries to appropriate something of the work for himself. According to Algonquin mythology the Devil often appears in human form, and because he brought death to this world God turned him into an animal which they named the Coyote.

In "News Behind the News" I published evidence which strongly indicates that Satan cursed our first parents to defect from God, causing Eve to indulge in "perversions" of sex, on the promise that if she accepted his advances and followed his advice, he would teach her the secrets of procreation, thus making her and Adam the equal of God in power. I pointed out that the Luciferian Creed teaches that Satan initiated her into the pleasures of sexual intercourse. We used the word "perversions" in the sense that what the Devil taught Eve in regard to sex and sexual behavior were practices contrary to sexual relationship as God intended should exist between a man and his wife.

While reading the book *Satan*, we found that other people, accepted as authorities, quoted evidence and opinions which support the belief that perver-

---

1 The author is indebted to Mr. Richard M. Passil, Poughkeepsie, NY, who sent him a copy of the book *Satan*, published by Sheed and Ward. Readers wishing to go more deeply into this aspect of the W.R.M. would do well to read this book.

-sions of sex did enter into bringing about "the fall of man and subjecting him to death."

Certain ministers and priests wrote me to say that the assumption that Satan had physical intercourse with Eve is utter nonsense because Satan is a pure spirit and therefore incapable of indulging in sexual intercourse with a human being. As to these arguments I agree with the old woman who said, "Everyone to his own liking" as she kissed the cow.

In the book *Satan*, while discussing the "Adversary of God in Primitive Religions," Joseph Henninger, S.V.D. says that the Wintum tribe of California refer to God, the Creator, as "Olelbis" and to the Devil as "Sedit." According to the mythology of the Wintum tribe, Olelbis desired that the members of the human race should live together as brothers and sisters; that there should be no birth and no death, that life should be agreeable and easy, and the purpose of life should be to rejoining Olelbis in heaven and live with him for all eternity. To satisfy the hunger of the human body, Olelbis created a species of nut which has no shell and falls off the tree when it is ripe (this species of nut or fruit is still a staple item of the Wintum's diet). Olelbis ordered two brothers to build a paved road from earth to heaven to facilitate the tribe's reunion with their Creator. But Sedit appeared on the scene and persuaded one of the brothers that it would be better to engage in sexual intercourse and procreate the human species. The one persuaded by Sedit argued the other into agreement, so both defected from Olelbis and joined together to destroy the road they were building to heaven.

Sedit, horrified when he finds he has brought death to the human race and must die himself, tries to escape his fate. He makes himself a mechanism of boughs and leaves (a plane), by means of which he hopes to fly to heaven. But he crashes and is killed. Olelbis looks down from the heights of heaven and says, "See. The first death! From henceforth (all) men shall die."

According to the mythology of the Yakuts who live in the northeastern extremity of Siberia, in the beginning the earth was entirely covered with water. Ai-tojon (The Supreme Being) saw a bubble from which issued a voice. Ai-tojon asked the Voice, "Who are you? Where do you come from?"

The Voice replied, "I am the devil. I live on the earth that is under the waters." Ai-tojon says: "If that is true, bring me a bit of it."

The devil dived and brought up some earth. Ai-tojon took it, blessed it and then laid down on it, and rested on the waters. The devil tried to drown him, but the more he pulled and tugged to overturn the raft God had made of earth, the larger it grew, until to his amazement and discomfort, it covered most of the waters and became this world on which the human race lives today. The mythology of the Tartars of the Altai is very similar to that of the Yakuts, except that their legend says that after Erlik (the Wicked One) had brought up the first earth from the depths and the Creator fashions it into dry land, the Creator orders him to dive a second time and bring up more earth. Erlik determined to do what the Creator did, and brought up two lots of earth, one of which he concealed in his mouth. But it swelled in size until he had to spit it out in order to prevent his choking. The earth he spat out God formed into the mountains and marshes and the waste lands. Then the Creator told Erlik, "You are now in a state of sin. You wanted to do me an ill turn. All men who also harbor evil thoughts shall be your people; but the good men shall be my people."

We hope to prove our point that the division between "Good" and "Evil" started before this world began and was transferred here by the Devil we Christians call Satan.

When Lucifer, working through one of his Princes of Darkness, whom we have named Satan, caused our first parents, Adam and Eve, to defect from God, they and their progeny automatically belonged to Lucifer and remained children of the flesh until they, of their own will and accord, prove they desire to reestablish their friendship with God by being born again spiritually. The manner in which the Luciferian conspiracy, which challenged God's RIGHT to exercise supreme authority over the entire universe, was transferred to this earth in order that the King of Hell might add it, and its human beings, to his domain, will be dealt with in detail further on.

At this point it is necessary to produce evidence to explain what really did happen in that part of the celestial world we call heaven at the time of the Luciferian revolution. This is necessary because the Forces of Evil, which have directed the continuing Luciferian conspiracy SINCE it was transferred to this earth, have caused the TRUTH to be hidden, and made the TRUTH so difficult to obtain, that the average man-in-the-street can't be blamed for knowing little, if anything, about the truth, even though his eternal salvation may depend on knowing these TRUTHS.

The greatest stumbling block the average person has to overcome before he, or she, can understand and believe in the continuing existence of the Luciferian

5

conspiracy is to erase from his mind the false conception of devils, because he has been taught to believe that Devils are hideous creatures, with ugly faces, horned heads, cloven hooves, and forked tails, etc. St. John of the Cross says: "The Devil is the strongest and the wiliest of our enemies and the most difficult to unmask." St. John says: "The Devil is skillful enough to turn the world and the flesh to his own account (the possession of the souls of men) as his top most faithful acolytes." This saint says that the Devil caused the ruin of a great multitude of religions which set out on the life of perfection.[2]

The reason most human beings mentally picture the Devil as a hideous, deformed, abominable creature is because artists have caricatured him as such in order to bring us their conception of ALL that is evil and horrible. In doing this they did the human race (probably at the instigation of the Devil himself), a great disservice.

Theologians of the early Christian church, and those of the Catholic and Protestant Churches in more modern times, agree that the Devil is a very different type of creature from what most people believe. This misconception of what the Devil really is, must have resulted from the Devil's own cunning and guile, and from his ability to make human beings do his will.

According to the Holy Scriptures, the creature who challenged the RIGHT of God the Creator to exercise supreme authority over the entire Universe was Lucifer. Lucifer was so named because he was and still is the brightest and most intelligent of all God's creatures. His name is "Prince of the Dawn," "Holder of the Light." He is a pure spirit. As such he is ageless and indestructible. He has abilities and capabilities beyond the understanding of the human brain. He uses these for selfish and evil purposes.

The Holy Scriptures tell us that because of "pride," i.e., his inflated ego and false belief in his own perfections, he led the revolt against the supremacy of God, and because of his power and great influence, he caused ONE THIRD of the brightest and most intelligent of the heavenly host to join him in rebellion. If telling the truth shames and confounds the Devil (Lucifer), it is my own opinion, as confirmed by St. John of the Cross, that, due to the Devil's wiles, none of the numerous Christian denominations teach their congregations suffi-

2 On page 2 of *Pawns in the Game* we stated that most, if not all religions, started out on a more or less uniformly high level, in which the worship and love of God ... formed the basic principle. "I have been severely taken to task because of this statement, but from what St. John of the Cross has to say, it would seem that I am in good company".

-cient of the TRUTH regarding devils and fallen angels, of which there are in existence multitudes who wander through the Universe, including this planet, seeking the ruin of souls.

Humanity has been brainwashed into accepting mental restrictions in this matter until today, even the vast majority of those who profess to be Christians believe only in some sort of mythical supernatural evil spirit whom we call Satan, and a personal good spirit we call our guardian angels. Millions outside the Christian religion refuse to believe there is a celestial world, and devils, and angels. Many modernists claim that belief in the supernatural is a sure symptom of insanity.

But if we are to understand the W.R.M. we must know, and believe that even the very lowest choir of angels consists of multitudes of pure spirits, each possessing more perfections than the next in that substantial way. To complete this first hierarchy we must mount through the numerous multitudes of the Archangels, and then go on to the even greater multitudes of the Principalities. There is still the second hierarchy consisting of the Powers, Virtues, and Dominations; and the third hierarchy consisting of the Thrones, the Cherubim, and the Seraphim. Of this whole galaxy of heavenly beings created by God, Lucifer is the greatest. He stood at the very peak of God's created perfection.

There are many things God has not as yet permitted the human mind to understand. We are on this earth on trial. We have been given an intellect and free will to decide for ourselves whether we wish to love and voluntarily serve God for all eternity or literally go to the Devil. If we knew all that has happened since Lucifer led the revolt against the supremacy of God there would be no test. By Faith, the teachings of the Scriptures, the Prophets, and Christ, we must believe and accept TRUTH which is beyond the comprehension of our human minds to understand. We must exercise HUMILITY instead of PRIDE. Those who remain humble, and believe, will see God. Those who become proud, and inflate their egos, until they lose all sense of their own littleness and limitations will go to the devil.

It would be impossible for the average human being to even begin to surmise why Lucifer "Fell from Grace," and WHY he defected from God, and influenced so many of the heavenly host to join him in rebellion if it were not for the fact that the Scriptures teach us that God, when He created both angels and human beings, gave them the sovereign will to do as they pleased.

It would seem logical to suppose that if God had NOT given His creatures an absolutely FREE WILL He wouldn't have obtained much satisfaction from His creation. God's pleasure, it would seem, is derived from the love of His creatures who remain loyal, faithful, and true, voluntarily, out of respect for His infinite perfections.

Thus we see the truth in the old saying, "The greater the pride, the greater the fall." Lucifer's pride caused him to fall from his pinnacle of greatness. He was second only to the actual God head. His defection caused him to become ruler of that part of the universe we term Hell. The fall of Lucifer proves that all angels and all   human beings can become evil if they so choose. The foregoing is intended to enable the average person to understand, and believe, that since the heavenly revolution was ended by St. Michael, the Archangel, the Universe has been dominated by two supernatural POWERS. God rules over those of His creatures that remain loyal to Him, while Lucifer is King of the regions of darkness, and rules the multitudes who voluntarily defect from God and join him in rebellion.

The next big stumbling block which prevents the average person accepting the TRUTH that the Luciferian conspiracy was transferred to earth in the Garden of Eden, and has continued here ever since, is the fact that the Scriptures don't explain clearly on what grounds Lucifer challenged the RIGHT of God to exercise supreme authority over the entire Universe. None of the great theologians has ventured to declare a definite opinion on this matter.

Knowing only too well the truth of the old adage, "A Fool will rush in where angels fear to tread," I still feel it my duty to express my own opinion on this all important matter, arrived at after many years of concentrated thought and study.

If God bases His plan for the rule of the universe on the premise that Lesser Beings can be taught to know Him, love Him, and to wish to serve Him voluntarily for all eternity out of love and respect for His own infinite perfections, then it seems reasonable to suppose that Lucifer challenged God's Right to exercise supreme authority over all the Universe on the grounds that His plan was weak and impractical. If this is so, then obviously Lucifer's ideology must be based on the premise that MIGHT is RIGHT, and rule must be totalitarian.

Considering that one-third of the highest and brightest of the heaven host joined him voluntarily in rebellion against God, it seems also reasonable to suppose that Lucifer founded the further totalitarian principle that beings of

8

vastly superior intelligence have the RIGHT to rule those less gifted.

In other words, God's plan is to derive pleasure and glory from the love and service voluntarily given him by His creatures who remain loyal despite the lies, deceits, and temptations to which they are subjected by Lucifer's Satanic agencies, while they are undergoing their period of trial. The Luciferian ideology is that all lesser beings must be forced to obey supreme authority by application of absolute despotism. Therefore, we would seem entitled to believe that we now are faced with the same alternatives on earth. Those who favor totalitarianism are determined to enslave those who favor freedom and voluntary service.

When I investigated the hidden, as well as the public life of Albert Pike, I learned the following facts which throw a great deal of light on my belief that we are experiencing on this earth similar conditions which accompanied the Luciferian revolution in heaven. I find plenty of passages in the Holy Scriptures to support my contention that the Luciferian conspiracy will end here on this earth, EXACTLY as St. Michael ended it in heaven. If this comes true, those souls who remain loyal and faithful to God Will join him in heaven, and those who defect from God will join Lucifer in Hell.

According to the Luciferian doctrine as expounded by Weishaupt and Pike, Lucifer, the greatest and most intelligent of the heavenly host, challenged God's "right" to exercise authority over the entire Universe on the grounds that only a totalitarian dictatorship could ensure permanent peace and prosperity by forcing ALL lesser beings to obey the edicts of the Supreme Being by use of absolute (Satanic) despotism.

Further, the Luciferian doctrine teaches adepts in the highest degrees of Grand Orient Lodges, and the Councils of Pike's New and Reformed Palladian Rite, that God had two sons. They refer to God the Creator, as Adonai, or Adonay. They identify His sons as Satan and St. Michael the Archangel. They claim that Satan accepted the Luciferian ideology because he considered it more practical than his Father's plan for the rule of the Universe. The Luciferian theologians claim that Satan is the elder brother of St. Michael. They admit that St. Michael, whom they term "the upstart," and "Le Parvenu," did cause Lucifer to be cast out of heaven. But the Luciferian doctrine also claims that by this very act Lucifer was elevated to become God of that part of the Universe we commonly designate as HELL, and that he is therefore the equal of Adonay. Students must never forget that words are only a means used to explain certain sets of circumstances or to designate some person, or place, or thing. Thus it is that hundreds of tribes, races, and nationalities use hundreds of different names to designate exactly the same God, the same Devil, person, place, or thing. For this reason we will discuss what some words in general use REALLY mean when considered in their relationship to W.R.M.

UNIVERSE. Means the totality of existing things, including the earth, the heavenly bodies, and all else throughout space. Thus we see that the Universe includes Heaven and Hell, as well as this earth.

HEAVEN. The abode of God; the supernatural beings we call angels, and the spirits of the righteous who enter heaven after death terminates their period of trial here on earth, and/or on other planets.[3]

In studying the W.R.M. we must never forget that this earth is in itself an infinitesimal part of the galaxy of planets and stars we call the solar system. It is still more important that we remember that the solar system is an infinitesimal part of the Universe. On a clear night we can see with our naked eye thousands of galaxies of solar systems far larger, and greater than our own. Each has its sun, each its planets and stars. Each sun exercises perfect control over its subordinate bodies. When we realize that far beyond reach of our eyes there are millions of other solar systems, many of which scientists declare are bigger than anything we can see, then it becomes possible to begin to realize the greatness of the Creator of all these worlds regardless of whether they be

3 It is a matter of interest to note that when Pope John XXII was a young priest, he wrote articles in which he stated his firm belief that he did not believe that the souls of ALL human beings saw God during the immediate judgment which takes place after it is released by death. These writings proved to be a bone of contention amongst the Church's theologians, and after the writer was made Pope he called together a special Council of those he considered to be the most learned Elders of the Church. They ruled against him, and he accepted their ruling because he had never made his personal beliefs the subject of a Papal Bull, or to declare such a belief was to be the dogma and part of the teaching of the Church over which he presided.

This throws a great deal of light on the general public's idea of Papal infallibility. The Pope is considered infallible only when, after consultation with all his advisors, long periods of contemplation and prayer, asking for the spiritual guidance of the Holy Ghost, he makes a definite ruling on a question of Faith or Morals. Such a pronouncement then becomes Canon Law, and must be accepted by all those who wish to remain members of the Roman Catholic Church. Such a pronouncement in recent years was belief in the fact that Mary, the mother of Jesus Christ, was taken into heaven body and soul, and now occupies the seat of the highest of the angels who defected from God at the time of the heavenly revolution. But a Catholic can still hold his own opinion regarding his soul seeing God immediately after death, or when it attains the necessary spiritual perfection to deserve the Beatific Vision.

earths similar to ours, or what we term celestial worlds.

The point we must understand and remember is that the word HEAVEN means that part of the Universe in which supernatural beings we call angels, and the spirits of these who have PROVED they wish to love, honor, obey, and serve God voluntarily, reside for all eternity. Heaven is a place of bliss, the pleasures and joys of which are beyond the capacity of the human mind to comprehend. Christ told us, "My Father's house (heaven) is a place of many mansions (worlds)." He told us also that he went from our humble abode (earth), to prepare a home for us.

The Scriptures devote a great deal of space to events connected with the Heavens. It is sufficient for our purpose therefore to say that the Scriptures and Jesus Christ are our authority for saying here that there are seven heavens, the dimensions of which are also beyond the comprehension of the human mind. That should be a comforting thought to people who think, even if they don't say, of their early associates, "If I thought Himmie Jones was going to heaven I'd quit trying to get there." These people need not worry. God's creation and His plan for the rule of the Heavens is perfect. You won't be crowded; you won't have to associate with those who are incompatible. Conditions will be happy, peaceful, joyous, and all sufficient for our heavenly natures.

HELL. Is that part of the Universe in which Lucifer and the angels who defected from God at the time of the heavenly revolution, reside, together with those who defected from God during their period of trial served on this earth, and possibly in other parts of the Universe.[4]

The Holy Scriptures tell us that Lucifer is a pure spirit. Thus he is indestructible. He must live on for all eternity. The Scriptures also tell us that there is a judgment immediately after death, and a final judgment.

---

4 The frantic efforts being made at this period of the world's history to conquer space is primarily to find out if forms of life similar to our own exist on other planets. The Satanically-inspired men who direct this probing into the hidden parts of God's Universe are attempting to do and to find out things which God didn't intend us to do or find out until revealed to us by Him. One would have to draw heavily on one's imagination to interpret the present research into atomic energy for destructive purposes, as being the work of those who believe in God as opposed to Lucifer. It appears pretty obvious that those who direct and finance atomic research out of public funds seek knowledge of outer space which they don't intend to share with the general public unless it will serve their own totalitarian plans to do so. But it is comforting to know that even the Devil will hang himself if given enough rope. It would appear to me that those who do the Devil's work on this earth are coming very close to the end of their tethers, i.e., the ropes with which they will hang themselves.

According to Revelations it is after the Final judgment that ALL the creatures God has made will be separated into two camps. Those referred to as the "Sheep," will go to Heaven, while "The Goats" will go to Hell where Lucifer will reign for all eternity.

The Scriptures inform us that Hell will be a place where the totalitarian rule of Lucifer will be one of utter chaos and confusion. We are told that everyone will hate everyone else, because all in Hell will realize that they were deceived by Lucifer and his agents into defecting from God. The flames of Hell, which burn but do not consume, consist of the knowledge that those who are damned have lost the love and benefits, the joys and companionship of God for all eternity.

LIMBO AND PURGATORY. Many who profess the Christian religion don't believe that there are any in-between places where souls may serve a further period of trial or purification after termination of the period of trial on this earth in order to prove that they deserve the Beatific Vision. They are perfectly entitled to their own opinions on this matter. My personal opinion is that the Scriptures indicate that there are other worlds on which spirits undergo further periods of trial to decide their ultimate and final fate. The fact that absolute knowledge regarding this matter has not been revealed to human beings is a blessing. If we all knew that there were intermediary stopping off places before we arrive in heaven or hell as our final destination, we might not try hard enough to earn our eternal reward while on this earth. It would seem logical to suppose that those who serve God as nearly perfectly as is humanly possible, will go to heaven when they die. It is just as logical to suppose that those who serve Lucifer to the best of their ability while on earth will join him in hell when they die. The vast majority of people don't seem to be able to realize that upon this earth there are considerably more people who serve the Luciferian Cause than there are trying to put God's plan for the rule of the Universe into effect upon this earth.

LUCIFER. This greatest of all the angels, created by God, challenged his Creator's RIGHT to exercise supreme authority over the Universe and all on and in it, yet he is mentioned only once in the Holy Scriptures. Isaiah 14:12 (King James Version). There are two other places where it seems reasonable to suppose the words used refer to Lucifer. Those are Luke 10:18 and Rev. 9:1-11.

The Holy Scriptures' lack of revelation regarding WHY Lucifer challenged the supremacy of God, and the fact that in the Holy Scriptures Lucifer is

THE DEVIL, THE WORLD AND THE FLESH

identified with Satan, makes most people believe that Lucifer and Satan are one and the same supernatural being. Study of the secret writings of men, who have at various periods of history directed the W.R.M., definitely prove that those who direct the W.R.M. AT THE TOP are Luciferians. Letters of instruction dealing with Luciferian doctrine and dogma have from time to time fallen into the hands other than intended while being circulated for instructional purposes, between those who direct AT THE TOP and their immediate subordinates. In my humble opinion, the revelations concerning the Luciferian doctrine and conspiracy are just as much "Acts of God" as are the revelations and inspirations which make the Holy Scriptures the inspired and revealed Word of God. I believe that because God (Adonay) is just and Merciful, He intended that all His creatures on this earth, whom He put here to work out their own eternal fate, should know every detail regarding both sides involved in obtaining possession of our souls for all eternity.[5]

Study of the W.R.M. indicates that it is very important to decide whether or not Lucifer and Satan are one and the same supernatural being. Search of the Holy Scriptures will not reveal a definite ruling. The most famous theologians who have lived since Christ, have shied clear of making a definite pronouncement on this particular question. But men who have directed the W.R.M. AT THE TOP are very definite in their belief that Lucifer is God, the equal of our God (whom the Luciferians refer to as Adonay). They claim that Lucifer is the "Holder of the light," "The God of Goodness," who struggles for humanity against Adonay, the God of Darkness and Evil and ALL wickedness. Albert Pike, who worked out a military blueprint of wars and revolutions which he calculated would bring the Luciferian conspiracy into its final stage upon this earth, stated definitely in his letters to fellow conspirators, that Satan, although Prince of this world, is definitely inferior and subordinate to Lucifer.[6]

5 While we recognize the truth that the Devil (Lucifer) is the "Father of Lies," as told to us by Jesus Christ; and the Synagogue of Satan (S.O.S.), who direct the Luciferian conspiracy here on this earth, are sons of the Devil, and masters in the art of deception, I still maintain, however, that a great deal of truth can be learned from the secret writings of men who were the High Priests of the Luciferian Religion in their day, because they never intended that their pronouncements on this all important subject should fall into hands other than intended. As will be proved in other chapters, many men have directed the ceremonial and dogmatic executives of the Synagogue of Satan and the Luciferian religion since Weishaupt died in 1830. They include Moses Hofbrook and Albert Pike of the United States of America; Mazzini and Lemmi of Italy, and, most recently, Alister Crowley of England.

6 Pike and his direction of the Luciferian conspiracy are dealt with fully in other chapters.

SATAN. The Scriptures use the word Satan quite often and tell us about his evil purpose and works. He is, as the word implies, the adversary of God. Satan is invariably associated with Lucifer. Most Christians accept the fact that Lucifer and Satan are one and the same supernatural being commonly referred to as the Devil. Those who have directed the Luciferian Conspiracy upon this earth have been very definite in pronouncing the doctrine that Lucifer is God, and Satan his "Prince of the World." There is Scriptural support for the belief that there are five or more other worlds over which Lucifer placed "Princes," and several others, in addition to claiming that Satan is the eldest son of God (Adonay), and the older brother of Jesus Christ, also claim that Jesus Christ is one and the same person as St. Michael the Archangel. They claim that when God decided to inhabit this earth Lucifer made Satan "Prince of this world." This claim is confirmed partially by the Scriptures, which refer to Satan as Prince of this world. John 14:30,16:11, Eph. 2:2.

The Luciferian doctrine teaches that Satan, using human agents, developed the Luciferian conspiracy so well that God (Adonay) decided to send St. Michael to earth in the form of Jesus Christ, to halt the conspiracy as he done in heaven.

Those who worship Satan as "Prince of the World," and Lucifer as God of the celestial world, claim that Christ failed in His earthly mission. They claim that when Christ refused to accept the overtures of Satan, his betrayal and death were arranged in such a manner that the Romans acted as judge and executioners for the S.O.S., while the High Priests used mob psychology to make the Jews reject Christ as the Messiah and then to assume the guilt for His crucifixion. Study of history indicates very strongly that those who have directed the Luciferian conspiracy upon this earth have made it their special business to make as many Jews as possible defect from God, reject Jesus Christ, and have used them to serve the purposes of the High Priests of the Synagogue of Satan, which Christ Himself informed us, is composed of "Them who say they are Jews, but are not, and do lie."

The Synagogue of Satan has hated the Jews from their beginning because God wished them to carry His banner here on earth. The S.O.S. warped the Jews' knowledge of God's wishes while they were in captivity in Babylon. They have since warped the Gentiles' knowledge of Christ's wishes in this regard also. It is because the Synagogue of Satan hated the Jews, and had treated them so badly in trying to obtain control of their minds while they enslaved their bodies in captivity, that Christ told us His mission here on this earth was to release both Gentiles and Jews from the bondage of Satan and his Satanic agencies.

In my opinion the agentur of the Illuminati who put out the Synagogue of Satan propaganda and lies, have deliberately hidden from general knowledge many things which would prove that it was the members of the Synagogue of Satan who caused the prophesies regarding Christ's betrayal and death to come to pass. Judas and the Jews were only instruments they used to accomplish their diabolical purpose, and then cover their own guilt by placing it on the shoulders of the Jews who, unfortunately, because of lies and deceits, have been made to wear that cloak of guilt ever since.

It must be admitted that the betrayal of Jesus by Judas was real and disastrous, particularly as it affected Christ's efforts to convert the Jews and release them from the bonds with which they have been bound by the Synagogue of Satan. But why is it that so many ordained ministers of Christ's religion preach that God intended that the Jews should bring about the death of His Son, our Lord and Savior? Why do they make the members of their congregation believe that Christ surrendered himself meekly to His fate in order that the prophesies of Scripture might be fulfilled? My study of this phase of history gives me an entirely different view of what really happened.

The Holy Scriptures tell me that Christ knew what was to happen. He went about His Father's business by day because He knew that because of His popularity with the masses the authorities would not dare arrest Him during the daylight or in public. The Scriptures say that Christ hid Himself at night. This proves that, despite His prophetic knowledge of what was to come, he in no way acted to bring about fulfillment of the prophecies.

The absolute contrary to general belief appears to be the truth. Christ exposed Judas' treacherous intentions, obviously in the hope that such denunciation would defer him from committing such an abominable crime which would lead him to suicide and eternal damnation. Christ condemned Judas precisely because his betrayal was to prove disastrous. His career was cut short at the very beginning of His mission. It is interesting to speculate on what might have happened regarding history since then if Christ had been allowed to live another fifty years. It is a strange thing that those who serve the Synagogue of Satan seem to live almost invariably into their eighties. Here we have the most outstanding example of those who direct the Luciferian conspiracy making human beings serve their diabolical purpose; God knew what would happen, but He didn't want it to happen.

Christ knew what would happen, but He didn't want it to happen. He even prayed to His heavenly Father in the Garden of Gethsemane, and begged to be saved from His pending fate, but at the same time Christ did as many of us have done since. He said, "Not my will, but Thy Will be done."

I believe it was the Synagogue of Satan who plotted, financed, and directed the betrayal, trial, and crucifixion of Jesus Christ, and used Judas as their tool, and caused the Jewish mob to assume the guilt for their sin against God, and crime against humanity, in order that they could retain the hold which Christ Himself told us He had come to earth to break.

What the Synagogue of Satan, those who, as Christ told us, "are them who say they are Jews, but are not, and do lie," did was to make it possible for them to use the Jews as tools, agents, and whipping boys from then to the present day. Tell this truth to the Jews as well as to the Gentiles, and perhaps the course of history may be changed sooner instead of later. What happened to Christ nearly two thousand years ago has been celebrated as a Luciferian and Satanic victory in every Black and/or Adonaicide Mass ever since. The horrible, revolting ritual claims that the Synagogue of Satan defeated Christ's mission to earth by bringing it to an early and sudden end, when they were able to engineer His betrayal, conviction on false charges, and death. I can find no mention of this as a Jewish victory in the documents I have studied which deal with this aspect of the Luciferian conspiracy.

Those who direct the Luciferian conspiracy AT THE TOP have also encouraged and even financed anti-Semitism, and used it to serve their secret plans and diabolical ambitions. But they have also deceived Gentiles into serving their diabolical purposes in exactly the same way. It is utterly ludicrous to say the W.R.M. is a Jewish plot designed to give the Jews ultimate control of the world, because study of the Luciferian plot proves clearly that ALL forms of government and religion are to be destroyed in the final stage of the Luciferian conspiracy, so that when "No power or cunning can prevent us, we (the high priests of the Luciferian religion) shall crown our leader King Despot of the entire world."

According to the writings of those who have directed the Luciferian conspiracy, their purpose is to enslave ALL Lesser human beings absolutely, physically, mentally, and spiritually, and force them to accept the Luciferian ideology by application of Satanic despotism. This being a fact, those who claim that the W.R.M. is a Jewish, Roman Catholic, Communist, Nazi, Masonic, or any other kind of conspiracy, talk utter nonsense, because evidence in this book will PROVE HOW the conspirators intend to destroy all forms of government and religion.

As far as our investigations have gone, the evidence indicates that those who have directed the Luciferian conspiracy secretly, have always masqueraded as champions of another established religion. We have the Luciferian who headed the Jewish Sanhedrin during Christ's mission on earth; we have Weishaupt, who taught Canon Law by which the Christian missionary efforts were governed in his day; we have Albert Pike-who was head of the Masonic religion (for Masonry is a religion), in his day, etc., etc.

GOD. The Supreme Being, Creator of the heavens and the earth (Universe). God is known as Jehovah, but this form of address dates only since 1518. The name given to God by the human race in pre-Mosaic times was Jahweh, sometimes spelled Yahweh, meaning Creator. God the Creator is also known as Elohim. But it is interesting to note that after Moses had been given the Commandments by God the fact that they forbade any person to take the name of God in vain caused the religious leaders of the Jews to substitute the word Adonai or Adonay. This is the word used by the high Priests of the Luciferian Creed when making any pronouncement or defining any dogma.

PROTOCOLS. The word means original written draft of a plan designed to achieve a definite objective. The protocols of the Luciferian conspiracy were written as soon as human beings had mastered the art of putting their thought and intentions regarding the future, on parchment, or other suitable material, so they could be preserved for the information of those who came after them. The Luciferian conspiracy (to prevent the Human Race from putting God's plan for the rule of the Universe into effect upon this earth so that a totalitarian Luciferian dictatorship may be imposed on ALL Lesser Beings in the final stages) has constantly been revised and modernized, BUT NEVER CHANGED. It has been revised and modernized so that those directing the conspiracy can take full advantage of rapidly changing social, economic, political, and religious conditions, and also to take full advantage of the advances being made in applied science. Men who refuse to give God credit for their superior intelligence invariably become Satanists, and as such, serve the secret plans, and further the diabolical ambitions, of those who direct the Luciferian conspiracy.

This TRUTH is made abundantly clear in the writings of both Adam Weishaupt and Albert Pike. They say that when the Luciferian conspiracy is finally imposed on what remains of the Human Race, the King-Despot will be served by a FEW millionaires, economists, and scientists, who have been proven to be devoted to the Luciferian Cause, assisted by sufficient soldiers and police (the United Nation's International Police?) to enforce the will of the dictator upon the masses (Goyim). All the Goyim, without exception, are to be reduced to the state of human cattle by a process of integration on an international scale. After the human race has been turned into a vast conglomeration of humanity, breeding will be limited to types and numbers considered sufficient to fill the requirements of the State (God). Artificial insemination will be used to accomplish this purpose. Less than 5% of the males, and 30% of the females, will be selected and used for breeding purposes.

The purpose of this book is to expose the conspiracy designed to accomplish these diabolical purposes. We explain how the conspiracy has been developed, until today it is in its semi-final stage. WE then tell what will happen if the TRUTH regarding the existence of the continuing conspiracy against God and the Human Race, isn't made known far and wide, as quickly as possible. The Scriptures promise that if we make the TRUTH known to all the people of all the remaining nations, the (knowledge of) Truth will set us free from the bonds of Satan with which we are being more and more securely bound as the years roll by. Satan is still Prince of this world. Our task is to shorten the time when the prophesies related in Revelations are brought to pass. It is our duty to bind Satan by making his evil plans known, so that he may be cast back into Hell for a thousand years (as foretold in the 20th chapter of Revelations), and so hasten the day when Satan again breaks his bonds and brings chaos, tribulations and further abominations to the people of this earth. It is then that God will intervene for the sake of the Elect. These things will not come to pass until people who consider themselves the Elect PROVE they are sincere. In order to prove our sincerity we must, in my humble opinion, become DOERS of His Holy Will, and not HEARERS ONLY, of His Word. I feel that mass action can shorten the days of our tribulation. If we parents have any true paternal affections, we must think of the welfare of the future generations also.

Revelation tells us that when Satan escapes from Hell he will introduce abominations the like of which the world has never known, and will never know again. Of this period Mark 13:20 says that if it were not for the intervention of God on behalf of His Elect, "there should no flesh be saved." St.

Matthew confirms what Mark says in Chapter 24, verses 3 to 32.

Like many others who have tried to find out who causes wars and revolutions, and why, I groped around in the Red Fog of Luciferian propaganda for many years. I gathered together thousands of pieces of evidence. I traced down hundreds of clues all over the world. At one time and another I blamed selfish Capitalism, Communism, Nazism, and political Zionism. Others I consulted were equally convinced that one or another of these evil forces were the SECRET POWER that worked behind the scenes of governments, and made them adopt policies which ultimately forced them into wars and revolutions. Some blamed the Roman Catholic Church; others Freemasonry; still others Judaism, the World Federalists, Bilderbergers. But when I used the Holy Bible, the inspired Word of God, to test the truth or fallacy of each piece of evidence, I began to realize the TRUTH. That TRUTH is that the Luciferian revolt against the right of God to exercise supreme authority over the entire universe was transferred to this earth in the Garden of Eden. It has continued to develop here ever since until it is now in its semi-final stage. Those who have directed the conspiracy have used every guile and form of cunning to set sections of the human race against each other, by dividing them into opposing camps, then arming them, and making them fight over one issue or another. When I considered how those who were enemies in one war were allied in the next; how Capitalists financed alleged "Workers' Revolutions;" how those who call themselves Jews, but are not, and do lie, sacrificed just as many of the lesser Jewish brethren as was necessary to serve their own diabolical purposes; how devilish propaganda divided millions of Christians into opposing armies, and made them fight and kill each other off by the tens of millions, without anyone engaged having the slightest personal animosity towards the other; then I became convinced that the Holy Scriptures are the inspired Word of God, and that Jesus Christ carne on earth to warn us of the existence of the Luciferian conspiracy. He lived, suffered, and died in order to make known the truths which will release us from the bonds of Satan so we can enjoy eternal happiness with His and our Heavenly Father. It is up to us now. We can accept or reject the truth. (John 8:32)

Chapter 2

HOW THE W.R.M.
WAS TRANSFERRED TO EARTH

We have seen that primitive people believed in a supreme being whom we refer to as God. They believed in an evil adversary whom we call Satan because he tried to interfere with God's creation and with His creatures which inhabit the earth. The Bible tells us that, at a much later date in the world's history, the Hebrews thought of the Heavens as concave, above a flat earth, supported on pillars, erected on foundations. (2 Sam. 22:8, Prov. 8:27-29) They believed that there are seven heavens inhabited by varying grades of superhumans, the highest Aravoth, being reserved for God. St. Paul tells us he was caught up into the third heaven. (2 Cor. 12:2)

The Scriptures don't tell us much regarding what happened in heaven after Lucifer and his fellow rebels had been cast out; nor are we told definitely WHY God decided to create this earth on which human beings decide their eternal fate. But God did give us intelligence so we can reason things out for ourselves. If He hadn't done things in this way we wouldn't have been subjected to much of a test, which is obviously designed to make each individual prove whether or not he honestly and sincerely desires to love God and serve Him voluntarily for all eternity.

Interesting light is thrown on this subject by several theologians who make reference to the fact that the cause of Lucifer's revolt against God could have been jealously aroused when God announced it to be His intention to create human beings and give them the chance and opportunity to develop into the highest ranks of the celestial beings. But it would appear more logical to assume that God came to His decision to create this world and populate it with human beings AFTER St. Michael had suppressed the Luciferian revolt.

This reasoning opens a line of thought which could lead us to believe that God is infinitely merciful, as well as just, and therefore created the world (worlds) and populated it, or them, with human beings because He did not hold all who had joined Lucifer in revolt equally guilty. It doesn't seem unreasonable to suppose that God decided to give those angels He judged to have been deceived into joining Lucifer, another opportunity to decide for themselves whether they wished to accept Him as their God and supreme authority, or Lucifer. This theory could explain why there is a definite affinity of a spiritual entity with each individual body. We commonly refer to this entity as the soul, and associate it with our personal guardian angel.

Carrying this theory to its logical conclusion, it would seem reasonable to suppose that God intended to place human beings on earth by a method of birth that prevented their having knowledge of other worlds beyond what He decided to reveal to our first parents personally, and to future generations through His prophets and the Scriptures. We are told that He did walk with Adam and Eve in the Garden of Eden, talking with them, and explaining to them His Holy Will and His plan for the rule of the Universe which He wanted to be established on this earth, as related in Genesis.

This being true, our first parents had first-hand knowledge of God; His wishes; His plans and intentions for them in the future.

He promised that if they respected His wishes and obeyed His commandments, they would, after a period of trial, rejoin Him in Heaven and live forever in perfect happiness. The Scriptures confirm that part of primitive man's mythology which says God made living easy for them by providing for their needs. Then again, it is possible, as some theologians claim, that the correct explanation is that God created this world and inhabited it with human beings, into whose bodies He "breathed" a soul, in order to give them the opportunity to fill the vacancies left in Heaven after Lucifer and those members of the Heavenly Host who joined in his revolt, were cast into Hell. They teach that God creates an individual soul for each individual body.

If this is the case, then it is also probable that there are as many worlds as there are many choirs of angels, and that each world is inhabited with human beings which compare in intelligence with the fallen angels they are designed to replace in Heaven. If this is so, it does not seem unreasonable to suppose that our spiritual advancement, or deterioration, could be progressive as well as immediate, after the death of our mortal bodies.

Millions of human beings believe in reincarnation. It could be that this belief originates with the knowledge that God's heaven consists of seven levels; that God's angels were made up of many choirs of varying degree, and that angels of lesser degree advance from one heaven to another. If this is so, it would appear that God intended human beings to exist in various degrees, and also intended that those on the lower plane could, by application, diligence, and attention to spiritual matters, advance themselves to higher levels on earth and higher degrees in heaven. This is what rugged individualism really means, and rugged individualism is what the enemies of God are determined to destroy.

Obviously human beings can, and do, deteriorate spiritually until they reach the stage when they are engulfed in Hell. This line of thought would offer some explanation to references made to Limbo, Purgatory, and the fact that Christ, after His resurrection, descended into some part of Hell, where He released souls who were waiting their redemption.

If God created human beings to fill the gaps made by the apostasies of the fallen spirits, then it is logical to assume He wants us to prove definitely that we wish to know, love, and serve Him voluntarily for all eternity. If we develop this line of thought to its logical conclusion, then it is our spiritual condition, when we emerge from the struggle going on in this world for the souls of men, which will determine whether or not we are considered "of the Elect" or "of the damned." Reference in the Scriptures to the "immediate" judgment at the moment of death, and the "final" judgment, when a definite division of the Universe is made into Heaven and Hell, would indicate that there are intermediary places where souls could be tested further until they have definitely decided their eternal fate. There are a number of theologians who maintain that the Elect of the human race are absorbed into the very hierarchy of the angels, into the ranks of the Cherubim and Seraphim, and all other orders. The theologians to whom I refer believe that "The Elect of the human race will not be only the outside fringe of the spirit world, but will, on the contrary, be the shining stars in every one of the spirit planes." This line of thought seems to be supported by St. Luke in Chapter 20, verse 36: "Neither can they die anymore; for they are equal unto the angels, and are the children of God, being the children of the resurrection." As Abbot Anscar Vonier O.S.A. stated in his treatise on the Angels: "We are not concerned here directly with demonology; our scope is a more consoling one. Whatever height a fallen angel may have occupied in the scale of being, it is possible for the grace of God to raise man to that height, so that even the throne vacated by Lucifer himself may become the congenital inheritance of some holy soul." The learned Abbot say further: "It is possible for the grace of God to raise man to that height." I feel it would be better to say, "The grace of God, used as He intends it to be used, can enable man to raise himself to such a height of spiritual perfection that it is possible for a human soul to occupy the vacancies left by the highest of the fallen angels."

Every 'living soul' knows that God did give us an intellect and the unrestricted use of our wills. If God hadn't intended to put us to a test there would have been no sense in His allowing an 'adversary' to oppose His plans, ridicule His wishes, and try to wean us away from God so that we could be possessed by Lucifer, the King of the Empire of Darkness, whom we commonly term the 'Devil.' Study of the opinions expressed by early Christians, and later by both Catholic and non-Catholic theologians, provides evidence which supports the reasoning set forth above. We find that several make reference to the fact that Lucifer and his followers expressed the lustful desire to have sexual relations with, and physical control over, the bodies of human beings God planned to create. Quite obviously they could have developed such desires only as the result of their rebellion against the supreme authority of God the Creator in order that they might foul up His plan to have human beings fill the gaps their rebellion had caused in the choirs of angels.

Several early Christian theologians believed that the fallen angels lusted for the people of this world. St. Augustine claimed that the perverted and depraved interpretation of sexual relations adopted by the human race at the instigation of Satan, are contrary to God's purpose and intention. He calls this 'concupiscence'. It would therefore seem logical to suppose that if 'concupiscence' is contrary to God's will it was introduced by Satan to help further the Luciferian conspiracy upon this earth. The above opinions are based on the authority of the *Book of Enoch*. But these opinions have been ruled 'in error' by the more modern theologians. St. Thomas, and the decree of the Council of Trent claim that because all angels (those who remained loyal and those who defected from God), are pure spirits, it is impossible for them to lust or have sexual relations with human beings. Again, on the other hand, there is evidence in the records of exorcism, practiced by ordained ministers of the Christian religion, which claim that victims released after having been possessed by devils, claimed they had been physically possessed sexually.

Be that as it may, we know that God did create this earth. He did inhabit it with human beings. We are told that we are made in His own image and likeness. Because there are so many degrees of bodily form and shape, a human being's likeness to God must of necessity relate to its spiritual entity, which we call the soul. The Scriptures support this conjecture. They tell us that until our first parents defected from God, and chose to accept the advice of Satan, their bodies shone like the sun because they were illuminated with the light of sanctifying grace. This spiritual illumination departed with the committing of what we term 'original sin.' But whatever happened in this regard, it is definitely established that our mortal bodies have their spiritual entities. To believe otherwise is to be atheistic.

We now come to the point in the world's history where God's adversary is named Satan. He caused Eve to defect from God. She afterwards persuaded Adam to join her in rebellion. Without stressing the point of HOW Satan deceived Eve into defecting from God, it must be apparent to most thinking people that perversion of sex definitely entered into the deception.

By perversion of sex we mean that Satan taught Eve how to use sexual relations to gratify animal passion and carnal desires. Study of this phase of the Luciferian conspiracy would indicate that God intended sexual intercourse to be a holy union between a man and his wife, entered into for the purpose of creating another human being into whom God could infuse a soul because He desired to have an opportunity to fill one of the vacancies left in Heaven as the result of the Luciferian rebellion. There must be some merit to this line of thought, otherwise there would not be such a clash of opinions regarding the use of contraceptives and so-called planned births. If there isn't merit in this point of view, why is it that those who work to prevent God's plan for the rule of Creation being established on this earth are secretly determined to replace God's plan for the reproduction of the human race by artificial insemination practiced on an international scale.

The teaching of Christ and many Scriptural quotations tell us that God made human beings greater than the angels in as much as he gave them the power to reproduce their kind according to His Will. The waste of human seed is condemned over and over again. Every sensible human being knows that because God is God, i.e., the Supreme Being, Creator of Heaven and Earth (the Universe), He could, if He wished, have prevented Lucifer interfering with His plan to create terrestrial worlds and human beings, but if He had done so, we would have been subjected to no real test. Without wishing to be presumptuous, it seems reasonable to suppose that God obtains His pleasure from His marvelous creation out of love and fidelity given Him by those, both angelic and human, who remain staunch, loyal, faithful and true, despite all the evil machination of the Devil, and his angels, who wander through this world (and probably others), seeking the ruin of immortal souls.

In order to understand these things we must understand the facts concerning "Spirit tutelage." The word "tutelage" is used to mean "guardianship" and/or "instruction." Spirit tutelage is a divine ordinance. It permits man to be influenced by Good and Evil spirits who have the power to put 'thoughts' into our minds.

Temptations are what we term "Evil" thoughts. Temptation by evil spirits is not a "divine ordinance." It results from what theologians call "the permissive providence of God." If the human race were not subject to "evil" influences as well as "good," there would be no purpose in God having given us an intellect and free will. The intellect enables us to analyze the thoughts which enter our minds. We make a decision. Then, by use of our free will we make our bodies put the decision of the mind into action.

The most frequent question asked by people in all walks of life concerning this very important matter is "If God is GOOD, then why does He permit evil? If God loves the Human Race, WHY does He permit even innocent people to suffer the tribulations of wars, revolutions, sickness, etc.?"

Experiences in two wars and three revolutions taught me the answer to these questions. FIRST, I believe that it is God's intention to fill the gaps in heaven resulting from the fall of angels of many degrees from Grace with beings, including human beings, who positively and definitely PROVE by the nature of their prayers and works, the manner in which they deal with temptation; and the way in which they stand up under conditions of physical, mental, and spiritual stress, that, regardless of what happens to them on this earth, they still wish, with a burning and constant desire, to VOLUNTARILY love and serve God for eternity. This belief is justified in Matt. 10:28; Luke 12:4; II Kings 7:4; Ps. 44:22, etc., etc.

I base this explanation on the further belief that God, being the Creator of the totality of the Universe, can derive happiness only from the love, loyalty, devotion, and service given Him VOLUNTARILY by His creatures. He intends that we prove to Him that we have definitely and irrevocably made this decision before He allows us to enter the Kingdom of Heaven. In other words, we decide our own eternal fate.

St. Paul's text, 1 Cor. 6:3, says, "Know you not that we shall judge angels? How much more things of this world?" I take this to indicate that those human beings who come out of this earthly test "With God's colors flying" will be chosen to pass judgment on the fallen angels who used their powers to inspire us with evil thoughts, and deceive us into doing evil things. The fact that the elect put aside temptation and refuse to be deceived, even though the agents of the Devil work great wonders, prove they have won spiritual domination over the forces of evil. They will be permitted to exercise this domination on the day of final judgment.

In 1918, when I was helping remove rubble, resulting from a German air raid on West Hartlepool, England, to rescue an infant whose cries came from the dark interior of the collapsed building, I learned the answer to the second half of the question. As we worked I heard the anguished mother cry, "If God is ALL GOOD how can He permit such evil?-How can He allow innocent little children to suffer? Why does He punish me so? I have tried to love Him and serve Him."

As I worked, the answer came to me. Half an hour later we reached the baby. It was alive and uninjured. It was lying alongside the grandmother on a mattress on the floor inside a cupboard made by enclosing the space under the stairs which led from the ground floor to the upstairs rooms. The grandmother was dead.

When the baby was placed in its mother's arms, I asked her if I might accompany her. Friends standing by had offered her shelter. She gave me permission.

Over the cup of tea (the provision of which is an absolute necessity in time of joy or sorrow with the English people), the mother hugged her infant to her breast and murmured, "Oh God, forgive me. How could I have doubted your infinite Goodness?" I placed my hand on her arm and said, "God doesn't will that we, His creatures, suffer the abomination of war. Wars are a punishment humanity afflicts upon itself because the majority have obstinately and persistently refused to do His Will, obey His Commandments, and put His plan for the rule of the Universe into effect upon this earth." We punish ourselves because we permit Satan to remain "Prince of this World."

This line of reasoning I honestly believe to be the TRUTH. The incident I record here happened in April, 1918. Another World War and many revolutions have been fought since. The W.R.M. is directed AT THE TOP by the Synagogue of Satan to further the secret plans of the High Priests of the Luciferian Creed. It is they, human beings, diabolically inspired by the spiritual forces of darkness, who foment wars and revolutions, and in doing so they confirm the words spoken by Christ Himself when He said of the S.O.S., "Ye are sons, of the Devil, whose lusts ye shall do. He was a murderer from the beginning; etc." Yes, the Devil has been and still is a murderer. Wars and revolutions are his means of committing mass murder. In my opinion we commit a terrible sin when we even think that God wills wars, revolutions, and other forms of abominations. God did not wish our first parents to defect from

Him. They did so of their own free will and accord. God did not Will that human beings terminate this earthly existence by the death of our mortal bodies. When Adam and Eve sinned they suffered the loss of sanctifying grace. That automatically involved the death of their mortal bodies, contrary to God's Will and His original intention.

The same conclusions are correct if applied to physical and mental ailments. While human beings ate meats, fish, fowl, fruits, nuts, seeds, and vegetables as intended by God they lived healthy lives, and they lived to a ripe old age. If they died naturally, they died of old age, the gradual wearing out of the body's vital organs. It was not until the human race departed from God's Will, in respect to diet, and substituted "the Devil's Brew," consisting of food, drinks, and drugs which satisfy gluttony, the carnal appetite, and arouse lustful thoughts and sensual desires, that ailments of the flesh shortened our life-span and caused physical diseases and mental suffering. Don't take my word for this. In the Scriptures Romans 6:23 tells us, "The wages of Sin is Death." Why do those who plot our subjugation force us to eat denatured foods in this day and age, if it isn't to weaken us mentally as well as physically?

There is another fact that concerns the W.R.M. being transferred to this earth in the Garden of Eden. The Devil, Lucifer, Satan, or however you wish to designate the Secret Evil Power on this earth, which constitutes the "Adversary" to God's Will, occupied this earth BEFORE God created Adam and Eve. Satan was here and ready to tempt Eve, and through her, Adam, when both were still in a state of innocence, and enjoying the Presence and Friendship of God. Man's sin strengthened the hold the Devil had on this world. It did not create it. Theologians as a rule accept this as an "Insoluble mystery." I would like to point out that this fact indicates that this world was, and still is, part of the section of the Universe controlled by Lucifer, the Part we term Hell. There seems to be a lot of truth in some old saying, which dates back into antiquity – "This is Hell upon Earth". Human beings still have the opportunity to reunite with God, if they so desire, but the vast majority don't seem to do very much about it. The next question is this: "Are Lucifer and Satan one and the same supernatural being?" For reasons beyond my own comprehension the accepted idea of most theologians is that Lucifer and Satan are one. Yet the same theologians agree that there is evidence for believing that there are several principalities in Hell, each ruled by a supernatural being who is subordinate to Lucifer. Is it unreasonable to suppose that Satan is a different being who defected from God at the time of the heavenly revolt led by Lucifer?

Is it unreasonable to suppose that there is a certain degree of TRUTH in the teachings and doctrines of those who expound the Luciferian ideology on this earth. Even admitting that an angel, by reason of being a pure spirit, regardless of whether it is 'Good' or 'Evil,' isn't confined to any geographical limitations, and can use its influence for 'Good' or 'evil' in a dozen different places in less time than is used in the twinkling of an eye, it still seems reasonable to suppose that Lucifer is "King" of all that part of the Universe we term Hell, and Satan is one of his Princes. Does not Christ Himself designate Satan as "Prince of this World?" The conditions existing upon this earth would seem to indicate it is part of Hell rather than a part of Heaven.

If this world is part of Hell, then it is reasonable to suppose that the decision we make here is final. That may explain why He visited here as He did another part of Hell before his resurrection. He redeemed us, but whether we accept His redemption or reject it, it is our own business.

Be that as it may, the fact remains that the Luciferian doctrines expound what the Holy Scriptures neglect to say on this important subject. Christ made it very clear that Lucifer is the "Father of Lies," and that Satan uses lies and deceits to achieve their diabolical purpose. Is it unreasonable to suppose that Lucifer has inspired those who have directed his conspiracy here on earth, to tell only a little of the truth? If this line of thought isn't logical then where did the old saying originate that "Half a truth is more dangerous than a whole lie?"

If Lucifer was at the very top of the highest heavens, and nest in beauty, power, and glory to God Himself, and if the Luciferian mythology the eldest son of God and older brother of St. Michael, is based on truth, then the many and varied pieces of evidence concerning the transfer of the Luciferian conspiracy onto this earth, given previously, fall into place, and provide an exceptionally clear picture of this phase of the conspiracy.

There are volumes upon volumes of writings which indicate and/or prove that Freemasons are taught that the origin of their secret society dates back to the time of the building of the pyramids. There are just as many volumes that prove that adepts of the Grand Orient Lodges and Councils of the New and Reformed Palladian Rite are taught that their form of Masonry has continued since the fall of Eve. They claim that her seduction by Satan produced Cain and that Cain founded the Synagogue of Satan. This is the teaching which requires members of the lower degrees of the Grand Orient and Palladian Rite to become Satanists.

It is a strange coincidence that most men who stoutly protest they are 100% for God and refuse to accept the idea that Satan is different and subordinate to Lucifer, are supported in this opinion by those who openly acknowledge their allegiance to Satan. Evidence will be produced to prove that it is only when a confirmed Satanist in the Grand Orient or Palladian Rite is initiated into the High Priesthood of the Luciferian Creed, that he is told THE FULL SECRET, and required to accept its Creed, which says, "Lucifer is God the equal of Adonai (Adonay) and the worship of Satan is therefore a heresy."

General Albert Pike is accepted as the greatest modern authority as far as Luciferianism is concerned. As head of the Palladian Rite he wrote a letter of instruction dated July 14, 1885, and sent it to the heads of the twenty-six Councils located throughout the world. In this letter he not only confirmed the belief that Satan is subordinate to Lucifer, but stated that Lucifer is God, the equal of Adonay, and added that Lucifer is the God of LIGHT, the God of GOOD, who struggles for humanity against Adonay the God of Darkness and all Evil.

Pike has been built up by the press of the United States to the point that most Freemasons consider him one of their most illustrious brethren, and one of America's greatest patriots. But research reveals that Pike lived a double life. Secretly he was a worshipper of Lucifer. Between 1859 and 1889 he rose to be head of the High Priests of the Luciferian Creed.

Lower degree Masons are taught to believe different statements regarding the source of their Secret Society. The fact is that, when they are initiated into a higher degree they are told something entirely different by those conducting the initiation, telling them that as they advance to the higher degrees they are admitted deeper and deeper into the mysteries of the Craft. Not one Mason in a thousand even suspects that, far away above the Scottish Rite of Blue Masonry, and beyond the reach of any except those carefully selected for admittance into Grand Orient Lodges and the Councils of Pike's New and Reformed Palladian Rite, Satanism is practiced. In these secret societies Satan is worshipped as God and "Prince of this World." But above these Satanic Societies, specially selected members of the Synagogue are initiated into the FULL SECRET, which is the final TRUTH as exemplified in the Luciferian Creed, as we have just explained.

The reader may ask, "Why all this secrecy?" The answer is that those human beings who have literally sold themselves to the Devil, know that the final success of their diabolical conspiracy against God and His Human Race depends upon their ability to keep their identity and TRUE purpose secret. This book is published to expose their secret and to arouse public opinion so that an end may be put to this conspiracy, and thus bring about the prophesies contained in Revelations, which say Satan shall be chained and returned to Hell and remain there for one thousand years.

In the international lodges of the Grand Orient and Pike's New Palladian Rite, adepts are required to accept as TRUTH, that Masonry really originated with Cain. They are told that Satan, whom they name Ebilis, conferred on the human race the greatest benefaction possible when he defeated God's (Adonay's) plot to keep the knowledge of sexual behavior, and the secret of procreation, from our first parents. The initiates are told that Ebilis initiated Eve into the pleasures of sexual intercourse, and taught her the secret of procreation, and thus made her and Adam equal in power to God. The initiate is also told that, as the result of the sexual relationship Eve gave birth to Cain, who started the movement (Masonry), and put the Luciferian ideology into effect here as it is in that part of the celestial world over which Lucifer reigns. Thus, where the members of the lower degrees of the Scottish Rite are taught that Hirarn was the father of Masonry, those admitted to the highest degree are taught differently.[7]

Study of the Manichaean movement and doctrine informs us that in order to prevent God's plan to make Adam and Eve the first parents of His human race, Satan seduced Eve and possessed her, and was the father of Cain and Eve's first daughter also. The Manichaean doctrine teaches that Cain 'married' his sister, and that the progeny of this union (incest) have perpetuated Satanism ever since. Without wishing to labor this point too heavily, it is of interest to point out that Scripture relates there was something very displeasing to God about Cain's 'marriage'. Cain also murdered his brother Abel; and Christ in His day castigated those of the Synagogue of Satan as "Ye are sons of your father the Devil; his lusts shall ye do. He as a murderer from the beginning, and abode not in the truth, because there is no truth in him." (John 8:44)

"The Serpent" is the name by which Satan is known in the Holy Scriptures (Rev. 20:2; Num. 21:9). The Serpent is the symbol of Satanism in secret socie-

---

7 Those wishing further information on this particular phase of the conspiracy should read the books listed elsewhere, particularly *Copin-Albancelli's le Drame Masconnique*

-ties which worship him as Prince of the World. Scriptures refer to Eve and "the seed of the serpent" (Gen. 3:1-16). Therefore we may ask, "Where did the seed of the Serpent come from?"

Paul said, in II Cor. that Eve had been unchaste with the Serpent, (Lucifer, Devil, Satan) - (Lucifer means the Bright and Shining One). Right here is the origin of the Seed of the Serpent. In Gen. 3:15 God said, "I will put enmity between thee and the woman, and between thy seed and her seed." In saying this to the Serpent, (Lucifer, Devil, Satan), God stated that Lucifer would have a seed (just as physical as Eve's seed would be physical). In Gen. 3:16 God said to Eve, "and thy desire shall be to thy husband," which indicated plainly that her desire had previously been to another! In Cor. 11:2-3 Paul here was talking about "chastity," to present the Corinthians as a CHASTE virgin to Christ. In the very next verse, Paul said, "But I fear, lest by any means, as the Serpent beguiled Eve through his subtlety."

Paul here affirmed that Eve did not present herself a CHASTE virgin to Adam! Remember, there is only one way for a virgin to lose her chastity. In Gen. 4:1, Eve thought that Cain was her promised seed, but later acknowledged that she was mistaken and that Seth (not Cain), was her promised seed, when she said (Gen. 4:25) "For God hath appointed me another Seed instead of Abel, whom Cain slew."

Cain and Abel were twins (Gen. 4:3-4) for they became of age at the same time and presented their offerings on the same day. Abel was the son of Adam, but Cain was the son of Lucifer. Lucifer and his seed have been killers down through the centuries, and Christ accused them of having slain all the prophets from Abel to His time (Matt. 23:35). Lucifer begat a seed, as God said he would (1 John 3:12). "Not as Cain, who was of that wicked one."

Lust is sexual desire outside the Natural Law of God. Therefore Christ Himself seems to have confirmed that Satan was lustful and is father of the Synagogue of Satan as those who are Satanists teach and believe. Satanists have always used sex-bribery and the depravities and perversions of sex to obtain control of men and women they wished to use to further the secret plans of their diabolical conspiracy. Satanism makes a God of sex. They worship the human body because of its sexual abilities. When men and women prove they are unyielding to all other forms of devilish temptation, they often fall as the result of becoming involved in illicit relationships and perversions. Did not David commit abominable sexual crimes, including incest?

Then, Christ also told us that the father of the Synagogue of Satan was a murderer from the beginning. Who else could that person have been but Satan? Did he not inspire Cain, his son, to kill his own brother, Abel? Has murder not been the stock-in-trade of those who have comprised the Synagogue of Satan ever since? What is revolution and war if not murder practiced on a mass scale?

Another important fact concerning incest being used to start the Synagogue of Satan on this earth is the practice of Pagan kings, who worshipped the Devil. In order to perpetuate their line of succession, they insisted that their sons marry their own sisters. But regardless of what is 'right' or what is 'wrong,' the fact remains that when Christ did start His mission, He told us that the Luciferian conspiracy had reached the stage where Satan, as Prince of this world, had obtained control over all those in high places.

The words in Gen. 4:15 seem to indicate that after Adam and Eve defected from God, He willed that what has happened since should take place. He said, "Whosoever should slay Cain, vengeance shall be taken on him seven-fold." It would seem that after our first parents defected, God insisted that those who truly wished to love Him and serve Him voluntarily for all eternity, out of respect for His infinite perfections, should prove their sincerity. Without the 'Adversary,' and the Synagogue of Satan, there would be no real test. The Holy Scriptures give us enough information to enable us to decide for ourselves which way we want to go.

Satanism teaches that Jesus Christ is one and the same as St. Michael, and is the younger brother of Satan. Satanism also claims that God sent St. Michael to earth, in the form of Jesus Christ in order that He might end the Luciferian conspiracy here as he had previously done in heaven. Both Satanists and Luciferian adepts boast that Christ failed in His mission. They make the reacting of His defeat the major part in the celebration of the 'Black Mass.' Pike revised and modernized the 'Black Mass' and named his brainchild, "The Adonaicide Mass."

The word "Adonaicide" means the death, or end, of God. The death of God was the primary purpose of Nietzscheism.[8]

It would seem that because the enmity between Satan and St. Michael started in heaven, and because Christ, while on earth, rejected the overtures of Satan to join him in rebellion against the absolute supremacy of God, the enmity has been carried out so that Christianity has been, and still is honeycombed with Luciferian and/or Satanic cells.

Since Christ first picked His apostles, these agenturs always hide their true identity while they bore industriously from within. Today they are to be found disguised as "Modernists," weakening the various denominations so that they will be ready to collapse when those who direct the conspiracy AT THE TOP, decide it is time to provoke the final social cataclysm. Pike explained what is intended to happen in a letter he wrote to his director (Mazzini) of the W.R.M. August 15,1871. This letter is quoted elsewhere. It is catalogued in the Library of the British Museum, London, England[9] and has been quoted from and referred to by dozens of authorities and students of the W.R.M., including Cardinal Rodriguez of Chile. (See page 118 of *The Mysteries of Freemasonry Unveiled*, 1925. English translation, 1957.)

That the Luciferian conspiracy does exist, and has had unbroken continuity since its very beginning, regardless of whether we take its beginning in the celestial world, or from the Garden of Eden, proves it to be of supernatural origin and direction. Nothing conceived in a human mind could be so perfect, so diabolical, so titanic in dimensions, or so utterly destructive as the Luciferian conspiracy, which today we call the World Revolutionary Movement (W.R.M.).

Every time an attempt has been made by ecclesiastical and/or civic officials to expose Satanism as the inversion of God's plans and laws, and the antithesis of the Christian religion, the Agentur of the High Priests of the Luciferian Creed, who are located behind the scenes of all governments, both secular and ecclesiastical, have so far succeeded in turning the intended exposure into an actual and factual witch hunt. To prevent real Satanists and dedicated Luciferians from being exposed and punished, the Synagogue of Satan and the High Priests of the Luciferian Creed, who control the S.O.S. have always succeeded in throwing an ample number of substitutes into the hands of the investigators, who provided the executioners with enough victims to satisfy the outraged feelings of the Princes, both religious and secular, and the bloodlust of the angry mobs. Until recently, these substitutes were accused of being witches and/or sorcerers who worshipped the Devil. Believers in God will be next.

---

8 See pages 346-7 of *Satan*, by Sheed and Ward, New York, 1951.
9 The Keeper of manuscripts recently informed the author that this letter is NOT catalogued in the British Museum Library. It seems strange that a man of Cardinal Rodriguez's knowledge should have said it WAS in 1925.

Between 1486 and 1675, thirty-two ecclesiastical measures were taken against Satanism; and between 1532 and 1682, 149 witches and/or sorcerers were burned, 78 banished from their countries, and 124 punished in other various ways. These measures and punishments affected Americans. They were accused of being Satanists and furthering the Luciferian conspiracy against Christianity. Public attention was thus kept centered upon unimportant victims, most of whom had been charged, or betrayed by the high officials who kept their own identity with the Luciferian conspiracy secret.[10]

The Scriptures and writings of inspired men since the advent of Christ are full of incidents of demonic possession of individuals, but except in the Collect, read by priests celebrating the Mass on the 17th Sunday after Pentecost, one is unable to find anything very definite on the "Diabolica Contagis"--diabolical contagion- or the Devil's influence on the human masses. This is rather extraordinary because if wars and revolutions are, as I maintain, the destructive force being used by those who direct the W.R.M. to eliminate all other forms of government and religion, then the Devil's influence on the "Goyim" (human masses) is far more powerful, seductive and deceptive than is the possession of an individual.

There can be no logical denial that the Devil, through his earthly agentur, can and does influence the thinking of the masses in order to produce evil mass results including wars and revolutions. We refer to the manner the Secret Powers of Evil have of using propaganda and mass psychology to serve their diabolical purposes.

10 See pages 346-7 of *Satan*, by Sheed and Ward, New York, 1951

Chapter 3

LUCIFERIANISM

In order to be able to realize that the W.R.M. is a continuation of the Heavenly revolution, we must understand Lucifer; what Lucifer did in heaven, and WHY, BEFORE he and/or Satan caused our first parents to defect from God.

Being the highest, brightest, and most intelligent of God's creatures, he also had a Free Will. He could will to remain loyal, faithful, and obedient to God, and accept God (Adonay) as the Supreme Authority over the entire Universe, or he could challenge that 'Right.'

Lucifer, in Heaven, was next to God. He was intelligent, therefore it is obvious that he could not have envied Him. St. Thomas said, "Only a fool can be envious of what is so far above him as to be impossible of attainment." Lucifer is no fool!

Lucifer's pride in his angelic attributes, i.e., office, character, and personality could have caused him to desire to be in his own order as God is in the divine order. In other words, Lucifer's pride in his own perfections could have made him wish to become the ruler of His own order rather than remain subject to God, regardless of the exalted state to which he had been elevated by God. This line of reasoning does not infer that Lucifer was fool enough to wish to dethrone God. He simply wished to rule a section of the universe in his own right. Today many human beings suffer from the same kind of inflated ego. It could be termed an overwhelming desire for absolute independence or self-sufficiency. St. Thomas, Scotus, and Suarez agree that the sin Lucifer committed was "The sin of Pride," but they disagree with each other on exactly what constituted his sin of pride.

My studies have convinced me that Lucifer's sin of pride consisted of his determination to break from God and set up his own dynasty. I am supported in my conviction by Biblical authority and history-Lucifer got what he wanted by leading the heavenly revolt. He persuaded vast multitudes of various levels of the angels to join him. Among these were one-third of the highest, the brightest and the most intelligent of the heavenly host.

Lucifer got himself expelled from Heaven and cast into Hell, and this was exactly what he wanted to have happen. Since then he has struggled to wean as many others away from God as possible, so that they may come under his dominion. We know of his activities only on this earth, and we call this the World Revolutionary Movement.

My purpose in writing my last three books (I doubt if I shall be granted time to write others), has been to shed light on the W.R.M. and the S.O.S., a subject of such great importance that it affects the life of every human being and his or her immortal soul. Many priests and ministers have told me of their appreciation of my motives.

On the other hand, there are priests and ministers who, when asked by their parishioners to express an opinion on the hidden chapters of biblical and secular history as exposed and explained in Pawns in the Game and Red Fog over America, have said, "What he writes borders on heresy." What they don't mention is the great TRUTH expounded by the greatest theologians and philosophers of the Church of Christ, i.e., "ALL TRUTH borders on heresy." What really matters is that, when expounding the TRUTH, we don't step over the borderline as defined in the Scriptures. When ministers and/or priests close the door to a "mind" seeking further knowledge of the TRUTH, they serve the Devil's purpose. Isaiah 28:7; Mic. 3:11; Mall 2:7.

A Presbyterian minister in Ottawa said my writings were "unmitigated nonsense." A minister in Owen Sound published a pamphlet stating that I was anti-Semitic and spreading modern heresy. These men and several others both Gentiles and Jews have done their best to involve me in arguments and litigation. They probably intended, by so doing, to use up my time to such an extent that they would seriously interfere with my determination to throw as much light as I can on this subject before my own light has gone out.

In case readers run into this kind of criticism, I wish to remind them that the knowledge of ministers and priests is subject to the restrictions placed on them by the curricula laid down by those who control the seminaries of a particular faith. My studies, over a period of forty years, have never ceased. I have never allowed my mind to be subjected to limitations. This is the way I believe that God intended it should be. What I write, I believe to be the TRUTH. Readers should consider the hidden facts of history as detailed in my writings, to form their own opinions and reach their own decisions.

The curricula in many seminaries are seriously restricted for the simple reason that even theologians of the same faiths have been, and still are, openly divided in opinion on many matters dealing with the fall of angels. However, both Scotus and Suarez agree that none of the angels, including Lucifer, ever repented their defection from God. Both agree that repentance was a possibility to them, and that God gave them the time and opportunity for repentance, but during the interval of time Lucifer and his followers committed other sins. With these opinions St. Thomas disagrees.

It is nothing to be amazed at when theologians and philosophers disagree. Only God and the Devil know on whose side they are. Matt. 7:15 warns us of "False prophets in sheep's clothing." Even as far back as Jeremiah's day, priests were being denounced because of their unfaithfulness (Jer. 1:18). Many priests and ministers today teach because they are hired. They teach what those who hire them say they must teach (Mal. 2:8). The word "hire" used in this regard can mean more than "to obtain pay for services." It can mean to render service and give unlimited obedience to an earthly power in the hope of obtaining earthly and supernatural rewards.

When, as Staff Training Officer for the Canadian Naval Reserve Division 1943-4, I lectured to the officers and men on the subject of "Discipline and Obedience." I shocked some of the Divisional Commanding Officers by telling their subordinates that no officer or man was required to obey an order that is contrary to the Commandments of God, i.e., Natural Law or the Dignity of Man. Many of the most horrible atrocities committed in the name of God against the human race by Satanists, were committed by innocent men carrying out orders. How very convenient! If subordinates are required to obey ALL orders, then all the S.O.S. (who control all those in High Places) need do is see that orders are given to do things that serve the Devil's purpose.

Christians in Holy Orders should never forget that regardless of any consideration, including the oath of obedience they give to superior authority their first allegiance, like that of a soldier or sailor, is to God. No oath can bind them to commit sin. Keeping silence, or failure to tell the whole truth regarding the W.R.M., is a sin against God and a crime against God's creatures. "Tell the Truth and shame (confound) the Devil" should be the motto of every militant Christian. This truth was repeatedly emphasized by the late Pope Pius XII, when he told parish priests they are responsible for the secular as well as the spiritual welfare of their congregations, and should guide the members of their flocks on social, economic and political matters. He showed his will in this regard when, in 1957 he asked all faithful Catholics to pray for the "Silent Church." The word "Church" as he used it, means the "Whole body of Christian believers; the ecclesiastical organization or power as distinguished from the State." Don't let anyone tell you differently. If they do, they lie. If they lie, they serve the Devil's cause.

The Luciferian conspiracy could not have developed since our Lord died, to its semi-final stage if those who have pretended to be Christian clergy, dedicated to God, had not sinned against Him by maintaining "Silence" on this all important subject.

Let me remind my readers that NO ecclesiastical authority, Catholic or non-Catholic, has challenged the truth of what I say on this subject. Hundreds of ordained priests and ministers have admitted that I have convinced them of the TRUTH. The majority of them excuse themselves from helping me openly by saying "I am under discipline."

I am afraid God does not accept that as a valid excuse. God dispensed with all forms of compulsory discipline. Under God's plan for the rule of the Universe we are free to love and serve Him of our own Will, or go to Hell in our own way. It is time we stopped making excuses and proceeded to prove to God that we wish to love and serve Him for eternity.[11]

My slanderers have never had to worry about where their next meal came from. They have been babied along and encouraged to develop an inflated ego regarding their knowledge and importance. They may have suffered a few hardships, but they always knew they would be looked after provided they remained obedient to those their benefactors placed over them.

My life has been entirely different. Due to a serious accident, my father died in his forties. At the age of thirteen I was left to shift for myself. When fifteen I was at sea, working an average of twelve hours a day. I rose to be a Master Mariner, and a Commander in the Canadian Navy. I have written enough sense to have had ten books of non-fiction published and incorporated in reference libraries throughout the world.

---

11 I feel justified in making one further remark to protect my readers from those who slander me and my work. In addition to being mentally restricted by the curriculum of their schools and colleges, those who slander me were brought up in an atmosphere of social security. In the majority of cases their education, or indoctrination, was paid for by multi-millionaires who set up so-called Charitable Foundations so they could dictate the curricula of the educational institutions which they endowed. It has been proved that these millionaires belong to the international financial cartels who have financed BOTH sides in every war and revolution fought in the last two hundred years. It is logical to assume that this being the case, the curricula of the educational institutions they endow are not directed to making God's truth known, but to limiting knowledge regarding the truth, so that the Luciferian conspiracy can be developed to its final objectives.

I did all this by the Grace of God and my application to a dedicated cause. I was determined to find out, if possible, why human beings can't live in peace. It is only fair to mention that I rejected offers of fame and fortune, because such offers always had strings attached which would have prevented me continuing to see after, and publish, THE TRUTH. The only thing I ask from God is that He permit me to live long enough to pass on what I have learned about the W.R.M. to others.

While my traducers slept in warm beds and lived in comfort and security, carefully guarded from danger, I battled my way on the stormy seas and lived a life which brought me in intimate contact with all that is evil. I became intimately associated with Bolsheviks, Nihilists, and Nazi proselytes. But, notwithstanding that, I wanted to help the underdog, and had the urge to be a 'Do-gooder.' By the Grace of God, I never was convinced that by joining any so-called reform organization, I would be doing the will of God. It is beyond my comprehension how the hierarchy of many religions embrace men who have worked openly in the W.R.M. for years simply because they profess to have had a change of heart and mind. They lionize these men and make them professors in universities. But, to my knowledge, not one of them has shed any light on the "Secret Power" they must know is behind the various subversive movements which make up the WR.M. If Mazzini felt that secret control, surely they must have felt it also. But if they do, they never say.

I do not name my traducers because I don't think it charitable to do so. However, I feel confident that this book will be brought to their attention by some of my readers. Then, if they have any sense they will accept the truth and square themselves with God.

Because of its very nature, the Luciferian revolt must of necessity be designed to bring about the destruction of ALL other forms of government and religion, so that, in the final stage of the conspiracy, the Luciferian ideology may be imposed on what is left of the human race by Satanic despotism. Today we term this "Totalitarian dictatorship."

Obviously, it is much easier for a small but powerful group to subjugate one person, one group, one organization, one government, or one religion, than it is to subjugate dozens and even hundreds of individuals. Therefore the Synagogue of Satan introduced 'Internationalism.' The late William Lyon Mackenzie King, Prime Minister of Canada for nearly a quarter of the twentieth century, sold the Rockefeller family on this idea early in the 1900's, when he was Labor Minister in the Canadian government. Just as Albert Pike worked secretly to bring about a one world government, and a one world religion (Luciferianism), so did Mackenzie King. He specialized in bringing organized labor under control of the international authority because if those placed in control AT THE TOP are agentur of the Synagogue of Satan, organized labor could be used to foment wars and revolutions leading to the destruction of governments and religions. Then, after organized labor had been used to stir up strife between capital and labor and cause economic chaos and turmoil, it could in turn be subjugated in the final stage of the conspiracy. Obviously, an international organization controlled AT THE TOP by the secret agents of the Synagogue of Satan can be more easily controlled, than can hundreds of independent unions and guilds. Does any thinking person believe that the thugs, ex-convicts, and university graduates in economics who control organized labor AT THE TOP are not agentur of the Illuminati, otherwise known as the Synagogue of Satan, if this were true why are those in control trying to make it compulsory for all workers to join unions?

The same principle as Mackenzie King used in organized labor is used by those who direct the W.R.M. AT THE TOP to obtain control of all other fields of human endeavor including the sciences, professions, politics, business, industry, governments, and religions. Thus we see that, previous to the organization of the League of Nations (after World War One ended) the policy of those who directed the W.R.M. AT THE TOP had been to split up and destroy all powerful governments, religions, industrial, financial, capitalistic, and labor organizations, etc., in order that out of the resulting chaos, those affected would gradually accept the idea of Internationalism.

World War Two was fomented, and fought to further soften up nationalism and rugged individualism. The United Nations Organization was set up (on land provided by the Rockefellers, by whom Mackenzie King was employed 1914-1919). The U.N. is intended to give an air of respectability to Internationalism which Communism and Nazism had brought into disrepute. The Synagogue of Satan controls the United Nations as they controlled the League of Nations. Looking back we can see how this "Secret Power" has controlled every strong and powerful group, organization, movement, and government from behind the scenes, by means of 'Specialists,' 'Experts,' and Advisors,' whom they trained and placed in key positions, by using the power and influence their control of GOLD gave them. Every development of the Luciferian conspiracy led to the stage in which the world finds itself today. Its

40

progress can be traced back to the days when Christ told us bluntly and plainly that the Synagogue of Satan controlled ALL those in high places.

Christ spoke the TRUTH. BUT HE DID NOT SAY, NOR DID HE IMPLY, THAT ALL those in High Places realized they were controlled by 'The Synagogue of Satan.' It is for this reason that Christ showed us by the nature, manner, and place of His birth; by His early life of subjection to the lawful and parental authority; by the way He chose His Apostles-humble working men, and by His teachings during the last three years of His life, that if we wish to break free from the bonds with which we are bound more and more strongly every day by 'The Synagogue of Satan,' we must start at the very bottom, at the grass roots, to make known the TRUTH concerning the continued existence of the Luciferian conspiracy, to ALL nations, as quickly as is possible.

It is the perfect wisdom of Christ which justifies Christians' belief in Him as "The Son of God." The fact that Christians don't accept the TRUTH He taught, and follow His advice, illustrates exactly how clever, cunning, and unscrupulous are those devils incarnate who, inspired by Lucifer, comprise 'The Synagogue of Satan,' (S.O.S.). Only the S.O.S., supernaturally inspired, could have prevented the human race from putting God's plan for the rule of Creation into effect upon this earth. Instead, we have allowed those who direct the W.R.M. AT THE TOP to further the secret plans and diabolical ambitions of the High Priests of the Luciferian Creed.

Christ gave us the Lord's prayer so that, by repeating it daily, we would have the above truths impressed upon our minds. It must be obvious that if we did establish God's Kingdom here on earth, His Will would be done here as it is in Heaven. When Christ told those who persecuted Him, "My kingdom is not of this world," He did not say, nor did He imply, that it wasn't our duty to introduce God's plans for the rule of the Universe into our own forms of government.

God's plan requires that religious leaders, truly God's men, should advise our temporal Rulers, and prevent them straying from the true and narrow path. That is the relationship God intended should exist between church and state.

Instead of Holy men, we have allowed the S.O.S. to place evil men in control of ALL those in high places. Our earth is a very, very small potato when compared with the galaxies of heavenly bodies, the suns, stars, and planets which make up the Universe. The Holy Scriptures tell us that the Universe is now split into two parts. One part is Heaven, reserved for those who PROVE they wish to love and serve God voluntarily for all eternity; the other part is Hell, reserved for those who defect from God. Revelations tell us exactly how and when this division will be made definite and final. Then there will be only Heaven and Hell, and they will last for all eternity.

It must be obvious to all thinking people that the reason Christ told us we must start at the bottom and work up, using men and women whose minds have not been brought under control of the Synagogue of Satan (by propaganda introduced into our seats of learning and ALL other channels of public information), is because He knew that ALL those in "High Places" don't realize they are being controlled by the agentur of "The Synagogue of Satan." However, the Devil's agents keep the human race so busily engaged scratching for a living, or seeking riches and carnal pleasures, that the vast majority never have time for prayer and meditation. Our leaders, secular, and religious, never seem to have time to consider anything other than worldly problems ... and the Devil's agents see they are busy with problems which concern the world and the flesh to the exclusion of all spiritual interest and values.

But because the vast majority of those who occupy the HIGH PLACES are elected by the people, it is logical to say that until the people are subjugated it is possible for an enlightened and fully-informed public to create such a force of public opinion, that such force could seriously affect even those who occupy the very highest places in politics, government, economics, industry, the sciences, and religion. In my humble opinion, that is what Christ meant when He told us to "Go and teach the TRUTH to ALL people of ALL nations." Christ made us the promise that if we did so "The TRUTH would set us free." These are the reasons that those who direct the Luciferian conspiracy AT THE TOP keep THEIR true intentions, to enslave the people physically, mentally, and spiritually secret. They deliberately surround the TRUTH with a thick fog of lies, which we term propaganda.

While dealing with this phase of the W.R.M., it is essential to prove that the Synagogue of Satan does not permit even those they select to direct the W.R.M. to suspect they are being used as 'Tools' to bring the Luciferian conspiracy nearer to its final goal.

Gussepi (sometimes referred to as Guiseppe of Joseph) Mazzini has been represented to the people by the controlled press as a great Italian patriot, as were Mackenzie King of Canada and General Albert Pike of the U.S.A., and many others since proved to be hypocrites. These men pretended to serve God, their country and humanity, while in reality they knowingly furthered the secret Luciferian plans. Documentary evidence definitely proves that from 1834 until he died in 1872, Mazzini directed the W.R.M. throughout the world. He used as revolutionary headquarters the Lodges of the Grand Orient, established towards the end of the 18th century by Weishaupt, and the Councils of Pike's New and Reformed Palladian Rite, established the second half of the 19th century in all countries throughout the world.

Mazzini was closely associated with one Dr. Breidenstine. After Mazzini's death in 1872, a letter he had written to Breidenstine came to light. The contents fully illustrate what I mean when I say that not even the directors of the W.R.M. are permitted to know they further the secret plans of the Luciferian conspiracy, unless they have convinced those who constitute the Synagogue of Satan that they have finally and completely defected from God and are suitable and ready for initiation into the FULL, or FINAL SECRET.

Study of Mazzini's 'secret' life proves that he actually accepted Satan as "Prince of the World." He worshipped him as such. As Director of the W.R.M. he was admitted into the Synagogue of Satan, and yet, even as a member of that group, his letter to Breidenstine shows that he had not been initiated into the FULL SECRET, which is that Lucifer is God, the equal of Adonay (our God) and that the ultimate purpose of the W.R.M. is to bring about one form or another of a one world government, the powers of which the High Priests of the Luciferian Creed intend to usurp so they can then impose a Luciferian totalitarian dictatorship upon the people of this world. In the letter referred to, Mazzini wrote, "We form an association of Brothers in all parts of the Globe. We wish to break every yoke. Yet there is one that is unseen; that can hardly be felt, yet that weighs on us. Whence comes it? Where is it? No one knows, or at least no one tells. This association is secret even to us, the veterans of Secret Societies."

The fact that the FULL SECRET is known only to a very few people, is of the greatest importance. It means that as long as there is still time to make the TRUTH known. I proved this statement to be true by making known to Communist leaders in Canada in 1956 the fact that, according to Pike's plan for the final stage of the Luciferian conspiracy, Communism is to be made to destroy itself, together with Christianity in the greatest social cataclysm the world has ever known, to be provoked for that specific purpose by those who direct the Luciferian conspiracy AT THE TOP. This information caused the biggest split in the Communist International that has happened since Lenin usurped power on behalf of the Illuminati in 1917. During 1956-1957 the split in the Communist Party made headlines in the newspapers of the world, and explained WHY Molotov, Malenkov, and others were ousted. The same information has been made known to religious leaders of most Christian denominations, but so far as we know they still refuse to accept the warnings as the TRUTH.

When Mazzini died in 1872, Pike selected Adriano Lemmi, another alleged Italian patriot, to succeed him as Director of the W.R.M. He also was a confirmed Satanist. Pike had established the supervising or directing council of the Political Action section of the W.R.M. in Rome before Mazzini died.

When Pike made his selection a strange situation developed. Lemmi was such a confirmed Satanist that he insisted that all members of Pike's New and Reformed Palladian Rite worship Satan as "Prince of this World," and as their God. He went so far as to have his friend, Brother Carducci, compose a hymn to his Satanic Majesty entitled, The Goddeal Mirror, which, to the great annoyance of Pike, Lemmit ordered to be sung at all Palladian Rite Banquets. This situation developed to the stage when Pike, to end the matter once and for all time, issued a 'Letter of Instruction: Pike, speaking as Sovereign Pontiff of the Luciferian Creed, made this very profound, and from the Christian viewpoint, 'profane,' pronouncement. He addressed it to the heads of the 26 councils of his (Pike's) New and Reformed Palladian Rite, established all over the five continents as the secret headquarters of those he had selected to direct ALL aspects and phases of the W.R.M., so that Communism, Nazism, Nihilism, and every other enemy of God and of His creatures, could be used to further the secret plans of those who directed the Luciferian conspiracy AT THE TOP Pike's letter reads in part: (We quote a translation of it, taken from page 587 of A.C. DeRive's book dealing with this subject, La Femme et l'enfant dans la France- Maconnerie Universale.

"That which we must say to the 'crowd' is, 'We worship God' -but it is the God that one worships without superstition .... The Masonic religion should be, by all of us initiates of the high degrees, maintained in the purity of the Luciferian doctrine ... if Lucifer were not God, would Adonay, whose deeds prove His cruelty, perfidy and hatred of men, barbarism, and repulsion for science would Adonay and His Priests, calumniate him?

"Yes, Lucifer is God. And, unfortunately Adonay is also God. For the eternal law is that there is no light without shade; no beauty without ugliness;

no white without black; for the absolute can only exist as two Gods.... THUS THE DOCTRINE OF SATANISM IS A HERESY; (emphasis added), and the true and pure philosophical religion is the belief in Lucifer, the equal of Adonay. But Lucifer, God of Light and God of Good, is struggling for humanity against Adonay, the God of Darkness and Evil."

We wish to point out that Pike's letter, from which the above quotation has been taken, was translated into French by De Rive, and then translated back into English. Because I have studied this matter from many angles, I believe the word 'crowd' should have been translated as 'Goyim' or 'Masses.' I also believe the translator used the words Masonic Religion when he should have said, "the religion as practiced in the Lodges of the Grand Orient and the Councils of the New and Reformed Palladian Rite." By using the word 'Masonic,' one may be misled, because study of contemporary literature of that time proves that the head of British Masonry had warned the Grand Masters of English Masonic lodges that they, and their members, were not, under any pretext or circumstance, to affiliate with, or associate with Grand Orient Masons, much less Pike's New and Reformed Palladian Rite.

Dom Paul Benoit, recognized as an authority on this subject, and author of *La Cite Antichristienne* (2 parts), and *La France Maconnerie* (2 vols.), says on page 449 of Vol. I. Of FM, "The Reformed Palladian Rite has a fundamental practice and purpose, the adoration of Lucifer. It is full of all the impieties and all the infamies, of black magic. Having been established in the United States (by Pike), it has invaded Europe and each year it is making terrifying progress. All its ceremonial is full ... of blasphemies against God and against our Lord Jesus Christ." Such is the guile, the cunning and deceit of those who direct the Luciferian conspiracy that they not only tolerate, but encourage Satanism in all but the highest degrees. They direct their agentur to place the idea in the public's mind that Freemasonry, Judaism, Roman Catholicism, Communism, Nazism and any or all other organizations with international objectives, are secretly directing the W.R.M., while all the time documentary evidence, and the events of history, prove that the Synagogue of Satan, controlled AT THE TOP by the High Priests of the Luciferian Creed use any and all of the movements whenever it is possible to further their own diabolical secret plans and ambitions.

Lemmi, when head of Grand Orient Masonry in Italy and France, also belonged to Pike's New and Reformed Palladian Rite. Before he was initiated into the FULL SECRET by Pike, Lemmi tried to bring about the destruction of the Vatican by his anticlerical campaigns.

After his initiation, which is said to have been conducted personally by Pike, his attitude and activities suddenly changed. While he outwardly remained anti-clerical and anti-Vatican, he no longer advocated the violent overthrow of the Vatican by force. Pike did with Lemmi what Karl Rothschild had had to do little more than a decade earlier with other Satanists when they stirred up so much anti-Vatican hatred that the governments of France and Italy were on the verge of destroying it. Karl Rothschild, an initiate of the Full Secret, stepped in to act as "Peacemaker" between the Vatican and her enemies. History relates how his intervention 'saved' the Vatican and made Karl Rothschild the 'friend' and 'trusted adviser' of the Pope. He reorganized the affairs of the Treasury and State Departments.

But history has proved that Karl Rothschild was no true friend of the Vatican. Two World Wars, instigated by his family of moneylenders, and their international affiliates who direct the W.R.M., have seen Christians of all denominations divided into opposing camps, been made to fight and kill each other off by the tens of millions. This has been done to bring Pike's plan for the final social cataclysm nearer to fruition. Communism grew stronger as Christianity was weakened, until today, as Pike's plan required, Communism has darkened the entire earth.

While it would be inaccurate to deny that there have been 'bad' Popes, as there have been 'bad' Kings, it is only proper to point out that the 'bad' Popes and Kings were no worse than some of the other leaders of Christianity, when they became presidents of republics. Luciferianism demands that ALL temporal and spiritual authority be destroyed because of their alleged badness. Because the struggle in which we are involved, is against the spiritual forces of darkness, it stands to reason that there must be good and bad people in all walks of life; in all levels of government and in all religions. It is typical of all who serve the Devil's cause that they always use destructive criticism aimed at those in authority, to undermine the confidence and loyalty of the individual in the remaining governmental and religious institutions. This policy helps those who direct the W.R.M. to at first weaken, and then destroy ALL remaining governments and religions. Let us never forget that there is nothing wrong with Christianity. Many things done in the name of Christianity were done by men who, knowingly or unknowingly, furthered the secret plans of the Luciferian conspiracy. What we need to do is lean upon and strengthen Christianity as God would wish.

The above remarks are published to explain how it is that Satanists have always attacked the Popes and the Vatican, and advocated their destruction, while the High Priests of the Luciferian Creed have, to-date, always stepped in and prevented their doing so. The intervention of those who control the Synagogue of Satan AT THE TOP was not out of love or respect for the Pope of the Vatican. They intervened because, being initiated into the FULL SECRET, they knew that when their conspiracy reaches its final stage; after all temporal powers have been reduced in strength until they no longer remain World Powers; when a tired and weary people have been reduced to such a physical and mental condition that they became convinced that ONLY a One World Government can put an end to revolutions and wars, and give them peace, they must use the clash between Communism and Christianity to destroy ALL remaining religious institutions also.

Gen. Albert Pike revealed how this was to be done in the letter he wrote Mazzini August 15, 1871. That part which deals with this particular phase of the conspiracy reads as follows, "We shall unleash the Nihilists and Atheists, and we shall provoke a formidable social cataclysm which in all its horror will show clearly to the nations (people of different nationalities), the effects of absolute atheism, origin of savagery and of the most bloody turmoil. Then everywhere, the citizens obliged to defend themselves against the world minority or revolutionaries, will exterminate those destroyers of civilization, and the multitude, disillusioned with Christianity, whose deistic spirits will be from that moment without compass (direction), anxious for an ideal, but without knowing where to render its adoration, will receive the TRUE LIGHT, through the universal manifestation of the pure doctrine of Lucifer, brought finally out in the public view, a manifestation which will result from the general reactionary movement which will follow the destruction of Christianity and Atheism, both conquered and exterminated at the same time."

We ask the reader to study every word of this diabolically inspired document. According to Pike's military blueprint, drawn up between 1859 and 1871, three global wars and three major revolutions were to place the High Priests of the Luciferian Creed in position to usurp world powers. Two World Wars have been fought according to schedule. The Russian and Chinese revolutions have achieved success. Communism has been built up in strength and Christendom weakened. World War Three is now in the making. If it is allowed to break out, all remaining nations will be further weakened, and Islam and political Zionism will be destroyed as world powers. The reader must not forget that the Arab world is made up of millions of people, many of whom are Christians; many are of the Jewish faith; many are Mohammedans, but all subscribe to belief in the same God Christians worship as the Creator of the Universe. The Koran of the Mohammedan faith is practically identical with the Bible, excepting only that the Mohammedan religion, while accepting Jesus Christ as the GREATEST of God's prophets before Mohammed, does not permit its members to believe in the Divinity of Christ.

The point we wish to make is this: Those who direct the Luciferian conspiracy AT THE TOP realize only too well that before they can provoke the final social cataclysm, they must first of all bring about the destruction of Islam as a world power, because if Islam were not destroyed, it would undoubtedly line up with Christianity in the event of an all-out war with Communism. If that were allowed to happen, the balance of power would be held by Christianity, allied to Mohammedanism, and it would be very unlikely that both sides would conquer and exterminate each other.

It is of the greatest of importance that these facts, which explain the political intrigue and chicanery now going on in the near, middle, and far East, be brought to the attention of ALL political and religious leaders so they may take action to prevent the last phases of the Luciferian conspiracy from being put into effect, and bring to fruition the prediction made in Chapter 20 of Revelations, i.e., that Satan shall be bound for a thousand years.

The events of the past half century would indicate that we are rapidly approaching that period of the world's history when, if it were not for the intervention of God, "No flesh would survive" (Matt. 24:22, Mark 13:20). It is important that the general public know the diabolical fate being prepared for the whole of the human race. I cannot agree with some of the clergy of several denominations, with whom I have discussed this matter at considerable length, who say, "It is better that the public be left in ignorance of their pending fate. To tell them the truth will only alarm them and cause them to panic."

Even some Bishops, who are supposed to be the shepherds of their flocks, hold such views. This is beyond my comprehension. They are like physicians who advocate drugging a person they supposed to be dying at the first indication of pain. If the general public is told the whole TRUTH, knowledge of the TRUTH will certainly make the vast majority of people busy themselves about saving their immortal souls. Knowledge of the TRUTH regarding the diabolically inspired conspiracy will wake them up; it will put an end to lethargy and indifference. As Christ told us the TRUTH will set us free (spiritually) from the bonds with which we are being ever tighter bound, by the spiritual forces of darkness every day. What does it matter if Devil's incarnate kill our bodies provided we prevent them deceiving us into losing our immortal souls? (Matt. 10:28; Luke 12:4).

The TRUTH is that if World War Three is fought, the United States will be the only remaining world power after it is ended. Either ALL people will have to acknowledge that power, or they will clamor for, and demand a world government. And they will get it if the Luciferian conspiracy is allowed to be developed to its intended conclusion. Then, through the auspices of the United Nations, or some similar organization, a puppet King will be made World Sovereign, and he will secretly be under the influence and direction of the agentur of the Synagogue of Satan, who will have been appointed, not elected, to be his "Specialists," "Experts," and "Advisors."

The High Priests of the Luciferian Creed know they cannot usurp world power before the United States is ruined as the last remaining world power, so those who direct the W.R.M. AT THE VERY TOP are arranging matters so the United States will, as Lenin stated, "Fall into our hands like an overripe fruit." This is how events taking place today indicate the subjugation of the U.S.A. is planned.

Pike's plan requires that the final social cataclysm between the masses controlled by atheistic-communism and those who profess Christianity, be fought on a national as well as an international scale. That is the reason, and the only reason, that Communism is being tolerated, while being kept under restraint, in the remaining so-called Free Nations of the World. I have served in the higher levels of government, and in the naval forces, in positions that enabled me to realize that Communism in Canada and in the United States is tolerated, and is being controlled and contained, so its evil destructive force can be used on the national level, as well as the international level, when the final social cataclysm is provoked by those who direct the W.R.M. AT THE TOP.

I have tried to bring this great TRUTH to the attention of cabinet ministers since 1944, when I served on the staff of Naval Headquarters in Ottawa. The late Right Hon. Angus McDonald was then Naval Secretary. Admiral J.C. Jones was Chief-of-Naval Staff. I convinced both these chief executives regarding the TRUTH of what was going on BEHIND THE SCENES of government in Canada and the United States. I was ordered to submit these facts in the form of briefs, so they could be presented to the Canadian cabinet. I know these matters were presented to said cabinet, but Mackenzie King brushed them aside. Col. Ralston, Minister for the Army, and Major 'Chubby' Power, Minister for the Air Force, were so disgusted with Mackenzie King because of the manner in which he wielded autocratic power, that they both resigned from his government, even though it was war time. The Naval Minister told me personally, "Carr, the cabinet is full of the people you wish to expose. I intend to stick with the ship (Navy) until we win the war. Then I am going to resign from federal politics. What is going on is more than I can take …."

When I requested to be de-mobilized in May, 1945 (after Germany collapsed), in order that I might start writing Pawns in the Game and Red Fog over America, Admiral Jones shook my hand as we said goodbye, and said, "I wish you luck with your new books. Publication of the TRUTH, as you have explained it to the Minister and myself, could do more to prevent World War Three than any defensive plan based on armaments." Both of these men died suddenly shortly afterwards.

In 1955 it required six times as many members of the RC.M.P. and the F.B.I. to 'contain' Communism in Canada and the United States, as it did in 1945. In 1956 the Canadian Minister of Justice asked parliament to increase his budget by millions of dollars on the grounds that six RC.M.P. officers were now required to keep check on Communists, where only one was required 10 years before. This was a superlative illustration of the double talk used by men who are involved in the W.R.M. The Minister said: "To keep check on Communists." What he should have said was: "To keep Communism in check until the time is ripe to use it."

I personally knew Inspector John Leopold who for many years headed the anti-subversive department of the RC.M.P. We discussed these matters on many occasions. The RC.M.P and the F.B.I. could arrest every Communist in Canada and the United States within twenty-four hours of the order being given by the heads of the respective departments of Justice, provided the Communists were not tipped off previously. It isn't much of an exaggeration to say that John Leopold had one of his agents sleep with the Communist leaders every night. But the order to destroy the most destructive weapon the leaders of the Luciferian conspiracy possess, by legal means, was not given, and John Leopold retired from the RC.M.P. a broken man, worn out bodily, mentally, and, I am sorry to say, spiritually, because of sheer frustration.

The power of the United States can be destroyed only from within. The internal unrest now being fomented between citizens of different races, colors, and creeds is not so much the result of aggressive action taken by different groups as it is the result of rulings which have been passed by the Supreme Court. Their purpose was the creation of issues and troubles where previously no real issue or problem existed.

I say with all gravity, fully realizing the seriousness of what I say, that if the day is allowed to come when those controlled by atheistic Communism are thrown at the throats of those who profess Christianity, on an international scale, over some real or cooked-up' issue, then Communists in every one of the remaining so-called free nations will be released from the check-reins with which they are now being contained, and, as Pike boasted to Mazzini, the people will experience the worst social cataclysm the world has ever known. What I say is based on documentary evidence supported by historical facts, events which have taken place since the plans were laid. Everything Weishaupt planned between 1770 and 1776 to further the Luciferian conspiracy has developed EXACTLY as he intended. Everything Pike planned between 1859 and 1871 has occurred EXACTLY as he intended. We are now on the verge of World War Three, and about to enter the first stage of the conspiracy. But what is of even greater importance the Holy Scriptures confirm what I say. All a person needs to do, to convince himself of this TRUTH, is to read Matt. 24:1-35 and Mark 13:1-30, and Luke 21: 25-33.

What abominations could the human mind conceive worse than those we know from experience happen when human beings fight civil wars? What could be worse than to use the atomic weapons and nerve gas? It seems that human beings are turned into devils incarnate when engaged in war, particularly civil war, because they practice every abomination upon each other that Dante in his Inferno describes as being practiced in Hell.

Chapter 4

THE LUCIFERIAN DOCTRINE

The Luciferian dogma and doctrines as expounded by Pike and others who at one time or another have been High Priests of the Luciferian creed can be summed up in very few words. It teaches 'inversion' of the Commandments of God. It teaches the exact opposite to what the Holy Scriptures tell was God's plan for the rule of the Universe before Lucifer led the Heavenly revolt. How do we know this statement to be the TRUTH?

The answer is simple. At various times documents of a most serious nature have fallen into hands other than those intended, while being circulated by the High Priests of the Luciferian Creed, to those they had selected to be heads of the Lodges of the Grand Orient and Councils of the New and Reformed Palladian Rite, which have been the secret headquarters of the W.R.M. throughout the world. I call these incidents 'acts of God.'

Raids on Lodges of the Grand Orient and Councils of the New and Reformed Palladian Rite between 1784 and 1924 produced documents and other evidence which prove conclusively the continued existence of the Luciferian conspiracy to obtain ultimate world domination. The raids conducted by the Bavarian government in 1784-1785 produced documents which were published under the title, *The Original Writings of the Order and Sect of the Illuminati*."

The raids conducted by the police under orders of the Hungarian government in 1919 after Bela Kun had usurped power and been deposed, are typical of what we mean.

Further evidence of the Luciferian plot to destroy ALL remaining governments and existing religions is to be found in the book, *Proofs of a Conspiracy to Destroy All Governments and Religions in Europe by Professor John Robison*, of Edinburgh University in 1797. Prof. Robison had been approached by Weishaupt and his leading Illuminists and asked to assist them infiltrating Luciferian ideas, disguised as Illuminism and Progress, into educational institutions and the Lodges of Freemasonry in England and Scotland. He was asked to tour Europe, and, as a 32nd. Mason of the Scottish Rite, he was introduced to leading Illuminists who had set up Grand Orient Lodges throughout Europe. John Robison suspected there was something behind Illuminism as it had been explained to him, but kept his suspicions to himself. He was entrusted with a copy of Weishaupt's revised and modernized edition of the age-old conspiracy as compiled by Zwack, for his study and comments. When the French Revolution broke out in 1789 as part of the conspirator's revolutionary program, Professor Robison decided to publish the information he possessed in support of what the Bavarian government had exposed in 1786.[12]

The investigations of dozens of historians have turned up further evidence which they found in national archives and those of universities. There is no lack of documentary and other kinds of evidence to prove what we are going to say.

The truly amazing thing about the Luciferian conspiracy is the way those who directed it down through the centuries have been able to cause officials of both church and state to brush aside the evidence of proof even when it has been put before them by men whose lives had proved their honesty and integrity and desire to serve God voluntarily. The fact that those who direct the Luciferian conspiracy are able to hold this control over people in high places in politics and religion simply confirms the words of our Lord and Savior Jesus Christ. It illustrates in the clearest possible manner the supernatural characteristics of the conspiracy. It proves that supernatural beings, "Angels," both 'Good' and 'Evil,' exert a great influence on human beings while we are here on earth undergoing our period of trial. It proves that the wiles, the cunning, the lies, and deceits of "Fallen Angels" often affect adversely the council (inspirations) of the "Good Angels." It proves that our human nature, because of the fall of our first parents, inclines more to 'evil' than it does to 'good,' until we are born again spiritually.

We don't want to labor this angle of the W.R.M., but we do want to make it easy for the man-in-the-street to understand what is going on. Those who direct the conspiracy have succeeded in keeping their existence so very secret that lack of knowledge on the part of the public enables them to develop their plot to its intended goal, and wean millions of souls away from God.

This is the Luciferian Creed:

1.   Where God requires a human being to PROVE it wishes to love and serve Him voluntarily for eternity, out of respect for His infinite perfections,

---

12 As these events have been dealt with in full in *Pawns in the Game*, we do not repeat the details here.

Lucifer says, "I will enslave the human race under a totalitarian dictatorship, and deprive them of their physical and mental liberties, and so negate their ability to use their intellect and free will as God intended." (This is the purpose behind the United Nations World Health and World Mental Health Organizations, both of which international movements were started by Dr. Brock Chisholm, of Canada.)

2.   Where the Commandments of God make perfectly clear what He considers sin, Luciferians and their agents teach the inversion of the Commandments of God. Pike and other High Priests of the Luciferian Creed state: "Everything God has made known to be displeasing to Him, is pleasing to Lucifer."

3.   God's plan for creation required everything to be made different. There are no two leaves exactly alike! No two snowflakes. The Luciferian ideology requires regimentation, so that everything can be centralized and made as much alike as possible. Integration is the most typical example of this theory being put into practice. Integration does not mean simply that the public shall accept the principle that people of different races, colors, and creeds shall enjoy the same privileges and considerations as white people. Integration means: "To bring together parts so they form one whole" (i.e., "To make up and complete as a whole").

The Luciferian ideology requires that the human race be integrated absolutely so that Reds, Blacks, Yellows, and Whites be mixed into one vast conglomeration of humanity without any distinctive features, cultures, racial traits, or other peculiarities. (The UNESCO man.)

4.   God's plan requires that there shall be numerous worlds. The scriptures speak of the Seventh Heaven (2 Sam. 22:8; Prov. 8:27-29; II Cor. 12:2). They name the different choirs of angels, their nature, office and characteristics.[13] They tell us that even in each choir, every angel is higher or lower in scale than another. We are told it is possible for those in the lowest choirs to work their way up so they achieve higher status by merit, or descend down the scale because of lack of merit. The Luciferian ideology requires that there shall be only two classes. First, those who govern, i.e., the 'Holders of the Light', the super-intelligent beings,[14,15] and, second those they enslave. Where

13 There are 22 passages in the Scriptures which deal with their nature.
14 That is the reason Weishaupt named his organization The Illuminati.
15 Pike to Mazzini, August 15, 1871

God permits, encourages and rewards individual initiative, Luciferianism does not tolerate it in any shape or form.

5.   God insists that in order to ensure perfect peace and happiness in Heaven, every soul He selects as one of His Elect must have proved that it honestly and sincerely, without qualification or revocation, desires to love and serve God voluntarily out of respect for His infinite perfections for ALL eternity. It is to produce PROOF of this desire that we human beings are being tested so thoroughly. God doesn't intend that there shall be a second revolt in Heaven. Luciferianism, on the other hand, says that permanent peace shall be assured by the King Despot, exercising absolute despotism over his subjects. The Luciferian Protocols say: The Luciferian totalitarian dictatorship when established on this earth will have at its head a King Despot, whose will is to be enforced by satanic despotism.

6.   Where God's plan required 'Love' to be the creative, and 'Charity' the governing force in Nature, the Luciferian Creed says 'Lust' shall be the creative force and 'Right or Might' the governing force.

7.   Where God ordered that each class of His creatures on this earth shall increase and multiply, each according to his kind, the Luciferian ideology requires that in the final stage of the conspiracy only the governing body shall have the 'liberty to enjoy the pleasures-'Lusts' of the flesh, and the 'Right' to gratify their carnal desires. All others are to be made into human cattle, and enslaved physically, mentally, and spiritually, in order to ensure permanent peace and social security. Procreation will be strictly limited to types and numbers determined scientifically as sufficient to fill the requirements to the State, (God). According to Bertrand Russell on pp. 49-51 of his book, *The Impact of Science on Society*, less than 5% of males and 30% of females, will be selected from the Goyim to be used for breeding purposes, and reproduction will be achieved by artificial insemination practiced on an international scale. Investigation has proved that experiments are now being conducted in both Canada and the United States to determine if the semen of human males cannot be preserved and kept fertile indefinitely, the same as the semen taken from prize bulls. Recent discoveries have made it possible to keep semen taken from bulls indefinitely be freezing quickly to a temperature of approximately 130° below zero. Already huge banks have been established in which several million samples of graded semen are stored. Orders received for a particular type or strain can be flown to any part of the world. Smaller banks are now being established in suitable locations to serve the needs of cattle raising states. This

statement is fact, not fiction.[16]

8.   Under God's plan, reproduction of the human species was, and is, intended to be the most holy and sacred function performed by a male and female, joined together in one flesh for the duration of their mortal lives. According to God's plan the primary motive to indulge in sexual intercourse is to procreate another human body into which God can infuse a soul which He wishes to give the opportunity of learning to know Him and love Him, and to will to serve Him voluntarily for all eternity.

Theologians admit that in giving the ability of reproduction 'in accordance to His will,' God gave us powers not even enjoyed by the angels. They are all, both 'Good' and 'Bad,' created beings. The powers God gave to human beings caused those angels who had joined Lucifer to become jealous. That is why Lucifer and/or Satan decided to 'foul up' God's plan as far as procreation of the human species is concerned. This is the reason women have had to present themselves for purification after the birth of a baby since as far back as we have been able to enquire. This is why Baptism was instituted as a Sacrament. This explains why women are required to cover their heads in Church. Because Satan fouled up God's plan, human beings who descended from Adam and Eve are children of the Flesh until they are born again spiritually.

9.   God's plan says that all human beings should love and be charitable towards their neighbors. The word 'neighbor,' as used by Christ, means, "a person who won't do another harm, but rather will go out of his way to do a good turn, even though the recipient be a stranger." The Luciferian doctrine says that in order to impose absolute power by Satanic despotism, those who are selected to rule must first prove they are utterly devoid of human sentiment. According to the pronouncement of Albert Pike, this ridding themselves of human emotions must be carried out by men selected to rule to the extent that they don't even feel love, or sympathy, or any sentimental feeling whatsoever, towards members of the opposite sex. Pike ruled that women initiated into Lodges of Adoption should be made common property. He said members of the Palladian Rite should use them frequently and without passion, but solely to gratify their sexual urges without allowing love or sentiment, "which lead so

---

16 The author has seen these deep-freeze semen banks, and had their present use and purpose explained to him. He was also briefed on the plan to eliminate the birch of crippled and diseased human beings by resorting to methods of procreation similar to those practiced by the best-informed cattle breeders.

many human hearts astray," entering into their sexual relationships. "Thus," he says, "men shall enchain women while obtaining absolute control of their own human weaknesses." So we see that everything that God considers 'Good,' Lucifer says is 'evil.' Everything God considers "Strength of character," Luciferians consider "Weakness of character."

10.   God's plan requires that human beings care for the sick, the disabled, the imprisoned, and the aged. The Luciferian ideology insists that ALL Goyim who become unable, or unfit, to serve the state efficiently shall be destroyed. This diabolical principle is being made acceptable in the minds of innocent human beings by being presented as "Mercy killing" the scientific name for which is euthanasia.

11.   God's plan for civilized society is based on the principle that two human beings of opposite sex shall establish a home and raise family. Luciferians say that the destruction of the family and home is absolutely essential to the success of their conspiracy.

12.   God's plan required the parents to provide for their offspring, and to educate them in God's Holy Will and the facts of life. Luciferians say the state shall regulate births and raise the children born as the result of planned selective breeding. They insist that ONLY the state has the right to 'educate' (forgive the use of the word by such devils in human form) those they intend shall serve the state.

13.   God's plan intends to elevate the dignity of man until he achieves a high degree of spiritual perfection. The Scriptures tell us that we can qualify for the highest vacant seats in Heaven. Luciferianism is insistent that every human being be reduced to its lowest possible level. It was to further this diabolical theory that Cromwell's "Levellers" drove in the thin edge of the wedge. Today it has advanced to the stage where women have demanded the 'right' to adopt the same immoral codes as men; the right to smoke, to do everything that does not elevate them above the filth, the dirt, and slime of decadent human nature. God sets up chastity as a virtue; Lucifer says we must be promiscuous to demonstrate our Godship. Christ proved by His devotion and love and respect for His earthly mother Mary, that God intended motherhood to be the greatest of all vocations. Christ's relationship to His earthly mother, and Mary's love and devotion to her Son, should tell us that, despite the Fall of Eve, He still wants woman to be a being of beauty, charm and grace, full of love, charity, and affection. He wants women to be real mothers, not just human incubators

who accidentally conceive due to human error. Luciferianism is determined to drag womanhood down into the gutter, and to the level of the natural state of the lower beasts of creation.

14. God provided everything we require for our use and benefit. He ordered that we use ALL things in moderation. The Luciferian ideology says, but doesn't intend, that man shall be a law unto himself and do as he pleases.

15. God's plan of creation placed everything He created in perfect balance. Those who are developing the Luciferian conspiracy to its ultimate objective are doing their level best to put God's creation out of balance, and the human race pays the penalty for the " sins of presumption" committed by Luciferians.

We could go on and on, proving that Luciferianism is diametrically opposed to God's plan for the rule of creation. The point we hope we have made is this: The Luciferian ideology has been drawn up to appeal to men who consider themselves intellectual giants. Lucifer knows that his totalitarian ideology is wrong. When he occupied the highest throne in heaven, and was subordinate to God alone, his pride convinced him that if he set up his own kingdom and ruled it with absolute despotism, every aspect and phase of his dominion would have to work peacefully, efficiently, and economically.

He used his supernatural powers to force the hand of Almighty God. Because God derives pleasure only from those of His creatures who love to serve Him voluntarily, because of their respect for His infinite perfections, He had to let Lucifer go to his eternal damnation or change the principle on which He had established His rule.

That Lucifer has realized his enormous mistake cannot be doubted. But his 'Pride' wouldn't allow him to admit it. How many, many human beings act like Lucifer in that respect today? The Hitlers, the Mussolinis, the Roosevelts, the Rockefellers, the Rothschilds, the Churchills - all of those who spread Luciferianism from their seats at the top levels of our civilization. How many of our lower orders ape them and follow them? They lead us, as Lucifer led so many of the heavenly host, to our destruction!

Now that I have studied this subject for so long and from so many angles, I don't find it difficult to understand how Lucifer's supernatural capacity to LOVE God, his Creator, turned into an equal capacity to HATE God, all of

God's creatures, and all His wonderful creation. I don't find it hard to understand that after Lucifer put his totalitarian ideology into practice in his Kingdom of Darkness, which we term Hell, and found out that what he considered PERFECT in theory, didn't work out as he expected in actual practice, his disappointment caused his hatred to mount until it has reached astronomical dimensions beyond the understanding of the human mind.

I no longer find it difficult to accept the definition of Hell as given to us in Revelations. In fact, I find it easy to understand that after the final judgment, every one of the Fallen Angels and every human soul who has been deceived by Lucifer and his other Princes of Darkness, into defecting from God, must of necessity hate not only Lucifer, along with his ruling princes, but also themselves and their neighbors. If it is true that selfish, foolish PRIDE has led the vast majority of those in Hell to their own damnation, it is not difficult to understand WHY the conditions in Hell are conditions of utter HATE, chaos and confusion. If it is true that the inhabitants of Hell are there because they accepted and practiced the inversion of the Commandments of God then it should not be difficult for the person of average intelligence to understand that all abominations, those who directed the Luciferian conspiracy introduced to this earth of ours, are being practiced in Hell and will continue for all eternity.

There can be no doubt that this world of ours has been turned by demonic forces into a 'Little Hell.' Due to the fact that we refuse with a blind obstinacy, to accept God's law, and put His plan into effect on this earth, conditions have been bad enough, and there can be no doubt that if we remain blind to the TRUTH, and obstinate in our refusal to PROVE our desire to love and serve God voluntarily for all eternity, then conditions must of necessity deteriorate until, as the Bible states, they will reach the point that if it were not for the intervention of God, no flesh would survive. (Matt. 24:22; Mark 13:20.)

That conditions here, and in Hell, are what they are is not the Will or intention of God. They exist because of Lucifer's selfish, foolish pride, and his determination to be self-sufficient. He defected from God. He took multitudes of others with him. It is only logical to suppose that after he realized his mistake, his hate reached the proportions that he was determined to continue to be revenged on God by deceiving His creatures. God wished to fill the vacancies left by Lucifer and his angels. Lucifer cares not what befalls those he deceives, or even what is in store for himself. This utter lack of further interest in anything is real despair!

Artists, preachers, authors, and others have depicted Hell and its inhabitants in such an exaggerated way that, instead of making people believe in it, they have caused untold millions, particularly in the last two centuries, to discredit its very existence. These so-called intellectuals have served the Luciferian cause well indeed, because when one rejects God, he automatically rejects the idea of Heaven and Hell.

Chapter 5

SATANISM BEFORE AND
AFTER THE ADVENT OF CHRIST

My personal experience proved I was unable to piece together the many thousands of pieces of information and evidence, I had gathered since 1918 concerning the World Revolutionary Movement, (W.R.M.) until quite by "accident" I picked up a Bible in 1943 and started to glance through it because, I am now ashamed to confess, I was bored stiff lying on a hospital bed, with no other literature within reach which I hadn't already read.

Ever since that day I have been convinced that what the vast majority of people call "accidents" or mere coincidence, are in reality "Acts of God." I don't go so far as to say that the Creator of this universe personally does things to us which will, if we heed what happens, seriously affect our lives, but I do believe that He wills such things to happen and his angels, who are associated with this world of ours, put His Divine Will into effect. Be that as it may. As I glanced through the Bible I could not help but see that many statements seemed to have a direct connection with events of history and events which were happening in this the 20th Century. This aroused my interest. Further study convinced me that in the Bible was to be found the "key" which would unlock the mystery which surrounds what so many authors have referred to in the past as The Secret Power which rules from BEHIND the scenes of ALL governments and causes them to adopt policies which ultimately lead to their own destruction. I therefore began to seek in the Bible the explanation of human events with which I had become familiar, but couldn't fathom the "CAUSE" or "REASON" for their happening. With this explanation I will proceed to explain "Satanism" as I understand it.

Satanism is the manual of action which puts the Luciferian conspiracy into effect on this earth. The Old Testament, trimmed down to its greatest simplicity, is nothing more or less than the "History of Satanism." It tells us how it has been directed since the Fall of our first parents to the Advent of Christ who came to set us free from the bonds of Satanism with which the human race was being more securely tied generation after generation. The Holy Scriptures refer to Satan sixty-seven times and to Christ only sixty-three. But what concerns us most is the fact that the Holy Scriptures tell us, and prove, that "Satan is Prince of this World" (John 12:31; 14:30; 16:2). Because Satan is

"The Adversary" of God and his human creatures, he must, as "Prince of this World," be related to the W.R.M.

The word "World" has admittedly different connotations. We can define the word in a "favorable" or "neutral" sense and use it to mean "The earth where men dwell" or by metonymy "men themselves." (John I. 9-10; III. 16, 17, 19; Genesis 27. etc.)

The word "World" can also be used, in the unfavorable sense, to mean "The reign of evil on earth." Those who constitute the "Reign of evil" are the Synagogue of Satan. What they inspire and do, and have done, is diametrically opposed to the WILL OF GOD; they set up a barrier between this world and Christ and his followers. To illustrate this, Christ is recorded by John as saying "I am not of this world ... I pray not for this world ... me it hateth." And to his disciples "You are not for the world ... the world hateth you," and so on. (John VIII. 23; XVII. 9; VII. 7; XV 19; etc.; I John III. 13,14).

Thus we can understand that, ever since the advent of Jesus Christ, Satanism has waged a perpetual war to prevent God's children on this earth from putting God's plan for the rule of the entire universe into operation upon this earth. By preventing us putting God's plan into effect; and by preventing us living "The way of life" as taught to us by Christ, and summarized in the words of "The Lord's Prayer," Satanism prevents the masses from doing God's Will on earth as it is done in Heaven.

This brings us to the interpretation of the Lord's Prayer. The preamble and middle require no explanation but the words, "And lead us not into temptation but deliver us from evil," most certainly do. How can we conceive that God would "LEAD" the members of the human race into temptation? He may, and undoubtedly does, permit us to be tempted by those who direct or serve Satanism. The Scriptures tell us God will not permit us to be tempted beyond our powers of resistance. Thus temptation enables us to PROVE whether we are "For" or "Against" God.

I have, as the vast majority of Christians have also done, repeated the Lord's Prayer daily since I could talk. But I never studied the words until I was on the flat of my back with a fractured spine in 1943. As the result of studying the words in their relation to Satanism, and the W.R.M., I reached the conclusion that the words would have had a better relationship had the interpretation into English been "And let us not be led into temptation; but deliver us from the Evil One (Satan)." I was pleased to discover, long afterwards, that the Greek fathers of early Christianity; the ancient Roman fathers; and several liturgies were strongly in favor of the masculine rather than the neutral use of the words "A malo." The importance of this question is to be found in the FACT that if we should be saying "But deliver us from the Evil One (Satan)" it would automatically mean that Christ considered Satanism the author of ALL temptation and all the evil (sin) we can commit and, at the same time, be the director of all the evils we can be made to suffer as a means of weaning us away from Faith in God.

These thoughts caused me to do further research, and I found in the New Testament, and in the texts of the "Desert Fathers," that Satan, and those of the Synagogue of Satan, exercise a general direction or superintendence over ALL the evil, temporal, and spiritual, which is committed, or experienced, in this world.

In support of this very interesting revelation, as far as the W.R.M. is concerned we find that "He that committeth sin is of the devil" (1 John 3:8) and according to the Gospels and Epistles of St. John and St. Paul, it is Satan's empire Christ came to overthrow, and Satan and his agents (agenturs) are the root and cause of all evil, both spiritual and temporal, which ravages humanity. Much nearer our own time St. Augustine supports this line of reasoning when he likens what is going on in the world to "The city of sin, the devil, born as the result of the rejection of God (by our first parents) as being in eternal opposition to the "City of God." St. Thomas doesn't entirely agree with this definite and exact interpretation so, as happens so often, it is just another case of everybody to their own liking.

But, when we study the W.R.M. in its relationship to Satanism as being practiced on this earth, it is important to remember that if Satan, or his agents in human form, can and do influence the decisions of individuals so they commit sin, it stands to reason that individual human beings so influenced can and do extend Satan's power for evil over the collective. Thus I found my reasoning to be based on a sound premise when I stated in *Pawns in the Game* and *The Red Fog Over America* that individuals who knowingly or unintentionally serve the cause of Satanism are responsible for stirring up dissensions which enable them to divide the masses into opposing camps on political, racial, social, economic, religious, and other issues, in order that they can then be armed and made to fight wars and revolutions, on an ever increasing scale, so that, if this destructive policy is permitted to continue, it must lead to the final destruction of ALL forms of remaining governments and religions, and thus leave the field wide open for those who constitute the Synagogue of Satan, to impose the Luciferian totalitarian dictatorship upon what remains of the human race.

This brings us to another very important question. We might ask, as so many priests and ministers do, "If the Gates of Hell shall not prevail against the Church of Christ, and if God is going to cast Satan and his followers down into Hell following the final judgment, what is there to worry about?"

In my humble opinion, there is nothing "to worry about," but a great deal remains to be done before that blessed event happens in order to save as many souls as possible from being deceived into defection from God. We can prove, as individuals, that we honestly and sincerely desire to love and serve God voluntarily for all eternity. We must work tirelessly to bring other souls to join us in that desire. In other words, we must become, as Christ admonished us, real soldiers of Jesus Christ and active enemies of the Synagogue of Satan. If lies and deceits are the stock-in-trade used by the forces of evil, then we must shame the Devil and confound his knavish tricks, by telling the TRUTH, as far, as wide, and as quickly as possible. If individual assassinations, and wholesale murder (wars and revolutions) are the means by which the Satanic forces remove all obstacles from their path which delay them in usurping absolute world domination, then we must use every legal means to prevent wars and revolutions.

Why does Satanism work to bring about a One World Government when powers of which they plan to usurp?

Today the power held by the Synagogue of Satan is neither general, nor complete, nor absolute. The Forces of Evil conspire to make their power absolute so they can enslave what remains of the human race absolutely, body, mind, and soul. Satanism believes in no half measures. When it comes to using lies and deceits, for the purpose of winning our immortal soul for Lucifer, they operate on the principle, "winner takes all."

The Scriptures in Revelations tell us exactly what the final results will be. But the Synagogue of Satan does not accept the Scriptures as the inspired word of God. Therefore, those who serve the Synagogue of Satan will continue to develop the Luciferian conspiracy in the belief that they will be able to establish a totalitarian dictatorship. They believe that if they can usurp world power they can establish physical control over our bodies. They believe that this physical control will enable them to obtain mental control also (Psychopolitics). They believe that mental control will enable them to erase all knowledge of God from the human mind and thus give Lucifer control of our souls for all eternity.

Thus we arrive at the point which reveals what is meant by the phrase (used so often by Communist writers, or I should say Satanist authors who write to promote Communist and other subversive movements), "the battle going on is for the minds of men." This proves that the ultimate objective of the W.R.M. is not materialistic, as is generally supposed, but definitely spiritual, which so few authors and historians seem to have suspected. Reasoning along this line of thought brings us to the understanding of how the words "World Revolutionary Movement" are only the deceptive words Satanists use to conceal the existence of the continuing Luciferian conspiracy. They make the vast majority of people, ordained ministers as well as Christian Laymen, believe that Communism is the root of all existing evil, that it is atheistic and materialistic, and that control of temporal power is the ultimate objective. This HALF-TRUTH is the biggest lie ever circulated by those who serve the Father of Lies. The TRUTH is revealed in Ephesians 6:10-17 which tells us among other things "our wrestling (struggle) is NOT against flesh and blood but against Principalities and the Powers, against the world rules of this darkness, and against the SPIRITUAL forces of wickedness on high." The other half of the truth concealed from the general public is the fact that the Synagogue of Satan control and use the destructive force of Communism to further their secret plans to achieve world domination. The Principalities, and the Powers, are sections of the Heavenly Host from which Lucifer undoubtedly recruited many followers.

The world ruler of darkness, is the Synagogue of Satan who is inspired by "the spiritual forces of wickedness on high" to put the continuing Luciferian conspiracy into effect. Thus we are able to understand exactly what we are up against. As we live our period of trial on this earth, we have to contend with:

1. The High Priests of the Luciferian Creed. We will prove that human beings who have been head of the Priesthood admit they had the powers to contact and consult members of the celestial world who had joined Lucifer in his revolt against the absolute supremacy of God.

2. The Synagogue of Satan, who put the Luciferian conspiracy into effect.

3. The secret societies who believe in and practice Satanism and whose members are the "Agentur" who serve the Synagogue of Satan.

4. All those who, because of the lies of those who constitute the "World Rulers of this darkness," have defected from God and follow a "Destructive" way of life as opposed to the "Constructive" way of life Christ taught us is God's Holy Will.

We will now study Satanism as it is practiced in this world. The vast majority of people, due to the manner in which they have been taught, cannot seem to make themselves believe that Satanism is actually practiced on this earth. Let us ask these good people a very simple question: "How could Satan be Prince of this World if he didn't have a government and the means of deceiving millions upon millions of human beings into serving him and furthering his intentions?"

They don't seem able to realize that Christ came on earth to expose the existence of the continuing Luciferian conspiracy such as it is directed on this earth by Satan, and by those who serve him who are, in reality, devils in human form. Christ made this very clear when he said to his Apostles: "Have I not chosen all twelve of you? And one of you is a devil." (John 6:70) And at the Last Supper do we not read, "The devil had already put it into the heart of Judas, son of Simon the Iscariot, to betray Him," and a little later, "The morsel once given, Satan entered into him; and Jesus said to him, "Be quick on thy errand." Judas was used by the Synagogue of Satan not by the Jewish people, and by accepting the thirty pieces of silver he opened the door of his heart and Satan entered into it.

Then it is interesting to note the words Christ used when being arrested. He said: "But this is your hour and (the hour of) the power of darkness." (Satan and/or Lucifer) - (Luke 22:53).

It has puzzled me a great deal to try to find out whether we are in the stage of the Luciferian conspiracy when Satan is about to be bound for a thousand years, or if Satan was bound for the thousand years, as mentioned in Revelations, at the time of, and by the death of Jesus Christ. As I have pointed out before the words "Day" and "Years" have more than one meaning; so could the words "A thousand years" simply mean "a period, or a long period of time," as expressed in the common saying "Not in a thousand years."

If the words "A thousand years" mean "A period of time," then the Scripture most definitely tells us we are fast approaching the time when God will intervene on behalf of His elect. This means that the day of final judgment is fast approaching also.

66

We can take it that the death of Our Lord, and his triumphant resurrection is to mean "sentence is now passed on this world (the principality of Satan); now is the time the Prince of this World (Satan) is to be cast out." (John 12:31 etc.) And while those who accept the Luciferian doctrine don't agree, the Scriptures assure us that Christ did succeed in his mission. And then we come to an extraordinary thing concerning the Bible. The part that should have declared, and explained, Christ's victory over Satan, as Prince of this World, seems to have been badly fouled up. I refer to Colossians 2:14. Translators such as Douay, Westminster, Knox as authorized and revised versions will show, give different and in a way contradictory meanings to the original words, which I "think" best interpret the TRUTH as St. Paul wished it to be understood. Speaking of Christ's triumph over the forces of evil, who governed this world until his advent, he corrected the false teachings of those who taught education and religion; He exposed laws and decrees which were opposed to God's Law and/or the Laws of Nature; He lifted the curtain behind which the Synagogue of Satan directed the Luciferian conspiracy, and He exposed the lies and deceits they used to cause human beings to defect from God. He "nailed the truth to the Cross," for all to see who wish to see. The Rev. Bernard Flemming in an article "The Adversary" gives as his translation of Colossians 2:14, "Christ ... blotted out the handwriting that was against us, with its decrees; lifted it clean away, nailing it to the cross, and despoiled the principalities and powers, put them to open shame, and led them away in triumph through the cross."

The task we are trying to perform is to convince the general public that Satanism is a very real and active force on this earth, whose purpose it is to try to defeat God's plan for the rule of creation being put into effect upon this earth.

We are trying to prove that Christ defeated the Luciferian conspiracy here as he did in Heaven. We are offering evidence which indicates we are living in the period of the world's history when Satan broke or was released from the bonds with which Christ had bound him for a "thousand years." He is now using the Synagogue of Satan to bring about the wars and revolutions, and other abominations which would, if not stopped by the intervention of God, on behalf of His elect, destroy all flesh. Atomic and H-bombs, nerve gas, and other secret weapons developed recently by those doing research into chemical and bacteriological warfare, have made it possible for a diabolically minded, satanically controlled mind to launch us into the final social cataclysm as planned by Pike by simply pressing a button. We call it "push button war."

And to assure my readers that those who bear witness to the TRUTH, as God has revealed it in Holy Scriptures, and as Christ explained it to us, are of the elect, we will quote Apoc. 12:9-12: "The great dragon, serpent of the primal age; was flung down to earth; he whom we call the devil, or Satan, the whole world's seducer, was flung down to earth, and his angels with him. Then we heard a voice crying aloud in heaven; the time has come; now we are saved and made strong, Our Lord reigns, and the power belongs to Christ, His anointed; the accuser of our brethren is overthrown. Day and night he stood accusing them in God's presence; but because of the Lamb's blood, and because of the truth to which they bore witness, they triumphed over him, holding their lives cheap till death took them. Rejoice over it, Heaven, and all you that dwell in Heaven."

The fact that the Kingdom of Satan in this world is surrounded by darkness (secrecy) as is the Luciferian Kingdom in the celestial world; and the further fact that the High Priests of the Luciferian Creed, and the members of the Synagogue of Satan, hide their identity and true purpose from the masses; and the further fact that they worship Satan and conduct their diabolically inspired ceremonies in secret chambers in Lodges of the Grand Orient and Councils of the New and Reformed Palladian Rite, doesn't detract from its power and influence over the affairs of this world and its people, in the slightest. On the contrary, the fact that those who direct the Luciferian conspiracy AT THE TOP can, and do, keep secret their identity, and their ultimate intention to enslave what is left of the human race, body, mind and soul, contributes to the success of their evil plans.

The fact that Christ did expose and condemn the Synagogue of Satan, its existence, and evil influence and purpose in this world has never been denied by theologians and leaders of religions. But such is the power of Satan that he has prevented a true and realistic impression being made on the human mind. The average person has been taught to think of the Devil as the most horrible creature imaginable; they have been taught to believe that Hell is an abyss or pit filled with fire and brimstone in which Lucifer, his fallen angels, and lost human souls simmer and sizzle for all eternity without ever being consumed. This misleading teaching of what constitutes Hell, Lucifer, and his fallen angels, has caused multitudes of people to defect from God and land in the very Hell they were deceived into believing a myth.

Notwithstanding the fact that the Fathers of the early Christian Church fully realized the enmity existing between Christ and Satan, and knew that Satanism

68

would continue to work in the dark and use lies and deceits to wean human beings away from God in order that their souls would be damned, they did not seem able to get the TRUTH regarding this all important matter across to the masses of the people. They taught the "Greatness and Perfections" of God and the "Goodness and Meekness" of Jesus Christ. They told of the wickedness of Satan and the Devil, but they didn't trouble to explain how the forces of evil upon this earth have operated since the fall of our first parents. Thus it was that Satanism, disguised in a thousand ways, and operating under a hundred different names, grew stronger and stronger without the general public knowing what was really behind the scenes causing all the evil things they had to suffer.

While we don't wish to labour this matter there is evidence which indicates that with the death and resurrection of Jesus Christ, Satan was cast back into Hell and there bound, as far as his being Prince of this World is concerned, for a thousand years. We believe according to the Apostles' Creed that Christ descended into Hell immediately after the death of his mortal body. Couldn't it have been to see that Satan was secured as well as to release the souls of the just who had been detained in that part of Hell called limbo until Christ had redeemed them?

Then, again, the Luciferian conspiracy seems to have had very poor direction on this earth from the time Christ left us until about A.D. 1,000. Christianity had flourished. It was progressing, church and state were trying to get along together. The Church was advising rulers in regard to God's plan for the rule of the universe, and the rulers were seemingly trying to put that plan into effect. Paganism was dying a natural death under the glare of the Light of Holy Scriptures. But as the thousand years ended Satanism broke out again in all its diabolical force and fury, and Satan again became Prince of this World. He and his agentur made "good" men pave their paths to hell with good intentions never put into practice. They split the Christian religion into a thousand fragments. They caused the Church and state to fight each other. They caused the human race to start dividing and fighting each other, till the heads of both Church and state seemed agreed on one point: Satanism was the root of ALL EVIL being inflicted upon the world and its inhabitants.

Satanism was so apparently the cause of all evil that in the 13th Century the Pope introduced the Inquisition in the hope the inquisitors would be able to root out the evil. How the High Priest of the Luciferian Creed must have doubled up with demoniacal laughter! They sat back and watched the Princes of the Christian Church and Kings of Christian countries tormenting human beings with the very tortures of the damned, and doing this diabolical task in the sweet and holy name of Jesus Christ. All the Inquisition did was torture and kill hundreds of human beings who, if they hadn't defected from God before they fell into the hands of the inquisitors, would almost certainly have lost their belief in Him before death ended their sufferings, considering their tortures were inflicted in the name of God.

Can any person with a sane mind believe God wishes His priests to commit such atrocities as the Inquisition?

The Inquisition was demonically inspired. It served the Luciferian cause in as much as it enabled Satanists to turn thousands of people away from the Church of Christ. The Inquisition enabled the enemies of Christ to split the Church of Christ wide asunder; it enabled Satanism to divide the united power of Church and state. It was the origin of those things which led to the Reformation and from the Reformation on enabled Satanism to split the Christian religion into more than 400 different denominations. The Inquisition enabled those who directed the W.R.M. AT THE TOP to put their principle of "first divide and then conquer" into full operation.

What a difference there would have been if, instead of persecuting a few thousand people who were accused of heresy and/or sorcery, the heads of Church and state had joined forces and taught the masses the TRUTH regarding Satanism, its diabolical direction, and purpose. If the masses had been told by their priests and rulers that the purpose of the Luciferian conspiracy was to ultimately enslave the whole of the human race, body and mind, in order that they could ruin their immortal souls, Satanism would have ended right there and then. A fully informed public could not be led from one evil to another. A fully informed people could not have been led into wars and revolutions.

But such is the power and cunning of the Devil that those who served him caused the heads of both Church and state to torture and kill those judged guilty of Satanism instead of making publicly known the details of the Luciferian conspiracy and thus depriving the agents of the devil of their opportunity to deceive a gullible and ignorant people.

By the 16th Century Satanism had obtained such a tremendous control over the thinking, and actions of the world's leaders that thirty-two ecclesiastical and twelve civil measures were passed against Satanism between 1484 and 1682.

The power of those who direct the Luciferian conspiracy, AT THE TOP, can be fully appreciated when it is pointed out that despite the knowledge and awareness of the leaders of Christianity, both ecclesiastical and secular, the Synagogue of Satan were able to restrict inquisition to individuals who were accused of witchcraft or sorcery. Thus between 1532 and 1682, 400 individuals were accused of practicing Satanism all over the Christian world including Nemesis, Carolina, U.S.A. Many of those accused were betrayed by enemies. They knew no more about Satanism, as it is practiced and directed AT THE TOP, than did their judges and executioners.

In 1776, the Synagogue of Satan was comprised of men of great intellect-mental giants-who because of their acquisition of wealth or achievements in the fields of finance, science, literature, the arts, and industry became literally "AS PROUD AS LUCIFER" whom they secretly worshipped as their God. These evil tycoons controlled Satanism AT THE TOP They plotted how they could best use the masses to place ultimate world domination in their hands, or the hands of their Luciferian successors. While individual Satanists including witches and sorcerers were busy dragging weak-minded, spineless victims down into Hell, the real leaders of Satanism were plotting to obtain mass control of the bodies and minds of the human race so that they could deprive them of their God-given gifts of an intellect and Free Will.

Those who directed the conspiracy threw many a hare to the hounds of justice so that they went chasing a single hare and overlooked the real massed enemy. The conspirators sacrificed just as many Jews and Gentiles as were needed to safeguard their own identity and hide their own diabolical purposes. The Powers of Evil even caused ecclesiastical and civil authorities to become involved in the prosecution, and persecution, of innocent children. These cases brought both ecclesiastical and civil authorities into disrepute. They furthered the secret plans of the conspirators to bring about the destruction of all forms of government and religion.

Such is the Power of Satanism that it extends not only over civic governments but, unfortunately, into religious government as well. It extends over secret societies, industry, finance, science, the professions, etc., etc. While remaining invisible itself, it holds a control that can scarcely be felt but is absolutely dominating as Mazzini so truly said.

Satanism controls also all that is evil in this world: all that serves the Devil's negative purposes. Take drug peddling! Only the pushers, never those who control it AT THE TOP are prosecuted Satanists could not control illegal traffic and trade, and use that control to enslave thousands of victims, and blackmail other thousands of influential people, if the traffic and trade wasn't made illegal in the first place.

What we are trying to say is this: if legislation, supposedly passed to protect humanity against the powers of evil, had never been passed, a few individuals, who lacked the self-control would suffer the result of their immoderation.

But once legislation makes the selling or possession of a commodity a crime, the Synagogue of Satan can then form syndicates which operate to defeat the ends of justice while making millions of dollars profit for themselves. Thus they extend their powers from individuals to organizations, societies, and governments. I realize some readers will think this is a terrible thing to say, but prohibitory legislation is against God's plan.

Everything He created can be used for our benefit. If we abuse what He gave us, we pay the penalty. It is a fact that nobody ever has, or ever will be, legislated into heaven. Legislation never kept a Satanist out of hell.

Prohibition enabled the Synagogue of Satan to establish a government within a government. The Synagogue of Satan established a Kingdom in the underworld. It enabled those who direct the W.R.M., AT THE TOP, to make billions of dollars while advancing their control on society as well as over the underworlds of all big cities. Today, exactly as the Protocols say would happen, the Princes of the underworld are lords of society. Ex-gang leaders now own fabulous resorts and legalized gambling palaces in the sanctuaries in which the S.O.S. intend to hide in case of war and/or revolution. They set the pace and fashions in so-called society. The proper procedure should be for proper authority to arrest and restrain, and try to cure individuals who sin against God to the extent that their actions prove dangerous or harmful to society.

If God hadn't forbidden Adam and Eve to eat the fruit on the Tree of Life they couldn't have sinned. But God made it possible for Adam and Eve to sin in order that they could prove they sincerely wished to love and serve Him voluntarily for all eternity. Death, as punishment, fitted their crime. Satan caused Eve to sin because she believed him when he promised to initiate her into the secret of procreation and make her equal in power to her, and his, creator. Eve learned to procreate, but God proved only He could create creatures which live forever. That is why we, the children of Adam and Eve must die. That is why we must be born again of the Spirit before we can be reunited with God.

Chapter 6

SECRET SOCIETIES AND
SUBVERSIVE MOVEMENTS

Nesta Webster published a book named *Secret Societies and Subversive Movements* to expose how they were used to further the W.R.M. She did not, however, come right out and say "The Secret Power" which controls all secret societies and subversive movements, AT THE TOP, is the Synagogue of Satan. She does not carry her subject beyond its materialistic and temporal characteristics.

She threw a great deal of light on Adam Weishaupt's secret life. She credits him with being the author of *The Original Writings of the Order and Sect of the Illuminati* and the founder of the Illuminati. With these statements I cannot agree.

My studies and research satisfied me that Weishaupt only revised and modernized the Protocols of the Luciferian Conspiracy in order to enable the Synagogue of Satan to take full advantage of the progress being made in applied science, and the rapidly changing social, political, economic, and religious conditions. He didn't originate Illuminism!

The Illuminati simply means "Holders of the Light" just as the word "Protocols" means "Original written draft of a plan designed to achieve a definite stated purpose." The Illuminati has existed since Cain defected from God. The Protocols were written just as soon as man mastered the art of expressing his thoughts, and recording his future plans by writing on material which could be preserved. The Protocols were written long before Zion was ever heard of.

Adam Weishaupt was at the age of 28, a professor of Canon Law at Ingolstadt University. He was a mental giant, commanding great respect in educational circles. Because he was Jesuit trained, many non-Catholics claim the Jesuits are "The Secret Power" which puts the Pope of Rome's plan, to win ultimate world domination, into effect. Following this line of reasoning the enemies of the Roman Catholic Church claim that it is this religious institution which is "The mystery, Babylon the great, the mother of harlots and abominations of the earth." (Rev. 17:5)

My studies have convinced me that Illuminism, under the name "Perfectionism," was practiced within the Jesuit Order long before Weishaupt defected from God and became a Luciferian. Both movements, Illuminism and Perfectionism, were started to encourage human beings to become as near perfect as possible. There is an old saying "The road to hell is paved with the good intentions of those who failed to put them into practice." The Jesuit Order was the greatest teaching order during the 17th and 18th Centuries. The Synagogue of Satan, quite naturally, infiltrated its agentur into the order as they infiltrate into every level of society. Their agentur hid their true identity. They were clever enough not to be openly critical of the curriculum of the Jesuits. They simply advised those who set up the curriculum not to teach too much about the existence of the Luciferian conspiracy or tell the students how and why it was directed.

Just so Catholics will not become antagonistic because of what I reveal regarding this aspect of the conspiracy which we call "The conspiracy of silence," I wish to remind them that even the Popes have blamed the rapid development of Satanism upon the manner in which priests have neglected to inform their parishioners on this all important matter.

The Bull "Summis Desiderantes" of Pope Innocent VIII issued December 6, 1484, was for a long time considered to be the papal declaration of war against witchcraft, which is only another word for Satanism. Why the ordained ministers of the Christian religions won't call a spade a spade when dealing with Satanism, and its ultimate purpose, is difficult to understand. Is it that they too are controlled AT THE TOP by Satanists who insist that they use the words "witchcraft" and "Sorcerers"? But when we study thoroughly what this Pope said, we find he added nothing new to the subject of Satanism. He certainly made no dogmatic ruling. I am supported in this opinion by Emile Brouette in his *Sixteenth Century and Satanism*, and a dozen other Catholic priests and authors. This papal Bull first recalls that the care of souls ought to be the ceaseless concern of pastors. The Pope expresses his sorrow that neglect on the part of pastors caused many of the faithful in the dioceses of the Rhine to defect from their religion and accept Satanism, including carnal relations with devils. The second part treats with witchcraft in detail; the third part authorizes the inquisitors, Sprenger and Institoris, to prosecute offenders with "the rigours of ecclesiastical justice." This document fell far short of the Decretals of Pope John XXII.

Because Weishaupt played such an important part in modernizing the

Luciferian conspiracy, it is advisable that the reader be given a few facts to enable him to understand how, and why, a brilliant young scholar can be caused to defect from God and literally sell his soul to the devil.

Born in 1748, Adam Weishaupt became professor of law at the University of Ingolstadt, Bavaria, Germany in 1776. He specialized in Canon Law, the law that is intended to keep Christianity on the straight and narrow path of TRUTH.

He was lionized by false friends. He was inculcated by so-called intellectuals and modernists: he was taught to accept "realistic liberal ideas." Then Satan, in the form of his own sister-in-law, took a hand. Either he seduced her, or she seduced him. This sexual perversion proved his undoing. Letters, among his correspondence, prove that he became so distraught when he found his sister-in-law was pregnant that he appealed frantically to his so-called friends. He implored them to help him procure an abortion before the birth of the child would overwhelm him with disgrace.

Weishaupt's letters prove he was literally as proud as Lucifer. He wasn't penitent because he had sinned against God, betrayed his brother, and broken his vow of chastity. Oh no! His letters prove his panic was caused by his fear that exposure would cast him down from the pinnacle of learning to which he had been elevated at such an early age.

Weishaupt found he had many "friends." But those who responded to his frantic appeal for help made him pay the full price. Under the guise of friendship they introduced him to a medical specialist; they supplied him with all the money he required: Truly the devil's ways ... first sexual depravity then gold! He was then brought under the influence of the newly formed House of Rothschild. He was retained to revise and modernize the age-old Luciferian "Protocols." His pride was given further inflation when he was asked to, or it was suggested, that he organize the Illuminati to put the revised version of the continuing Luciferian conspiracy into effect.

Weishaupt wrote many books and pamphlets dealing with the Illuminati, and "The New Order" which was the deceptive name modernists gave to "Totalitarianism," which is only another name for Luciferianism. In his *Code of Illuminism* he gives detailed instructions to be followed by recruiters delegated to bring learned and wealthy and influential men into the Illuminati. People often wonder WHY lawyers dominate in the field of politics. We will explain. Weishaupt told his recruiters that the success of the movement (conspiracy) depended on their ability to bring about the "conquest" of professional people, lawyers in particular, who have the ability as speakers and are astute and active. To quote his own words, Weishaupt told those he instructed: "These people (lawyers) are true demons, most difficult to handle; but their conquest is always good when it can be obtained."

He recommended as next on their list of conquest, "teachers, university professors, and the superiors of seminaries whenever possible." Doesn't this explain the control the forces of evil now have obtained over our educational institutions, including our seminaries? When students studying for the Ministry of the Christian religion can have the TRUTH withheld from them, and ordained ministers, who learn the TRUTH can be forced by their superiors to keep silence, the Devil has made tremendous strides in developing the Luciferian conspiracy towards its final goal.

To prove that lies and deceits are the stock-in-trade to be used by agentur of the Illuminati, Weishaupt told his recruiters: "If there is any man of great reputation, of his own merit, cause it to be believed that he is one of us."

This advice was followed in the case of General George Washington. He was claimed to be a Mason of the Highest Degree by the Illuminists after Illuminism was introduced to America. This claim has been proved to be a deceptive lie. Illuminists have claimed, but never proved, that even Popes have been initiated into their Order. It is regrettable, but it must be admitted that there is a great deal of evidence to indicate a number of priests and ministers of Christian denominations are now being initiated into the Illuminati, the Lodges of Grand Orient Masonry, or Pike's New and Reformed Palladian Rite. A letter I received November 11, 1958, from a member of the Roman Catholic hierarchy frankly admits he has noticed things about his associates which indicates this statement is a fact.

Weishaupt also wrote *The Cause*. He emphasizes the importance of conquering public officials so they can be used to monopolize public offices and bring about centralization of governments. Is this not what is happening in what is left of the so-called Free Nations today?

Even kings and princes are considered by Weishaupt as preferred objectives. When Mazzini took over the direction of Weishaupt's program for wars and revolutions in 1834, under the guise of "Director of Political Action," he reiterated what Weishaupt had said in this regard and we quote: "The assistance of the influential is an indispensable necessity to bring about reform in a feudal country." In the jargon of the W.R.M. leaders this word "reform" means "subjugation." Today we find Prince Bernhard of the Netherlands and Prince Philip of England active in the Bilderbergers and other international groups.

Today, Weishaupt's revised and modernized version of the Luciferian conspiracy is being furthered by the intellectuals who comprise the controlling influence in the Bilderberger Group, the World Federalist Movement, and the Council of Foreign Relations located in the Henry Pratt Bldg., NY. These pressure groups force remaining national governments, and their representatives in the United Nations Organization, to further the idea of "A ONE WORLD GOVERNMENT," the powers of which the Luciferians, not the Communists, nor the Political Zionists, intend to usurp.

So that good Christian people may be better able to judge which of their spiritual advisers are real Soldiers of Jesus Christ and which are wolves in sheep's clothing, we will prove that Satanism's infiltration into the clergy of ALL religions and religious orders is nothing unusual or modern.

In 1500 Pope Alexander VI wrote to the Prior of Klosterneuburg and to Institoris seeking information regarding the progress of sorcery (Satanism) in Bohemia and Moravia. This letter is important because Germany and Bohemia have long been headquarters of Satanism and remained so until after Weishaupt died in 1830.

Satanism revived under the influence of Nietzsche's teachings. The Councils of Cologne 1536 and 1550 reveal that members of the clergy had defected from their belief in God and were teaching and practicing Satanism. Those who comprised the membership of these councils ordered such clergy to be excommunicated.

In 1583 the Council of Rheims excommunicated sorcerers: "who make a pact with the devil; who pervert sexual relations; who practice deviltries, and pretend to heal through the powers of Satan."

From 1580 to 1620 the disciplinary and dogmatic assemblies of the Protestant religion often discussed the question of Sorcery and Satanism, both as it was being practiced individually and in general.

But to get back to Weishaupt and his writings, and to prove that he had defected from Christianity and embraced Satanism when he revised the "Protocols." He finished this task in 1776. He announced this to the Illuminati May 1st. This is the real reason why May 1st of every year since has been celebrated by revolutionary organizations, and even labor organizations, without the vast majority of the membership even suspecting the truth. This is why May 1, 1776 is printed on American one dollar bills under the great pyramid. On top of the pyramid is the all-seeing eye of the Illuminati.

Weishaupt established the Lodges of the Grand Orient to be located in the principal cities of Europe, and to be the headquarters of the Illuminati which he reorganized to put the revised and modernized version of the Luciferian conspiracy into effect. The members of the Illuminati were at first restricted to about 2,000. They were men who, because they possessed exceptional mental abilities, had advanced to the top of their particular fields of human endeavor. They were financiers, such as the Rothschilds and their affiliated international financiers; they were scientists, such as Scheel; and educationists and encyclopedists such as Voltaire. Those who comprised the Synagogue of Satan all assumed nicknames to hide their identities. The term "nick-name" was first used to indicate a man who took, assumed, or was given another name to conceal the fact that he had become a worshiper of the Devil who is often referred to as "Old Nick."

We don't want to labor this point. It is sufficient to say that the men chosen to become adepts in Satanism were members of the Illuminati, who, by their lives, words, and deeds, proved they had defected from God.

Some were avowed atheists. But the majority willingly accepted "Totalitarianism" (the Luciferian ideology) as presented to them by Weishaupt, as their creed. Only a fool can be a convinced atheist. Only a fool can believe that the Universe, and all it includes, just happened. Even evolutionists with brains admit that evolution could be part of God's plan of creation under which creatures can develop into a higher plane or deteriorate to a lower plane.

The Illuminati have one thing in common; they agreed that those who use their brains to win success in this world have the "RIGHT" to rule others with less brains on the grounds that the Goyim (the masses or common people) just don't know what is good (best) for them. As Voltaire stated so clearly in a letter he wrote to a fellow Illuminist, in order to lead the mob out of their present oppression into a new subjection, those who directed the conspiracy must order those they control to lie, "not timidly, or for a while only, but like the very devil, boldly and always..." Voltaire is also on record as having advised those Illuminists, with which he was associated, that they should use high sounding phrases when addressing the Goyim, and make them lavish promises. He added, "the opposite of what is said and promised can be done afterwards ... that is of no consequence."

The Goyim were encouraged to destroy established government and religions in order to establish democracies. Democracies were defined (deceptively) as being government, and religion, of the people, by the people, for the people.

Thus the vast majority understand the word democracy even today. In actual fact the word "democracy" means demoniacal or mob-rule. Those who direct the Luciferian conspiracy, AT THE TOP, use the "mob" to do the fighting and destroy their governments and religions, then they subjugate the mob.

As far as the High Priests of the Luciferian Creed are concerned, it doesn't matter if Americans and British destroy the governments of other countries as long as the citizens of other countries ultimately destroy the governments of Britain and the U.S.A. by wars and revolutions. According to the Luciferian principle wars always lead to revolutions. That is why Communist leaders adopted the Luciferian slogan; "Revolution to end all wars." The Luciferian policy is: Wars to weaken governments; revolutions to complete their destruction.

After every revolution, revolutionary leaders tell their followers it is necessary to establish a "Proletarian dictatorship" in order to restore law and order. Then in due time will come the Socialist Republic. That is another lie. The so-called proletarian dictatorship is ALWAYS turned into an absolute dictatorship. When Lenin was asked "How long will it be before your absolute dictatorship gives way to a Soviet (workers) government?" He replied, "That is a question I cannot answer, Who knows how long it will be before the workers, 'Goyim' learn enough to be able to govern themselves efficiently? Unfortunately the 'Mob' don't know what is best for themselves." "Mob" is Communist jargon; "Goyim" is Luciferian. There is really no difference. All lesser beings are considered "Human Cattle."

In order that the Illuminati could obtain control of the Goyim and make them fight wars and revolutions to further the secret plans of those who direct the Luciferian conspiracy, AT THE TOP, Karl Marx was instructed to write the books *Das Capital* and the *Communist Manifesto*. He advocated atheism. Weishaupt and Pike and other Luciferian preached about the equality of man, liberty, and fraternalism, etc., with their tongues in their cheeks. Pike had to explain his support of atheistic Communists to his associates by telling them Communism, like Nazism, was only a passing phase of the over-all movement to world power.

Satanism was encouraged in the lower degrees of the Grand Orient Lodges established by Weishaupt, as it was in the lower degrees of the New and Reformed Palladian Rite as organized by Albert Pike nearly a hundred years later when he took over the direction of the Luciferian conspiracy. Satanism was, and still is, celebrated at the Black Mass. This has often been referred to as "The Witches Sunday." The Black Mass perpetuates Sataris initiation of Eve into the pleasures of sexual intercourse and the secret of procreation. Adepts are reminded that Satan thus conferred the greatest benefaction possible upon the human race.

At the Black Mass the celebrant represents Satan and a young priestess represents Eve. The seduction and possession of Eve is performed before the eyes of the worshippers. The second part of the Black Mass perpetuates the defeat of Christ by Satan. Adepts are taught that Satan is the eldest son of God (Adonay) and the brother of St. Michael. The Luciferian dogma teaches that St. Michael, the archangel is one and the same celestial being as Jesus Christ and states that God (Adonay) sent St. Michael to earth in the form of Jesus Christ in order that he could halt the Luciferian conspiracy on this earth as he had done in heaven. We proved in preceding chapters how wrong and deceptive these teachings really are.

The Luciferian doctrine does not admit that St. Michael defeated Lucifer in heaven. It claims that Lucifer won his independence from God and now rules his own section of the universe. Pike said that, "Lucifer" is the equal of God (Adonay). We will deal with this at greater length elsewhere. The Black Mass illustrates how Satan made overtures to Christ, and tried to make friends with him by even offering him rule of this world if he would join the Luciferian cause. It depicts how Christ's refusal made it imperative that he be destroyed. During every Adonaicide Mass a victim is sacrificed, to symbolize the immolation of Christ at the instigation of the Synagogue of Satan. The victim can be human, fowl, or animal according to circumstances and the risk involved. Research dug up documentary evidence which indicates that in the Middle Ages several hundred youths who disappeared in Central Europe were used as sacrificial victims during the celebration of Black Masses. Rosecrucianism was closely associated with these ritualistic murders of male and female youths. But Rosecrucianism and Illuminism are now being introduced to the general public as movements based on the highest of ideals.

Much more recently, British, French, German, and even American police authorities have investigated similar crimes where the bodies have definitely been branded with symbolic figures used in rituals of satanic rites.

The third part of the Mass consists of the desecration of a host consecrated by a priest of the Roman Catholic Church. If an ordained priest can be hired, or blackmailed, into consecrating a host, he is well paid for his services. In 1513 Pope Julius ordered the inquisitor of Cremona to prosecute those priests who were abusing the Eucharist with the practices of witchcraft (Satanism) and who were worshipping the Devil.[17]

In more recent years Roman Catholic churches have been broken into, in order to procure consecrated hosts for this diabolical purpose. One Satanist in America forced his wife to attend Communion-rail in Catholic churches and save the host she received at Communion for him to use. She confessed this to a friend of mine before she died.

After a Black Mass, the worshippers, both men and women indulge in an orgy. The women who take part in these orgies are members of what are termed "Lodges of Adoption." They are used as common property by the members of the male organization.

There are several kinds of Black Masses as there are High and Low masses in the Roman Catholic and Church of England services. Satanism also includes a wide variety of sexual orgies organized for the purpose of placing influential people, whom they wish to control, in an incriminating situation.

One man told me that what took place at these orgies actually made him vomit. Satanism is introduced to stag parties in the form of what is known as "a Circus." These circuses are quite common in most large cities. They employ anywhere from one man and one woman to as many as twenty odd men and women who engage in every form of sexual indulgence and perversion. Satanism is spread insidiously by the distribution of motion pictures depicting every form of sexual abomination it has been possible for devils in human form to perform. Satanism is being introduced into our schools and colleges and training institutions by those so-called modernists who, posing as psychiatric specialists, teach Freudian theories to their students under the guise of modernism. Under this heading, medical students, and girls learning the art of

17 Mag. Mun BULL. ROM. Vol. I, p. 617: Pratt op. cit.; Hansen op. cit.

nursing, are made to believe that masturbation and the practice of homosexualism are perfectly normal practices in the development of a human body and are good for the individual.

Satanism today is advanced by a multi-million dollar output of pornographic literature and obscene pictures yearly. The sales of this mind-destroying filth is increasing steadily year by year.

Satanism is being promoted at parties given to delegates attending conventions in large cities, and in some private homes, where Bacchanalia is practiced today as it was in the days of pagan Rome.

But members of the public inveigled into attending the sexual fringes of Satanism are not permitted to know that, AT THE TOP, directing all the many phases of this abominable section of the conspiracy is the Synagogue of Satan.

They are not permitted to even suspect that the Synagogue of Satan is itself controlled AT THE TOP by the High Priests of the Luciferian Creed. At first those who proselytize for Satanism get their intended victims to witness sexual performances out of curiosity. Then they get them to practice Satanism by convincing them there is nothing wrong in nature. So their victims sin because they like to sin. Progress along these lines at first deadens and then kills the victim's conscience. When properly hog-tied the victim is used to serve Satanism's diabolical purposes.

The effect of Satanism is to be seen and heard at so-called parties everywhere. Dirty stories are now told to, and by, members of both sexes at every opportunity. Language which connects the name of Jesus Christ with unprintable four letter words is in common use. Juvenile delinquency is encouraged by Satanists and Satanism.

Satan doesn't bother men and women who serve him well. Usually he rewards internationally minded totalitarians with wealth and power enough to satisfy their selfish materialistic ambitions. The point to remember is this. EVERY form of internationalism, EVERY totalitarian idea, EVERY racket, EVERY negative organization and movement, serves to further the secret plans of those who direct the Luciferian conspiracy AT THE VERY TOP.

Many great men, including His Eminence Cardinal Caro Y Rodriguez of Chili, when exposing Satanism, as practiced in the Lodges of the Grand Orient and Councils of the New and Reformed Palladian Rite, refer to these two secret societies as "Masonry" and even "Freemasonry." This causes uninformed people to believe that many Masons of the Scottish Rite (also known as "Blue" or "Continental Freemasonry") are Satanists also. This is untrue and very misleading!

Not even members of the lower degrees of the Grand Orient and New Palladian Rite practice Satanism. Even those members who are selected to be initiated as adepts into Satanism are not told the FULL secret, i.e., that Satanism is controlled AT THE TOP by the High Priests of the Luciferian Creed. Only those initiated into the highest degree are shown "THE TRUE LIGHT of the PURE DOCTRINE of Lucifer" and required to worship him as their one and only God. Only a very few carefully selected candidates are allowed to know that it is the Luciferian totalitarian ideology which is to be imposed on what is left of the human race after the final social cataclysm involving Communist controlled people with the rest of the world is ended.

Weishaupt and Pike were both High Degree Freemasons but not one Mason in ten thousand even suspected they were also High Priests of the Luciferian Creed. Mazzini directed the W.R.M. from 1834 to 1871 before Pike acquainted him with the FULL secret.

Not one freemason in a thousand even suspects that Freemasonry, together with ALL other secret societies, is to be destroyed in the final stage of the conspiracy, together with all other religions, so that only the true light of the Pure doctrine of Lucifer will be used to influence the human mind.

Belen de Sarraga who initiated members of the Grand Orient into Satanism in Iquique explained to them that Satan is the "good" God, the Angel of Light who came to teach Eve the secret of how to make human beings equal to God. Sarraga taught that Satan possessed Eve carnally, a knowledge which she afterwards shared with Adam and passed on to the human race.

Benoit tells us that initiates into the 25th degree of Knights of the Brazen Serpent are required to adore the serpent (symbol of Satan) which is the enemy of God (Adonay) and the friend of man, who with his triumph, will make men return to Eden.

Benoit also says that in the 20th degree of the same order the initiate is required to say "In the sacred name of Lucifer cast out obscurantism." (Opposition to inquiry and enlightenment.)

Benoit quotes a leaflet, circulated among Grand Orient Masons, which says that when John Ziska and John Huss were proselytizing Satanism in Bohemia they represented Satan as the innocent victim of a despotic power (God Adonay) who made of him (Satan) the companion in chains of all the oppressed. These two replaced the age-old expression "God be with you" with this substitution; "May the one to whom injustice is done keep you." Proudhon, another Satanist, is recorded as invoking Satan with the words: "Come Satan, exiled by priests, but blessed be (in) my heart." (Benoit F.M.I. p. 460-462.)

Dom Benoit says Albert Pike's New and Reformed Palladian Rite has, as a fundamental practice and purpose, the adoration of Lucifer ... it is full of all the impieties and infamies of Black Magic. Having been established in the United States it has invaded Europe, and each year makes terrifying progress. All its ceremonial is full of blasphemies against God and Our Lord Jesus Christ. (F.M.I. p. 449-454.)

Domenico Margiotta wrote the life of Adriano Lemmi under the title *Adriano Lemmi Chef Supreme des Franc-Macons*. Lemmi was also head of Italian Grand Orient Masons. Only a very few people seem to know that he was a confirmed Satanist and was selected by Pike to become supreme director of the W.R.M. after Mazzini died. Lemmi is presented to the public, by the controlled press, as a great Italian patriot. But delve into his private and secret life and we find him an idol with feet of clay like Pike and Mazzini, Lord Palmerston, Churchill, F.D. Roosevelt and many others.

Margiotta says "Adriano Lemmi did not hide his worship of Satan. In Italy, all knew he is a Satanist. In the name of Satan he used to send out his circulars, although adapting himself at times to the opinion of the imperfect initiates, but it is enough to leaf through the collection of his diary (reserved for Grand Orient Masons) to know his sentiments concerning occultism and the wickedness of one who had delivered himself to the Devil. "Yes! As a Satanist he organized the anti-clerical movements and boasted of it from 1883 on!"

In his official organ *The Revista Della Massoneria Italiana* (Vol. I of the Masonic Yearbook from March 1, 1883 to February 28, 1884, p. 306) he makes this cynical declaration: "The Pope has said, 'Vecilla Regis Prodcunt Inferni.' Yes, indeed, the standards of the King of the Inferno advance, and there is not one conscious man who loves liberty; there is not one who will fail to enlist under those standards."

Thus he, like all other revolutionary leaders, used the word liberty while all the time he worked to lead the masses into the "New Order" which is the polite, but deceptive name they give the Luciferian totalitarian dictatorship under which they intend to enslave the human race, body, mind, and soul.

Lemmi goes on to say: "Yes! Yes! The standards of the King of the Inferno are marching forward because Freemasonry which by principle, by institution, by instinct, has always combated and always will combat without truce or quarter all that can impede the development of liberty, of peace, and happiness for humanity, must combat today more energetically and more openly than ever before all the artifice of the clerical reaction." (Margiotta, Adriano Lemmi, p. 168-169.)

Here we see Lemmi injects the word "Freemasonry" instead of Luciferianism. He again speaks of liberty when he and his kind intend to use absolute despotism to enforce their will on the "Goyim" as Lenin did in Russia, 1917, during the first big experiment used to test the Luciferian theories out in actual practice.

Copin Albancelli, another authority on how Satanism is practiced in modern times, says he obtained definite proof that certain societies, which profess to be Masonic worship Lucifer: "They adore Lucifer as the true God and they are so animated with an implacable hatred towards the God of the Christians, whom they declare to be an impostor, they have a formula which sums up their state of mind. No longer do they say, "To the glory of the Great Architect of the Universe," but "Glory and love to Lucifer! Hatred! Hatred! Hatred! To God be damnation! Damnation! Damnation!" Copin-Albancelli goes on to say "It is confessed in these societies that everything the Christian God ordains is disagreeable to Lucifer that, on the contrary, everything he forbids is agreeable to Lucifer and consequently it is necessary to do everything the Christian God fought and to guard against everything he ordains as if it were fire. Copin-Albancelli says and I quote: "I repeat, I have held the proof of all this in my hands. I have read and studied hundreds of documents belonging to one of these societies, documents I am not permitted to publish, and which came from members, men and women of the group in question. I have been able to prove that this pleases Lucifer, also that murder is practiced there (The Black or Adonaicide Mass) always because it displeases the Christian God and pleases Lucifer." (Copin, P.O. 291-292.)

Margiotta relates that Pike reproved Lemmi for his rabid Satanism and decreed that the God of Masonry (the New and Reformed Palladian Rite) ought to be given only the ineffable name of Lucifer.

At the International Congress of Brussels in 1886, La Fargus exclaimed:

"War on God! Hatred to God! In this is progress. It is necessary to crush Heaven as if it were a piece of paper." (The World Congress in Brussels 1958 was one of the most Godless exhibitions ever staged. One could find Satanism everywhere.) A Luciferian adept Brother Lanesan (Solstical Festival of the Clement Friendship Lodge on March 13, 1880) blasphemed with these words: "We must crush the infamous One. But that infamous One is not clericalism, that infamous One is God." (International Review of Secret Societies, #17, 1924, pp. 309-310.)

We have only quoted a few unrelated authors who in the second half of the 19th Century found out truths I confirmed as the result of my own research in the first half of the 20th Century. Those who direct the Luciferian conspiracy can keep this information locked up because they control the press and all avenues of public information. But is it not strange that the ministers of the Christian religion don't insist on making these truths known from their pulpits, set up in what they claim are Christian churches-the Houses of God?

In order to drive the final nails in the coffin of those who try to make the general public believe that ALL Freemasons are tarred with the same brush "Satanism" and/or Luciferianism, I wish to point out that both Weishaupt and Pike took particular care to provide for the total destruction of Freemasonry, together with all other secret societies, in the final stages of the conspiracy.

In the lectures delivered on the "Protocols" of the Luciferian conspiracy, as divided into chapters and paragraphs by Marsden, the lecturer said Masons and Freemasonry are to be dealt with as follows: (Chp. IV. Par. 2) "Who and what is in position to overthrow an invisible force? And this is precisely what our force is. Gentile masonry blindly serves as a screen for us and our objects, but the plan of action of our force, even its very abiding place, remains for the whole people an unknown mystery." Because this copy of the lectures was to be used for arousing anti-Semitism in Russia to boiling point the word "Gentile" was introduced.

Chap. IX:2 - "The Masonic watch words, "Liberty, Equality, and Fraternity: will, when we come into our Kingdom be changed to mean the "right of liberty, the duty of equality, the ideal of brotherhood-that is how we shall put it."

The lecturer then goes on to explain: "Nowadays, if any states raise a protest against us the Satanists and Luciferians who direct the W.R.M. AT THE TOP it is only proforma at our discretion and by our direction (because they control the policies of ALL governments from behind the scenes)." There is also a statement made which refers to "the management of our lesser brethren." This statement indicates the Directors of the Luciferian conspiracy intended to use Lower Degree Masons as they use Lesser Jewish brethren to serve their own secret plans and sacrifice as many as necessary to serve their own devilish purposes.

Chap. XI: 5-7, says: "we shall keep promising to give back (to the people) all the liberties we have taken away as soon as we have quelled the enemies of peace and tamed all parties. It is not worthwhile to say anything about how long a time they will be kept waiting for the return of their liberties."

"For what purpose then have we invented this whole policy and insinuated it into the minds of the "goys" without giving them any chance to examine its underlying meaning? For what, indeed, if not in order to obtain in a roundabout way what is for our scattered tribe unattainable by the direct road?"

"It is this which has served as a basis for our organization of SECRET MASONRY, which is not known to, and aims which are not even so much as suspected by, these GOY cattle, attracted by us into the 'SHOW' army of Masonic Lodges in order to throw dust in the eyes of their fellows."

The above reads as if Jews were directing the conspiracy but we must remember we are dealing with the High Priests of the Synagogue of Satan, The Masters of Deceit, whom Christ told us are them who say they are Jews but are not. Those who serve Satanism all over the world, seeking the ruin of souls, are just as much "the scattered tribe" as are the Jews (Hebrews).

Chap. XV tells what is going to happen to all Lesser Beings, Masons, Jews, Christians, etc. etc., "when we (the High Priests of the Luciferian Creed) at last definitely come into our kingdom by aid of a "coup d'etat" prepared everywhere for one and the same day, after the worthlessness of all existing forms of government has been definitely acknowledged."

This lecture was delivered between 1873 and 1901. The lecturer told his listeners it might take a century to place those who directed the conspiracy "where NO power or cunning can prevent us usurping undisputed world domination." He tells his audience that once in power they shall take the following steps to make certain they remain in power:

1. We shall slay without mercy ALL who take arms to oppose our coming into our kingdom.

2. Belonging to anything like a secret society will be punishable by death.

3. Those who having belonged to secret societies has served the S.O.S., are to be disbanded and sent into exile. (Exactly as was done in Russia and is now being done in China.) The lecturer adds, "in this way we will proceed with Masons who know too much."

4. Death will be the penalty of all who hinder our affairs. We execute Masons in such wise that none save the Brotherhood can ever have suspicion of it, not even the victims themselves of our death sentence. They will all die when required as if from a normal kind of illness.

Scottish Rite Masons would do well to investigate and expose who among them are secretly of "The Synagogue of Satan." By their fruits ye shall know them.

Because Christ told us Lucifer is the "Father of Lies" and "The Master of Deceit," we will examine General Albert Pike, alleged patriot, and considered one of the greatest doctors of Masonic Science, in the light of his own words, which were never supposed to see the light of day. He said: "The Blue degrees are no more than the outer door of the temple portal. Part of the symbols are explained here to the initiated, but he unintentionally deceived with false interpretations! It is not intended that he understand them, but rather that he imagine himself to understand them. Their true interpretation is reserved for the Initiated Ones, the Princes of Masonry."

"Masonry" continues Pike, "like all religions, all mysteries, hermeticism and alchemies, hide secrets from everyone except the Initiated Sages or Elects, and employs false explanations and interpretations of its symbols to deceive those who deserve to be deceived, and to hide from them the truth, which is called LIGHT and to separate them from it."[19]

It is only when we compare the above statement with the information contained in Pike's letters to Mazzini and others who became "Initiated Sages" and "The Elect" of the Luciferian Creed that we can understand and appreciate the terrible truth hidden behind the above quoted words. The word LIGHT which he emphasized is proved to mean "the TRUE LIGHT of the pure doctrine of Lucifer" as he explained to Mazzini in the letter he addressed to him, August 15, 1871.

18 We have the evidence of students who attended courses in Canada to prove this statement.
19 For confirmation of the above quotation read *Preuse* AF pp. 12-13.

I consider many Freemasons among my friends. During the 1930's I had the honor, and privilege, to be the guest speaker at numerous Masonic Lodges. I was so honored by the Ionic Lodge of Hamilton, Ontario (the oldest Lodge in Canada) on several occasions. It is with feelings of love and charity that I reveal that they are lied to and deceived, and that their society is used as a cloak to cover up the true identity and purpose of the members of the Synagogue of Satan who use their temples as their secret headquarters so they can work secretly and mysteriously, in the dark, promoting Satanism and directing the Luciferian conspiracy.

I know that Masons, in Blue Masonry, swear on the Bible when taking their oaths. That proves the vast majority believe in God, (Adonay) as the Creator of Heaven and Earth, whom they call the Grand Architect of the Universe.

I know the vast majority of apprentices mean every word they say when they swear by God they will never reveal the secrets; and I know that the God they swear by is the God they think of as that Supernatural Being who cast Lucifer and his fellow rebels out of Heaven and into Hell. I know that of the vast number of Freemasons, located throughout the world that, only a few, and a very few, deteriorate to the point they are considered "worthy' to be initiated into Satanism; I know that still fewer are selected to become members of the Elect of Lucifer. As far as my studies go, I feel that the insidious purpose behind Luciferian infiltration into Freemasonry and all other religions is to deceive them into directly and indirectly promoting the "Idea" of a One World Government and religion. As I said before, I repeat once more, "not one Mason in ten thousand even suspects that those who direct all aspects of the Luciferian conspiracy intend to usurp the powers of the first world government to be established and then impose the Luciferian ideology upon what is left of the human race."

I know that some of the very fine Masons I am proud to consider my friends would become violently ill if asked to utter the blasphemies against the God they worship and adore, and take part in the abominations practiced at one of Pike's modernized Black Masses to which he gave the name Adonaicide Mass.

Chapter 7

ADAM WEISHAUPT

With deceit as their chief weapon, those who direct the Luciferian conspiracy have caused Catholics to believe Freemasonry to be the main instrument the Devil uses to destroy them and Christianity. Using exactly the same deception Masons are taught to believe Roman Catholicism is Luciferianism in disguise. By the same token Communists are taught they are the champions of "democracy" while the people of the so-called remaining democratic nations are being convinced Communism is the root of all evil and the main threat towards the destruction of their governments and religions. Thus those who direct the Luciferian conspiracy kept the Goyim divided among themselves. They shift the blame for their own sins against God and their crimes against humanity and place it where they find it most convenient. In a most remarkable manner, which can only be explained by the power of the Devil, they manage to deflect towards others the finger of suspicion whenever it is pointed at them and, generally speaking, they preserve the secrecy of their motives and identity.

The Synagogue of Satan directs the Luciferian conspiracy. History proves the S.O.S. has used ALL internationalist movements organized since the beginning of time to further their own secret plans. The Bible tells us the 'idea' of a one world government was introduced to Solomon ten centuries before Christ was born. As happened to Nazism, all international movements are made to destroy themselves as soon as they have served the Luciferian cause. Thus it is that the few, who direct the World Revolutionary Movement move peacefully nearer to establishing a totalitarian state. They make those they plot to subjugate, fight, and destroy each other, their governments, and religions because they stand as obstacles in their path.

The "Protocols" are the original draft of the plan by which the Synagogue of Satan intend to obtain undisputed world domination. The Protocols are, as the saying goes, as old as the hills. Weishaupt simply revised and modernized them in order that those who comprise the Synagogue of Satan may take full advantage of rapidly changing conditions, and the advances being made by applied science. The manner in which the discovery of atomic energy is being used to frighten the masses into accepting the "idea' that a One World Government is the only solution to the world's many problems is typical of

90

what I mean. Those who direct the conspiracy carefully conceal, from those they use to serve their devilish purpose, the fact that in the final stage of the conspiracy they intend to usurp the powers of the first world government to be established, and then impose the Luciferian ideology upon what remains of the human race. Once One Worlders are enlightened in this regard, they will reject internationalism in any form.

Weishaupt organized the Illuminati to put his revised version of the conspiracy into effect. He also established the lodges of Grand Orient Masonry to be the secret headquarters of the Illuminati. When members of the Illuminati infiltrated into other secret organizations, including Continental or Blue Freemasonry, they organized their own secret society within the lodges of the secret society into which they infiltrated. The ordinary, "Imperfect", members were, and still are, kept in ignorance of this fact.

The most prominent Satanists, or Luciferians, who worked with Weishaupt were the famous German author Zwack, Baron Knigge, Baron Bassus-in Sandersdorf, the Marquis Constanza and Nicolai. In order to hide their identity, and real purpose, Weishaupt and his lieutenants used code names.[20] Weishaupt was "Spartacus"; Zwack was "Cato"; Baron Knigge was "Philo"; Bassus was "Hannibal;" The Marquis Constanza was "Diomedes;" and Nicolai the greatest scoffer of ALL religions which teach belief in a God other than Lucifer, became "Lucian."

Cities in which Grand Orient Lodges were established to be the secret revolutionary headquarters of those who directed the conspiracy also received code names. Thus Munich became "Athens;" Vienna became "Rome;" etc. It was an accident, or an "Act of God" which exposed these secrets. Zwack had put Weishaupt's notes into orderly manuscript form ready for publication for the information of revolutionary leaders throughout the world. Copies of this Luciferian Bible were placed in the hands of carefully selected trustees to ensure that some would survive if government authorities seized other copies. One copy was entrusted to the care of Prof. John Robison of Edinburgh University.

In 1784, another copy was sent from Frankfort-on-Main in Germany to Mirabeau in Paris, France. He had been selected by Weishaupt to foment the French Revolution scheduled to break out in 1789.

20 This practice continues to the present day as we proved in the story of the secret meetings held on Jekyl Island, and St. Simon Island, published in *Pawns in the Game*, and *The Red Fog Over America*.

Very few historians seem to realized that early in the 1700's, long before Weishaupt was retained, by the newly formed House of Rothschild, to revise and modernize the age old conspiracy to bring about a ONE WORLD GOVERNMENT, the so-called "Internationalists" had infiltrated into America. The works of those historians who do mention this fact have been suppressed. There is documentary evidence which proves these subversives were active as early as 1746. They celebrated May 1, 1776 as the day on which Weishaupt finished the revision of the age old conspiracy and gave the name "Illuminati" to those selected to direct the conspiracy, and put his revised plans into effect. Millions upon millions of people have celebrated May Day ever since, thinking it the anniversary of the day America and Labor gained independence. The Masses (Goyim) never dreamed May 1, 1776 was an epoch making day in the history of the Luciferian conspiracy which we refer to as the World Revolutionary Movement. It was the day Illuminati stabbed Britain in the back as part of their program to ultimately destroy the British Empire together with ALL other remaining governments and religions. May Day had been celebrated by the Roman Catholic Church for centuries as the feast day of the mother of Jesus Christ. It was for this reason that Weishaupt, a renegade Jesuit, picked it to announce to his fellow Satanists and Luciferians his revised plan to destroy Christianity and bring about what Nietzche afterwards referred to as "The death of God."

But to get back to our story. As the Illuminati's courier rode through the town of Ratisbon, on his way to Paris to deliver Mirabeau his copy of Weishaupt's revised plans, the courier was killed by a stroke of lightning. This event occurred in 1784. The police turned the documents found on the body over to Bavarian government authorities. Examination revealed them to be the "Protocols" of the order and sect of the Illuminati. The word "Protocol" means: "A copy of the original draft of a plan to achieve a definite purpose and reach a clearly defined goal".

The Bavarian government had got hold of the Protocols of the Luciferian conspiracy as revised by Adam Weishaupt between 1770 and 1776. They knew how Weishaupt intended to use "The Order and Sect of the Illuminati" to put his modernized plans into effect. The documents further disclosed that the Lodges of the Grand Orient were to be used as the secret headquarters of those who directed the conspiracy, to destroy all remaining governments and religions, throughout the world. They also revealed that the Illuminati intended to infiltrate into all other secret societies, but particularly into Continental

(Blue) Freemasonry, for the purpose of contacting wealthy and influential people over whom they wished to obtain control so they could be used to further the Illuminati's secret plans to bring about a One World Government.

The "Elector of Bavaria" ordered the police to raid the homes and meeting places of Weishaupt and his close associates. These raids added a wealth of additional evidence to what had already been obtained from the documents found on the body of the courier.

The Bavarian government was very thorough. By 1786 they had examined all available evidence. They published the information in a book entitled (English translation) *Original Writings of the Order and Sect of the Illuminati*. Zwack's manuscript containing Weishaupt's revised version of the age old Luciferian conspiracy was entitled *Einige Originalschriften*. Copies of the conspiracy were sent by the Bavarian government to ALL heads of Church and state in Europe. History proves these warnings were ignored because Weishaupt's Illuminati had already been placed in key positions behind the scenes of government, both secular and religious, as "Experts" and "Advisers." They denounced the evidence as a "forgery." They claimed it was part of a huge practical joke being perpetrated by those who wished to ridicule the heads of Church and state. But the French revolution broke out on schedule, and history proves that the conspiracy has been developed since 1776 EXACTLY as Weishaupt intended. Today, it is in its semi-final stage.

The Elector of Bavaria banished Weishaupt. He lost his "chair" in Ingolstadt University where he taught "Canon Law" He moved to Regensburg, Switzerland, where he reorganized his Illuminati. Switzerland was made into a neutral nation and remained the headquarters of the directors of the World Revolutionary Movement until the United Nations Organization was set up by the Rockefellers in New York. Then the "Brains," which work out the program to bring the conspiracy to its ultimate goal, moved into the Harold Pratt Building, New York.

Two Italians, the Marquis Constanza, and the Marquis Savioli joined Weishaupt in Switzerland. This explains why the Italian Guiseppe Mazzini was selected to direct the World Revolutionary program in 1834; and was succeeded by another Italian, Adriano Lemmi, in 1872 when Mazzini died. With devilish cunning Weishaupt and his fellow conspirators made those in authority believe that the Illuminati had died a natural death in 1786. The truth is the plot to bring what remains of the human race under a totalitarian dictatorship has never ended. It blossomed forth under new names and disguises in all parts of the world. It is the W.R.M. as we know it today.

Weishaupt himself tells us he planned well in advance of 1786 how to take care of the risk of possible discovery and exposure. Those who defect from God (Adonay) first become Satanists, then after long years of testing and trial, a few Satanists are selected for the initiation into the Luciferian Priesthood. From these are selected the High Priests and the Universal Sovereign Pontiff of the Luciferian Creed. Weishaupt (Spartacus) aspired to become Sovereign Pontiff. In a letter he wrote "Cato" (Zwack) dated February 6, 1778, he said "the allegory on which I am to found the Mysteries of the Higher Orders is 'The Fire-worship of the Magi' (worship of Lucifer). We must have some worship and none is so apposite- 'Let there be light.' This is my motto, and this is my fundamental principle."

In March the same year, Weishaupt again wrote to his friend "Cato" (Zwack). He said: "I have gone through the whole circle of human inquiry. I have exorcised spirits.[21] I raised ghosts; discovered treasures; interrogate the Cabale;[22] I have never transmuted metals. I would have executed much greater things had not the government (his superiors in the Luciferian conspiracy at the time) always opposed my exertions and placed others in situations which suited my talents."

21 The word "exorcised" means to expel a devil or devils from a person who has been possessed. The scriptures tell us how Christ cast out devils. But Satanists invite devils to enter into, and possess, their mediums and through them to speak to those who seek knowledge or advice from Satan and/or Lucifer. After the medium has served their purpose, the High Priests of the Synagogue of Satan then "exorcised" the devils from that person's body, and he or she becomes normal again. It is this practice which caused the Synagogue of Satan which wished to discredit Christ, to accuse him of casting out devils in the name, and through the powers of Beelzebub the Prince of Devils and not by the power of God. (Luke 11:14-15)

22 The Cabale (often spelled differently) as referred to by Weishaupt means "The Spiritual Powers headed by Lucifer in the celestial world:" the Holy Scriptures refer to them "As the spiritual Powers of Darkness." Human beings who direct the Luciferian cause often consult their spiritual directors in the celestial world, in exactly the same way as millions of Christians believe in the Communion of the Saints and pray to them to intercede with God on their behalf for spiritual insight and blessings. Mackenzie King while Prime Minister of Canada repeatedly tried to obtain advice and guidance from people who had already departed from this life. Pike is on record as having done so repeatedly also; the best recorded instance is his own report of the seance he personally conducted in St. Louis as reported elsewhere. Thus we see that "Truth" is much stranger than any fiction ever written.

Weishaupt was literally as proud as Lucifer. He was determined to become the Sovereign Pontiff of the Luciferian Creed. He was determined to be placed higher than any other person in this or the celestial world, excepting only his beloved Lucifer. This statement is proved by a letter he wrote "Cato" (Zwack) in 1778. He told his friend: "By this plan we shall direct all mankind. In this manner, and by the simplest means, we shall set all in motion and in flames. The occupations must be so allotted and contrived, that we may, in secret, influence all political "transactions".... I have considered everything, and so prepared it, that if the Order should this day go to ruin, I shall in a year reestablish it more brilliant than ever." There we have the key to the secret. The Bavarian government discovered and exposed the existence of the continuing conspiracy, but Weishaupt built it up and made it stronger than ever. All the Bavarian government actually did was prune the Tree of Evil and make it grow stronger. What they should have done was dig it up by the roots and burn it as the Holy Scriptures tell us we must do if we wish to destroy the Spiritual Forces of Darkness who roam about this world seeking the destruction of Souls (Matt. 7: 15-24). If the heads of Church and state had in 1786 followed the advice of the scriptures and cut down and burned the Evil Tree, of which the Illuminati is only one of many branches, "the womb would have forgot him (Weishaupt); the worm would have fed sweetly on him; he would be no more remembered; and wickedness would have been broken as an evil tree." (Job 24:20)

Before Weishaupt was banished in 1786, his 2,000 well educated, carefully selected, brilliant-minded, wealthy and well-bred Illuminists had established one or more Lodges of the Grand Orient in Munich, Ingolstadt, Frankfort, Echstadt, Hanover, Brunswick, Calbe, Magdeburgh, Cassel, Osnabruck, Wiemar, Saxony, Heidelbergh, Mannheim, Strasbourg, Spire, Worms, DusseldorfF, Cologne, Bonn, Livonia, Courtland, Franendahl, Alsace, Wienne, Deuxponts, Hesse, Cousel, Buchenwerter, Treves, Montpelier, Aix-la-Chapelle, Stuttgart, Barschied, Carlsruhe, Hahrenberg, Anspach, Neuweid, Mentz, Rome, Naples, Ancona, Turin, Florence, Warsaw, and Dresden. There were Lodges in Upper Saxony, Westphalis, Switzerland, France, Scotland, Holland, and last but by no means least, America.

Many, so-called, authorities have, since 1786, tried to convince the heads of Church and state in America and elsewhere that Illuminism is dead as the Dodo bird. These Luciferians produce what they claim is documentary evidence to prove what they say is the TRUTH, but they are careful to conceal the evidence which proves that Albert Pike reorganized the Palladian Rite between 1859 and 1889 to take over the direction of the Luciferian conspiracy from the Illuminati. They carefully conceal the evidence which proves that Illuminism began to stink in the nostrils of honest Americans. In the early 1800's 45,000 Scottish Rite masons handed in their charters in protest against the manner Illuminism had infiltrated into their lodges. This it is that few Americans know that Pike established twenty-six councils (triangles) of this New and Reformed Palladian Rite in every large city throughout the world to direct the Luciferian conspiracy as Weishaupt intended. We explain how this plot worked in another chapter.

We mentioned that Professor John Robison of Edinburgh University was one of those entrusted with a copy of Zwack's original manuscripts dealing with Weishaupt's revised and modernized version of the age old Luciferian conspiracy.

Robison was a 33rd degree member of the Scottish Rite of Freemasonry. As such he visited most Masonic Lodges in European cities, and took part in their rituals and initiations. He taught Natural Philosophy at Edinburgh University. He was secretary of the Royal Society. Weishaupt had been particularly anxious to obtain Robison's cooperation so that the "IDEA" of a One World Government could be introduced into ALL educational institutions. This objective has since been achieved as any parent of children of school age must admit. Weishaupt ordered his Illuminists to wine and dine Robison, and introduce him into the best European educational circles. He was flattered and hailed as one of the greatest educationalists of his time. But all the wiles and guiles of the Devil's servants didn't deceive John Robison. He recognized that behind the Illuminati's clever presentation that a One World Government could solve all our political, social, economic, and religious problems, the real intention of those who controlled the Illuminati AT THE VERY TOP was to usurp the power of the first world government to be established and then impose a totalitarian Luciferian dictatorship upon what remained of the human race.

After the heads of Church and state refused to heed the warnings given to them by the Bavarian government in 1786, and the French Revolution broke out as scheduled in 1789, John Robison published all the knowledge he had obtained regarding the Illuminati, and those who controlled it AT THE TOP, in a book containing 548 pages. It is entitled *Proofs of a Conspiracy Against all Religions and Governments of Europe*. On the front cover is the additional information "Carried on in the secret meetings of Freemasons, Illuminati, and

Reading Societies." Copies of this book are still in existence despite the frantic efforts of those who direct the conspiracy to try to destroy all that were published. I have the written statement of a friend who owns a copy that agents of the Rockefeller Foundation told him he could name his own price for his copy. He rejected the offer.

Another authentic source of information is M. Barruel who wrote *Memoirs of Jacobism*. This is a companion piece to Proofs of a Conspiracy. As I mentioned in *Pawns in the Game*, Sir Walter Scott also published two volumes on the subject under the title *Life of Napoleon*, both of which have been suppressed. This great work is not even listed by most libraries as being one of his works.

But again an accident, "An Act of God," enabled a friend of mine to obtain original copies of both volumes from a second hand book dealer in the U.S.A. for the ridiculous price of $17.50. Thinking I had these rare books in my personal possession, and intended to use them for reference while writing this book, thieves robbed me of all the books and papers I did have with me the very first night I arrived in Clearwater, Florida, November 1957 to start writing this book. It was a serious setback. It delayed my work a year, but it hasn't stopped me.

In order that good Christian people may be alerted to the depths of deception used by agentur of the S.O.S. we will quote the statement contained in a letter Weishaupt wrote to Philo (Knigge): "We must win (control over) the common people in every corner. This will be obtained chiefly by means of the schools. In like manner, we must try to obtain and influence the military academies, the printing houses, booksellers, shops, chapters, and in short, in all offices or even in directing the mind of the man; painting, and engraving are highly worth our care.

"Their (the Illuminati's) first task, and immediate aim, is to get the possession of riches, power, and influence without industry; and to accomplish this, they want to abolish Christianity; and then dissolute manners and universal profligacy will procure them the adherence of all the wicked, and enable them to overturn all civil governments of Europe; after which they will think of further conquests, and extend their operations to the other quarters of the globe; until they have reduced mankind to one indistinguishable chaotic mass."

In order to reach the type of people the Illuminati needed to further their own secret plans, Weishaupt organized an apprentice class for those the Illuminati's recruiters interested in internationalism. This apprentice state was called "The Minervals." These were introduced to, and brought under the influence of, "The Twenty-two United Brethren." On the surface this was a kind of writers' club exactly the same as are to be found in all large cities, and organized communities today. Out of them came the "Reading Societies." These led the minds of members into channels of thought which convinced them there is real merit in the "idea" of a One World Government. The same thing is being done today to confirm the public's belief in the value of a One World Government and the Universal Brotherhood of Man. The United Nations Organization is nothing more or less than a deceptive front, dressed in an air of respectability, to cover the activities of those who plan to usurp the powers of the first world government to be established.

The "Twenty-two United Brethren" told Minervals: "we have united in order to accomplish the aim of the exalted Founder of Christianity, viz. The enlightening of mankind, and the dethronement of superstition and fanaticism, by means of a secret fraternization of all who love the work of God."

The stating of this apparently idealistic purpose was proved to be a deliberate deception when some of both Weishaupt's and Pike's secret correspondence fell into hands other than intended. This correspondence proves that when the Luciferians say they wish to serve "the exalted Founder of Christianity" they have their tongue in their cheek. What they really mean is that they serve Lucifer. Pike told the heads of the Councils of the Palladian Rite that they were to use the words "we worship God" when addressing the masses, despite the fact "we worship Lucifer." This angle of the conspiracy is dealt with elsewhere.

Many outstanding students, professional men (particular lawyers) and civil servants in the higher levels of government, we deceived into allowing themselves to be initiated as Minervals. Thus, as initiates they were placed in a position which required taking an oath and swearing that under pain of death they would never reveal anything with which they became acquainted as the result of their induction into the secret society.

Why any person who intends to love and serve God would take a solemn oath not to divulge information about matters of which he has no personal knowledge is beyond comprehension. Why any sincere Christian would want to join a secret society, and work in the dark, behind the scenes, instead of in the open, spreading the LIGHT OF TRUTH as revealed by Jesus Christ, is also difficult to understand, but just about one out of every dozen adult males belong to Freemasonry while nearly as many belong to other secret societies. The Scriptures warn us that we must not hide our Light under a bushel. People who are honest and sincere and have no ulterior motives, don't go underground. They stand up to be counted and take the consequences, knowing the worst the agents of Lucifer can do is kill their bodies. (Matt. 10:28; Luke 12:4)

The truth, as revealed by secret documents, is that Minervals, who proved they had high moral principles and were incorruptible, were accepted into the Secret Society and commended for their fine ideals; but only those who were proved to be immoral, and open to bribery and/or corruption, were advanced to the higher degrees. The good were used as "Do-Gooders," "Reformers" and other types of tools; those who had sold their souls to the Devil were used as instruments of destruction. This explains why so many clergymen are deceived into becoming "tools of the Devil" without realizing they are serving the Luciferian cause.

If those who direct the Luciferian conspiracy AT THE TOP can get the majority of those they persuade to join secret societies, and social and service clubs, to accept the IDEA that nationalism is outmoded; and Christianity weak and poorly led, they have achieved their purpose. Their agentur within the societies and clubs then suggest that nationalism leads us into wars and causes revolutions; they suggest that Christianity has proved ineffective and unable to prevent these wars and revolutions. The secret agents then promote the IDEA that a One World Government, via the United Nations Organization; and a One World Religion could solve the many and varied problems bedeviling the human race today. What the agentur of the Synagogue of Satan keep carefully concealed is the fact that their masters are ready, and fully prepared, to usurp the powers of the first world government to be established exactly as they usurped power in Russia in October 1917. After they usurp power they will impose the Luciferian ideology upon mankind by use of satanic despotism to enforce their will and destroy ALL secret societies, ALL religions, and ALL who oppose their will as is so clearly set forth in the Protocols.

Chapter 8

HOW THE SYNAGOGUE OF SATAN
WORKS IN HIGH PLACES

The "idea" of a One World. Government can be presented in a manner which makes it sound reasonable, practical, and even desirable. Clever agentur of the Illuminati, belonging to clubs and societies, serve the purpose of the Synagogue of Satan by presenting what appear to be sound arguments in favor of a One World Government to those they can persuade to listen. Very few of the rank and file members of the clubs and societies suspect that beyond the end of the primrose path of liberalism, and social security, that leads to a One World Government is a precipice over which we are to be tumbled, into the abyss of absolute slavery of body, mind, and soul.

I am frank to admit that as late as 1945 I was convinced that a One World Government was the ONLY solution to the world's many problems particularly political, economic, social, and religious. It wasn't until I came in personal contact with men who advocated and helped organize the United Nations Organization that I began to suspect that something was wrong somewhere. When I was appointed to the staff of Naval Service headquarters in 1944, as the author of seven books already published, I was welcomed into the internationalist set. This I came in personal contact with men in the top level of government in Canada who were protégés of William Lyon Mackenzie King, then Prime Minister. His house was "real" close to the Soviet Embassy. His henchmen (Hatchet men would be a better word) were ruthless and unscrupulous. Mackenzie King himself was as inscrutable as the proverbial sphinx.

The Prime Minister was an extraordinary man. He was indefatigable. He required unlimited obedience and service from those he selected for his cabinet. He was a good deal colder than ice as far as his personality was concerned. If he had any human emotions he kept them in subzero storage. He rarely smiled. He had a typical "poker" face; his eyes were deep and penetrating, but if the eyes are the "windows of the soul" then Mackenzie King had lost his soul long before he ever became Prime Minister. In the course of his public duties he had to meet people and shake hands. Those who did shake hands with the Prime Minister say the experience reminded them of picking up a dead fish. It was said on Parliament Hill that he didn't have a close friend in all the world. If there was an exception it was his barber. And yet he had a secret power which enabled him to mesmerize the voters into voting him, and his liberal party, into power time after time for nearly a quarter of a century. He could command loyalty from his subordinates without giving friendship in return. He proved himself a radical during his days at Toronto University. He would set the tinder, supply the spark, cause a disturbance, and then leave others to take the blame. During his university days he was friendless, as he was later on in life. As one man who knew him when at University, and served him afterwards until he died, said in a puzzled tone of voice; "If Mackenzie King did have a friend close enough to confide in, it must have been the Devil." Another said: "He was so steeped in international intrigue he didn't dare marry for fear he might talk in his sleep."

While I was on the staff in Ottawa I was carefully sounded out to determine if my loyalty to the British Crown was so pronounced that I wouldn't be likely to accept the "idea' of a One World Government even if those who presented the "idea' emphasized the fact that national governments would be allowed to rule their own affairs. This presentation is so obviously a lie that I was extremely cautious from then on.

Knowing that there was in existence a "Secret Power" which had used Nazism and intended to use Communism to serve its own secret plans, and further its own ambitions to usurp undisputed world domination, I was determined to find out, if possible, who or what the secret power was. So I pretended to become an internationalist. I was then brought in personal contact with men at the deputy minister level of government, and also with some of the "Specialists," "Experts," and "Advisers" who served the government behind the scenes. Then I began to suspect the truth.

Generally speaking, the majority of these One Worlders were Satanists. They ducked attending church services. They ridiculed religion. The accepted the Freudian code of morals which means they didn't care what they did, or with whom they did it, provided they satisfied their own carnal pleasures and desires. If they used the name of God they always took His Name in vain. If they used the words "Jesus Christ" it was an injection in ordinary conversations or coupled with dirty four letter words. Without openly professing the fact, they were obviously adepts of Pike's Palladian Rite or Grand Orient Masonry. Close observation while they were drinking in the officers' messes, and elsewhere, showed they used signs that Masons and Knights of Columbus didn't understand.

I may be wrong but observation of men who had obviously defected from God and become Satanists, convinced me they could recognize and identify each other by the fold of their handkerchief which they wore in top pocket of their coats.

They obviously accepted Pike's dogma as far as women were concerned: Pike required that the members of all Councils of his New and Reformed Palladian Rite organize selected females into "Councils of Adoption." These women were to be used as the common property of the male members because, according to Pike's dogma, before a member became "Perfect," he had to obtain absolute control over the sentiments of the heart and desires of the flesh. He claimed that many men were led astray from the path of duty because they were weak enough to feel love and affection for women. He argued that in order for a member to become "perfect" he must obtain absolute control over his senses and sentiments, and suggested that the best way to obtain control over the sexual urges is to use women "Often and without passion and thus enchain women to their will."

I found that some of the top level internationalists "swapped" wives during parties. Professor Raymond Boyer, top level scientist, and Canadian millionaire, and E.V. Field, American millionaire, locked together in international intrigue and subversion as proved by both Canadian and American government investigating committees, carried this practice to the extent that they swapped each others' wives for good, and made the exchange legal in the eyes of civil lay by going through a ceremony the new papers called "marriage." What does God think of such practices? These people were all far too intelligent to be atheists. They know there is the supernatural as well as the natural, therefore, if they defect from God they automatically become Satanists as far as this world is concerned, and Luciferian as far as the next world is concerned. (For further details see pp. 212 and 213 *Red Fog Over America*.)

If these top level intellectuals who advocate the establishment of a One World Government intended to put God's plan for the rule of the whole of the universe into effect upon this earth it hardly seems likely that they would pack the civil services of ALL remaining governments with homosexuals. Any person who has had to live in London, Ottawa and/or Washington knows that as far as homosexualism is concerned all three are modern cities like Sodom and Gomorrah. "Burgess and McLean Case" is typical of what I mean. Professor Pitrim Sorokin of Harvard University published an exposure of this angle of the Luciferian conspiracy in a book entitled *The American Sex*

Revolution. The author states that perverted sexual behavior plays a major part in modern U.S. political life and that sex bribery and blackmail are now as prevalent as monetary corruption. He states "sexually infamous persons, or their protégé, are being appointed to ambassadorships and other high offices; profligates sometimes become popular mayors of metropolises, members of cabinets, or leaders of political parties. Among our political officials there is a vast legion of profligates both heterosexual and homosexual. Our morals have changed so notably that contingency, chastity, and faithfulness are increasingly viewed as oddities."

Professor Sorokin's book didn't get the same kind, or volume, of publicity as did Dr. Kinsey's books dealing with the alleged moral practices of males and females. According to Satanism, it is perfectly right, and proper, to encourage moral turpitude in all classes of society, and at all levels of government, by convincing the public that abnormal sexual behavior is normal; and that the moral code accepted by civilized nations, based on the Commandments of God and teachings of the Holy Scriptures, is old fashioned and introduced by Church and state for selfish purposes. But behind the building up of a WRONG conception of sex, and its purposes as intended by God our Creator, is the Satanic principle that "The best revolutionary is a youth absolutely devoid of morals." When Lenin stated this as recorded in *Pawns in The Game* he only confirmed what other Satanists had stated a hundred times previously. It is Satanism, as it is direct from THE TOP, which is responsible for the increase in juvenile delinquency, but those selected by the governments of the world to investigate this problem invariably give every CAUSE other than the right one. I have discussed the causes of juvenile delinquency with the heads of Church and state in Canada since 1923, but the Synagogue of Satan has always proved strong enough to prevent any TRUTHFUL public explanation of the cause, and the purpose, of those who direct the Luciferian conspiracy AT THE TOP. On the other hand, thousands of letters have been received from parents who read *The Red Fog Over America*, thanking us for explaining the causes which produce the effect we term juvenile delinquency. They tell us they find it much easier to counteract evil influences when they can explain clearly and truthfully to their children the reason Satanists work so hard to wean young people away from God by teaching them lies regarding sex. I repeat again, there is nothing wrong, nothing degrading, nothing to be ashamed of in sexual relationship as INTENDED BY GOD, but a great deal is wrong when multitudes deify sex, the promiscuous worship of the human body, and cunningly and slyly make each succeeding generation of human beings believe pre-marital experience, every form of sexual depravity and vice, is absolutely normal, providing pleasure is derived from such indulgences; and that contingency, chastity, and faithfulness are old fashioned.

The point I wish to make is this-the vast majority of men and women who sponsor and direct the campaign for a One World Government, other than Communism, are just as bitterly opposed to God as are the Communists.

The vast majority who promote the "idea" that a One World Government run by Luciferian intellectuals, rather than atheistic Communists, is the only solution to our problems are as devoid of morals as the proverbial mink. If they are against God and against atheistic Communism they must be Luciferian.

Confirmation of the above opinion was obtained when I discussed the relationship of changing public opinion regarding morals and spiritual values, and the increase of juvenile delinquency with a top level official of the Department of Health and Welfare in Canada. After a lengthy discussion, during which his attitude and facial expression showed he found it hard to believe that a man of my experience could still place spiritual values above material considerations, my companion literally snorted: "Well! What do you suggest we do ... clean every homosexual out of the civil service, and throw them in prison where they can indulge their queer ideas of pleasure to their hearts desire? Many of them are brilliantly minded men. When on the job they are efficient and work long hours. You seem to forget Oscar Wilde was a homosexual. Stop trying to save the human race. The vast majority aren't worth the time or the trouble. Most of them will be better off if they are forced to live under a totalitarian dictatorship; they will then get what the government decides is good for them."

Because I expressed "old fashioned ideas" regarding "Sin," "Morals," and "Marriage vows" some intellectuals I met decided I needed to have my mind cleaned. (Exactly what Weishaupt said was to be done in 1776.) I was brought in contact with the internationally famous specialist in mental health. This man was a graduate of the Freudian School of Psychiatry. He had studied in Vienna. He was on the staff of Dr. Broch Chisholm who was Canada's Minister of Health and Welfare at the time. Chisholm afterwards became the first president of the U.N.O.'s Health, and Mental Health Organizations. This man tried in a very friendly manner to change my ideas. I listened, I pretended to be interested, but I still remain to be convinced that God, who gave us the

Commandments, is "wrong," and Luciferianism which teaches the inversion of those commandments, is "right."

I read history, which mostly records wars and revolutions and therefore, the progress of the World Revolutionary Movement, to try to find out the "cause" which produced these destructive forces which result in such terrible sufferings. I thought at the time the lessons history teaches, if applied to past mistakes, could provide the solution to most of our problems. I was even then deceived into believing government was of the people, by the people, for the people. But a study of modern history showed that the younger generation is being taught to believe a pack of lies and deceits. Personal experience exposed this fact.

When in the hospital in 1945, I laid on my back and pondered over this strange truth. People who write history are not ignorant or fools. If they deliberately published lies and deceits with the knowledge and consent of our governments, then they must have a definite purpose. It was then I began to obtain books which recorded hidden history, and I delved and dug deeper and deeper, with the cooperation of one of Canada's leading librarians, until I was able to learn about the double lives men like Weishaupt and Pike had led. But although I continued studying and reading it was not until 1956, AFTER *Pawns in the Game* and *The Red Fog* had been published, that I finally realized that the Illuminati, whose secret plot and intentions I had exposed, were controlled AT THE TOP by the Synagogue of Satan. It wasn't until I was given information regarding Pike's dual personality, that I was able to dig up proof that the Synagogue of Satan is controlled by the High Priests of the Luciferian Creed. Once I had penetrated this secret it became obvious that the wars and revolutions which plague the world today are part and parcel of the Luciferian conspiracy, and that ALL aspects of the World Revolutionary Movement are part of that conspiracy.

Historians are restricted to recording events as they happen. They are not permitted to indulge in making deductions or surmises. My problem was to find out a way in which I could leave off recording history and obtain evidence which would enable me to project the course-line (party line in Communist and Illuminist double talk) into the future and on to its logical conclusion - the formation of a worldwide totalitarian dictatorship; and the imposition of the Luciferian ideology upon what is left of the human race. I could expose the conspiracy, its ultimate purpose, and objectives by quoting from the writings of Weishaupt, Mazzini, Pike, Lemmi, Lenin, Churchill, Roosevelt, and others, but I knew I would be accused of forgery and lunacy. I had to find documentary evidence. I had to find confirmation of the TRUTH, as it had been revealed to me, in a book or among documents, which the greatest encyclopedists wouldn't dare to challenge.

Then a strange thing happened. I was lying flat on my back on a fracture board. I had read everything within reach; I was tired thinking; I was bored. Then a thought entered my mind. I had read all the history 1 could get my hands on except BIBLE HISTORY I asked for a Bible and a King James version was brought to me. I glanced through the pages wondering if I had the will power and intestinal fortitude to wade through such an imposing volume. Then, after I had read a verse which threw light on present day conditions another thought entered my mind: "why don't you use the Bible as a yardstick to measure the correctness of the TRUTH or ERROR in the evidence you have gathered and particularly as regards the projections you are going to make, and the conclusions you are going to draw?"

That seemed a really good idea. It would save me the time it would have required to read both the Old and the New Testaments. From then on I used the Bible, the inspired word of God, to help me separate the wheat from the chaff as I browsed through the evidence which filled several trunks and filing cabinets.

Chapter 9

HOW THE SYNAGOGUE OF SATAN CONTROLS THE CHANNELS OF PUBLIC INFORMATION

At first I couldn't understand how the Synagogue of Satan (S.O.S.) could possibly control the publication and sales of newspapers, periodicals, and books throughout the world in order to keep the "Masses" from suspecting that the directors of the conspiracy plan to enslave them body, mind, and soul. Then the study of Robison's exposure of Weishaupt's "Twenty-two United Brethren" solved that problem. Weishaupt required that in every reading society, and in public libraries, the books to be read would be selected by the "Managers" who served the Illuminati. After they have molded public opinion, they make the "common" belief he is uttering his own sentiments when he is actually only echoing the thoughts put into his mind by the books, and articles, to which he is given access.

The booksellers in Weishaupt's day were also the publishers. When Weishaupt, through the Illuminati and their "Reading Societies," controlled the reading of the public, the publishers and booksellers, had to print what they wanted to have printed. Weishaupt even used his plan to FORCE authors to write material which directly or indirectly, furthered the plans of the S.O.S.

Today authors comply with this requirement or find it impossible to get their work published. To quote his own words Weishaupt wrote: "when we by degrees bring the whole trade of bookselling into our hands we shall bring it about that at least the writers who labor in the cause of superstition and restraint, will have neither a publisher nor readers." How true those words have turned out to be!

Then again he said: "when, lastly, by the spreading of (the influence) our fraternity, all "good" hearts and "sensible" men, will adhere to us and by our means will be put in a condition that enables them to work in silence upon all courts, families, secretaries, parish priests, public teachers and private tutors."

This it was that Weishaupt set up the plan to control ALL channels of public information. Can any unbiased person say that conditions today do not prove that newspapers, periodicals, books, play, TV. and radio only tell the public what those who direct the Synagogue of Satan want the public to know?

Was there ever a time when men and women over beer, liquor, and cocktails THINK they are voicing their own opinions when they are simply echoing what they have been forced to read or hear? Was there ever a day, since Weishaupt's time, that agentur of the One Worlders controlled the editorial policies of all types of publication, as they control editorial policy today?

While double tongued Illuminists boast about FREEDOM of THOUGHT, Freedom of Religion, Freedom of the Press, Freedom to speak, and Freedom from fear, just how much freedom does exist? Let any individual just try to argue against the propaganda put out by the agentur of the S.O.S. and he is immediately knocked down, smeared, boycotted, ridiculed, and represented as having a nut loose in the upper story, either that or he is accused of being completely insane.

Weishaupt adopted the six pointed star as one of the emblems of his Illuminati, not because it is the Star of David, but because his program consists of six main points. They are as follows:

1. Abolition of all existing governments.

2. Abolition of all existing religions.

3. Abolition of all private property.

4. Abolition of all inheritance.

5. Abolition of the family, as the "cell" from which civilized society shall develop.

6. Abolition of patriotism, as far as national government are concerned.

How can the above objectives form part of a Roman Catholic, Jewish, or Masonic plot to achieve world domination? Pike, Weishaupt's successor, has distinctly stipulated in his works written a century later that:

1. The first world government shall be turned into "A totalitarian Luciferian dictatorship."

2. The universal religion imposed upon those of the Goyim (human cattle) who survive the final social cataclysm, shall be "The True Light of the pure doctrine of Lucifer."

3. That all the Goyim shall be enslaved and turned into "one vast conglomeration of mongrelized humanity."

4.   That breeding will be strictly limited to types and numbers "required to fill the requirements of the state (God)."

5.   That all breeding, as far as the Goyim are concerned, will be done by artificial insemination practiced on an international scale, and limited to 5% of males and 30% of females specially selected for this purpose.

6.   That rigid control of the minds of the Goyim shall "erase all knowledge of the past, including religions, other than the Luciferian ideology, and of all other forms of government other than the Luciferian dictatorship."

Because bigotry is used by those who serve the S.O.S. to keep those they plot to subjugate divided amongst themselves on religious and racial issues, I wish to debunk those who claim the World Revolutionary Movement is designed to give Roman Catholics, Communists, Jews, Freemasons, Nazi, or any other political or religious group undisputed world domination. Don't for one moment think I am not fully aware of the fact that there are bigoted, narrow minded, foolish and utterly deceived Roman Catholics, Communists, Jews, Freemasons, Fascists and others who firmly believe that the world's problems will not be permanently solved until the organization to which they belong, be it religious and/or political, does rule the world.

Most of those who so believe have convinced themselves as Roman Catholics, Jews, Freemasons, Communists, or World Federalists, that if they hope, pray, and work hard enough the day will come when their organization will be able to establish a benevolent dictatorship and enforce rule in accordance with their own religious and so-called democratic principles. These deceived people indeed need enlightenment. The Third World War was planned by Pike nearly a century ago. It is now in the making. The final social cataclysm as he explained it to Mazzini August 15, 1871, and as it has been explained to members of the Palladian Rite and Grand Orient Lodges by lecturers ever since 1885, is to be made to involve not only Roman Catholicism but the whole of the so-called Christian world, and the masses who are now controlled by Communism in Russia and China. Freemasonry and Judaism are also to be destroyed in order that the Luciferian ideology... "The New Order" ... may be established on the ruins of ALL the old orders. Gentiles and Jews, Communists and Freemasons should not fool themselves. They and their beliefs are ALL marked down for complete liquidation, as are all other political, religious, social service, and similar organizations. It is intended that there shall be a clean sweep, a purification by "The Fire of the Magi."

To prove how ridiculous the charges against Catholicism really are, history proves the Vatican suspended the Jesuits as a teaching order after Weishaupt's perfidy had been made known. This suspension wasn't lifted for many years (I believe it was 30 years). While Weishaupt remained unsuspected, he was "happy" as a Jesuit. He wore a "cloak" that hid perfectly his diabolical activities. But when the Jesuits were disbanded by papal Bull, he showed his true colours and directed the Illuminati's hatred against all members of the Jesuit Order. This hatred has been continued by Illuminists against the Jesuits ever since. Jesuit schools and colleges have been closed and the members of the Order have been persecuted in every revolution since.

To prove how ridiculous it is to charge Freemasons with directing the W.R.M. we have only to study the efforts of Professor Robison of Scotland, the Duke of Brunswich in Germany, and the Grand Masters of British Lodges, and Captain Henry Morgan of New England, USA, made to try to stop Illuminists infiltrating into the Lodges of Freemasonry, and to prevent Freemasons fraternizing with Grand Orient Masons, and those of Pike's New and Reformed Palladian Rites. We must remember also that Copin-Albancelli was a 33rd degree Mason. He was selected to go beyond the 33rd degree into the mysteries of the Grand Orient Masonry and those of the Palladian Rite. He refused at the very last minute, just before initiation, because he had become convinced that on the other side of the dark curtain was Satanism which ruled with absolute despotism. Weishaupt's revised version of the Protocols says exactly how Masons, suspected of knowing too much, shall be disposed of. He sets forth clearly how ALL forms of Masonry, and other secret societies, are to be abolished once the leader of Luciferianism is crowned King-despot of this world.

It is equally absurd to contend Judaism is the root of all evil as it is to claim the "Protocols," as exposed by Sergy Nilus (1905) and Victor Marsden (1921), are those of the "Learned Elders of Zion." It is true many, far too many, Jews have been deceived into joining revolutionary organizations. But it is equally true that seven years after Lenin usurped absolute power in Russia, on behalf of the Synagogue of Satan, there wasn't a single Jewish member of the First International who hadn't been liquidated or imprisoned. We would also like to point out that a great number of real Jews today are not Zionists. They hate political Zionism because they can see clearly that it is designed to lead them to their own ultimate subjugation and destruction as a race. Lucifer is not concerned whether the souls he wins away from God are white or black, Gentile or Jew. All are fish in his net. There are just as few real Jews in the Synagogue of Satan today as there were in the days of Jesus Christ.

The Duke of Brunswick had been a member of Weishaupt's Illuminati. His "nickname" was "Aaron." But when he found out he had been deceived regarding Weishaupt's real intentions, he did his utmost to stamp Grand Orient Masonry out in Germany. In 1794 he issued a manifesto dissolving Freemasonry in Germany on the grounds that the Illuminati's secret agents had obtained such control of it that dissolution was the only remedy left.

In 1878 the head of British Freemasons ordered Masons to "withdraw completely from all connections with Grand Orient Masonry." Again in 1923 the heads of British Masonry issued the following manifesto regarding Grand Orient Masonry: "As recognition was withdrawn from that body by the United Grand Lodge of England in 1878 ... it is considered necessary to warn all members of our lodges that they cannot visit any lodge under the obedience of a jurisdiction unrecognized by the United Grand Lodge of England; and further, that under rule 150 of the Book of Constitutions, they cannot admit visitors therefrom."

Weishaupt and Pike are both on record as saying Jews, and also anti-Semitism, were to be used to serve their own secret plans and diabolical ambitions. This phase of the conspiracy will be dealt with more fully later.

We give the above information in order that people who are sincere in their search for the TRUTH may be on their guard against bigots and those who stir up strife based on differences of color, race and/or creed.

Time after time we have it dinned in our ears, in the press, on TV, by public speakers, by parliamentarians, from pulpits everywhere, all the time, that Communism is in reality a fight for possession of the minds of men, and therefore the root of all evil, and responsible for the mess the world finds itself today. That is the biggest lie the S.O.S. ever thought up and propagated. But that lie is not one iota different from the lie circulated to enable the S.O.S. to foment World Wars One and Two. We were told in America and Britain that Nazism was the root of all evil, and responsible for the chaotic conditions in the world. The masses in Germany, and the countries which were to be her allies, were made to believe the same untruths regarding the British and Americans.

Hitler wasn't an atheist. He most certainly wasn't a Christian; therefore he must have been a member of the Synagogue of Satan.

This allegation is supported by the fact that it was Hitler who said "tell a big enough lie often enough and it will be accepted as the TRUTH." Winston Churchill isn't a Communist or a Nazi, but he can't be much of a Christian either because he said, "I will join hands with the Devil if by so doing he will help me defeat that ----- Hitler."

Before we trace the perfect continuity of the Luciferian conspiracy, as directed and controlled by the human beings who have constituted the Synagogue of Satan since 1776, we will first prove that the conspiracy, as revised and modernized by Weishaupt, never did die a natural death as those who directed it since, would have the public, and their elected representatives, believe.

The TRUTH is that both Communism and Nazism consider only the materialistic concepts of world domination. They seek control of our bodies so that physical control will enable them to control our minds and make us accept their materialistic ideologies. The Synagogue of Satan, however, believes in the supernatural and use Communism and Nazism to further their own secret plans. The S.O.S. is determined to obtain control of our minds so that it can determine the destiny of our immortal souls. Satanism has been delivering millions of human souls to Lucifer every few weeks. During an all-out war or revolution, the Satanic harvest in souls reaches its peak. Don't let yourselves be deceived. Don't let those who serve the devil's cause, regardless of how they are disguised, pull the wool over your eyes. The eyes are the windows of the soul. Then don't let so- called Illuminists pull down the blinds over your eyes. Insist on looking out through the window so you can see not only to the horizons of this world but appreciate that the struggle going on in this world is to increase the size of the Devil's domains in the celestial world after God renders final judgment.

(Nesta Webster, and other historians confirm what I learned as the result of my own investigations. Directors of Naval Intelligence, and the late Inspector John Leopold, who was in charge of the anti-subversive branch of the R.C.M.P., 1943 to 1945, while I was in Ottawa, and other students of the World Revolutionary Movement, both clerical and secular agree that we are contending with the spiritual forces of darkness.)

Weishaupt, after he was banished, remained the Devil's agent in human form. He directed the Luciferian conspiracy so that it developed into the Great French Revolution and others, including the American Revolution. We will deal later with the reason Weishaupt's plan required the United States of America to become the last great nationalistic world power.

Weishaupt's Illuminati, and his Lodges of the Grand Orient, went underground. They were succeeded by the Jacobin Clubs and convents as has been explained in *Pawns in The Game*. Mirabeau directed the French Revolution. He was ably assisted by Adrien Duport, who was also an initiate of the Higher Degrees of the Illuminati. It was Duport who set before the Committee of Propaganda the policy of destruction they were to carry out on May 21, 1790.

When Weishaupt had destroyed France as a monarchy and a world power, and had Americans cut each other's throat because of alleged grievances which propaganda made appear very real, he then moved to Italy.

Illuminism was running hog-wild in Italy. Under various names and disguise, it was aimed at the destruction of the Vatican because it was both a spiritual as well as a temporal power. The Italian Illuminists reasoned, "how can we destroy ALL governments and ALL religions if we don't first of all destroy the Vatican." But this line of reasoning was not in keeping with Weishaupt's plans as we will prove.

Italian Grand Orient Masons and Illuminists, and Alta Vendita members had not been initiated into the FULL secret. According to Weishaupt's plan, as has been confirmed by Mazzini, Pike, Lemmi, and Lenin, the Vatican is to be allowed to survive, and control nearly 500,000,000 souls, until those who direct the Synagogue of Satan decide it is time to involve ALL Christian people in the final social cataclysm with all people controlled by atheistic-Communists. For this reason Weishaupt hurried to Italy to prevent a premature destruction of the Vatican. Nearly one hundred years later Pike had to take similar action to prevent first Mazzini and later Lemmi from upsetting the Synagogue of Satan's plans by doing exactly the same thing, All this proves that only a very few men who comprise the High Priesthood of the Luciferian Creed know the full secret and how their conspiracy is intended to reach its final goal.

Chapter 10

PROOF OF THE CONSPIRACY

Its Introduction into America

Those who directed the "Great" French Revolution used a preconceived "Reign of Terror" to put into effect the Luciferian principle that the Goyim are to be reduced to one common level in subjection. It is this principle that Cromwell's "Roundheads" demonstrated so effectively when they put the "Levellers" into action after the Synagogue of Satan had helped remove the Crowned Head of England and usurp dictatorial power.

Those who serve the Synagogue of Satan are still engaged in leveling the Goyim. Instead of raising women up to the high levels of morality and virtue once practiced by women who patterned their behavior on that of the Mother of Jesus Christ, Satanists have introduced "modernism" which dragged women down to the level of males. They call this "Women's Suffrage." The purpose was stated to be to "free women from slavery of body, mind, and soul," if we heed what Mrs. Pankhurst and others had to say. But behind the "window dressing" is the intention to brainwash women into a pattern of behaviors which will cause men to withdraw their respect and kill chivalry. This is all part of the conspiracy to reduce women to be either the play-things of the ruling classes or human incubators to supply the numbers and types of individuals the Dictator will decide are necessary to fill the requirements of the state.

Under God's plan for the rule of the Universe all His Creatures were born unequal. It is common fallacy to believe all men are born equal. It is a half-truth which is worse than a down right lie. The ONLY manner in which all men are equal is inasmuch as they all have a body and soul. As far as mental capacity, bodily stamina, physical beauty and spiritual characteristics are concerned no two people in the entire world are alike or equal.

God intended that every one of His human creatures could, if they so desired, develop spiritually until qualified to fill the highest places in Heaven. Because human beings, as well as angels, have intellects, and the use of their free will, they can deteriorate until they qualify for the lowest levels in Hell. Talk of a classless world is pure Luciferian doctrine. Lucifer's capacity for love has turned into a capacity for hate. He knows he was and is wrong, but he is determined to drag as many human souls down to his level as is possible; he is succeeding in a terribly efficient manner. The words of Our Lord "For many are called, but few are chosen," are so true that to think about what is going on in the world today, under the influence of Satanism, is truly terrifying. But that does not relieve us from the responsibility of putting an end to the diabolically inspired conspiracy. Far too many people just don't want to hear anything unpleasant. They don't want to meddle in dirty affairs. Like oysters they want to confine themselves within a shell. They are the real untouchables. Their motto is: "I mind my own business. Let other see to theirs, and may the Devil take the hindmost." I can't imagine Heaven being filled with such creatures, but they will surely fit nicely into hell.

We have dealt with how leveling was achieved during the French Revolution in *Pawns in The Game*, so we will now go with Weishaupt to Italy in order to show how the Synagogue of Satan controlled ALL aspects of the W.R.M. then as they do today.

In keeping with his intention to make authorities, in Church and state, believe the Illuminati was dead, Weishaupt arranged that the secret revolutionary society in Italy, known as "The Carbonari," be revived and reorganized to put the plans of the S.O.S. into effect. He needed a gang of assassins to liquidate individuals and movements which opposed internationalism. Carbonarism was revived in 1815. The Grand Secret Consistory held a meeting October 13, 1820. As a result the Carbonari became part and parcel of Grand Orient Masonry. Its members have committed nearly all political murders ever since. Like all evil groups, controlled by the S.O.S., the Carbonari operated under many names. One off-shoot was the Mafia which operated particularly in the United States of America. They direct "Gang" wars which put men selected by the S.O.S. at the head of organized labor, gambling, dope peddling, white slavery, and all other forms of vice. The Mafia is more powerful and active in the U.S.A. today than ever before.

Guiseppe Mazzini was initiated into the Carbonari and Grand Orient Masonry, in 1827. Weishaupt ordered him to go to America and secretly develop the part America was to play in the final stages of the Luciferian conspiracy. Many students of the W.R.M. express the opinion that it was Mazzini who became the mentor who controlled Pike until 1872 when he (Mazzini) died. With this opinion I must disagree.

I know it will hurt a great many good American people to learn that Thomas Jefferson was just another, publicity made, idol who had feet of clay. The Synagogue of Satan needed to obtain control of America so that they could use this new giant to enable them to bring the semi-final and final stages of their revolutionary plan to fruition. In order to do this America had to be separated from Great Britain. Despite all the agentur of the S.O.S. had done, Britain in some strange way, or by the grace of God, had rejected revolutionary action to bring about a change of government. Illuminist Manuilsky said when discussing Britain in a speech he made to the delegates attending the 18th Congress of the Communist Party (international) in Moscow in 1938: "Britain is the rock upon which the waves of revolution have so far dashed themselves in vain. *Britain and her people must be destroyed before we can reach our ultimate objectives.*"

Manuilsky is no more an atheistic Communist than I am. He is a top ranking member of the S.O.S. who succeeded Lenin as the Illuminati's director of political action which, as we have previously stated, in the jargon of Illuminism means Director of the W.R.M. As I explained in *Red Fog Over America*, the second World War was designed to reduce Britain to a third class world power. It started the following year. Manuilsky, although proved to be a director of the W.R.M., was made President of the United Nations Security Council as soon as the U.N. was born.[23]

The Synagogue of Satan's agentur were busy in America soon after Columbus discovered the lower parts of what is now the U.S.A. Contrary to general belief the northern part of America from Labrador to Virginia had been discovered and explored by the Vikings hundreds of years before Columbus was born.[24]

---

23 When I served in the Canadian Navy during World War Two, part of the time as Staff Officer Operations with headquarters at Shelbourne, N.S. and later as Senior Naval Officer at Goose Bay, Labrador, I had the opportunity to see the Runic messages the Vikings had cut into flat rocks along the shoreline as they worked their way south after landing on North America From Greenland. The Runic language, and characters, had fallen into disuse long before Columbus was born. I only mention this fact because it helps to prove that those who serve the Devil do control our educational systems so that children are now being indoctrinated and not educated.

24 For further particulars read pages 12 to 18 and 98 of *Pawns in the Game*.

Many people who have read *Pawns in the Game*, and *The Red Fog Over America* have asked me "why is it men sell their immortal souls to the Devil when they know they can't take material wealth and temporal power with them?"

The answer is this: They believe Lucifer will give them their eternal reward, just as those of us who believe in God believe He will give us our reward in Heaven.

It is belief in the supernatural which marks the difference between those who serve the S.O.S. and atheists.

Weishaupt told his close associates, when discussing atheists and nihilists, that organizing them into international communism, and using their destructive force to further their own secret plans and ambitions, was justified because Communism and atheism are only passing phases of the W.R.M.. He and Pike both provided that Communism will be completely erased in the final stages of the conspiracy. Pike confirmed this in his letter to Mazzini dated August 15, 1871.

Nobody explained why the S.O.S. provide for the perfect continuity of the direction of the Luciferian conspiracy better than did Voltaire. "It may last for years, perhaps for centuries. In our ranks a soldier dies but the war (against God) is continued."

Lenin went one step further. He said it might take three thousand years before the World Revolutionary Movement reached its final stage and the proletariat took over and established a classless world and socialist government.

Lenin was an adept of the highest degrees in Grand Orient Masonry. He knew the final secret as did Mazzini and Lemmi before him. He was using double talk to answer the question, "how long will you maintain an absolute dictatorship?"

Because the Master Satanists serve the Father of Lies, they invariably make the public believe what they do is for the honor and glory of God, and in the public interest. That has been their excuse for fomenting every war and revolution fought to-date. As history proves, the most horrible, and most terrible, atrocities have been perpetrated on individuals, and on the masses of humanity, in the Holy Name of God. Our Blessed Lord warned us this would happen when he said, "Yes, the time cometh that whosoever killeth you will think he doeth God service." (John 16:2) We Christians killed each other by the tens of millions in World Wars One and Two ... men... women ... and little children and both sides did what they did because the Synagogue of Satan had deceived us into believing we were serving God and our countries.

Because Lucifer is "Master of Deceit" those who comprise the S.O.S. use their agentur, working behind the scenes of government, to make our rulers, be they kings or presidents, adopt policies which start wars and/or revolutions. Sometimes those who fomented wars and/or revolutions used the flimsiest excuses. In the light of recent history surely few people remain so gullible that they can't see that wars and revolutions are planned a long, long time in advance. Every war and revolution fought since 1776 was designed to bring closer Weishaupt's conspiracy to destroy ALL governments and religions so the Luciferian ideology can be imposed on the human race. The very fact that nations who are enemies in one war are allied in the next proves the truth of the above statement. The S.O.S. line up nations so that a "balance of power" is maintained. This assures them that the utmost destruction can be accomplished in a given time. Then weight is thrown on the side of the S.O.S. wish to win. But the victor only wins an empty victory. As wars were developed into global wars the power and strength of the U.S.A. was twice held back two years, before being released to bring about the defeat of Germany and her allies. Nazism, just another name for Nierzcheism, had been organized and used just as Weishaupt and Pike intended. Having served its purpose of enabling the S.O.S. to foment World Wars One and Two it had to be destroyed. Those Nazi leaders, who knew too much, were liquidated by "due process of law" exactly as Weishaupt said was to be done away back in the 1770's.

But to get back to Pike and Mazzini, I wish to point out the fact that the High Priests of the Luciferian Creed control the Synagogue of Satan. That was true regarding the plot to crucify Christ. It is true regarding Mazzini, Lemmi, Lenin, and Manuilsky who, in turn, directed the revolutionary plans of the conspirators since 1834. The evidence already submitted should prove that neither Mazzini nor Lemmi were made acquainted with the Full Secret until long after they had been selected to be "Directors of Political Action." Pike reorganized the Palladian Rite to provide a secret headquarters for those who direct the W.R.M. because the Lodges of the Grand Orient were becoming more and more suspected as the result of Mazzini's and Lemmi's activities. Pike, working from his headquarters in Charleston, S.C. established two supervisory councils to govern the political and dogmatic activities of the other twenty three councils he and Mazzini had located throughout the world. In Rome, under Mazzini, the council supervised "Political action" against governments. In Berlin the supervisory council supervised the dogmatic and financial policies and activities of the S.O.S. The manner in which the director of dogmatic activities developed Nietzcheism into Nazism and then had it destroyed is typical of what I mean. But long before Pike became High Priest of the Luciferian Creed direction of the conspiracy, AT THE TOP, had been from Charleston, S.C. Pike succeeded Moses Holbrook and direction of the conspiracy, AT THE TOP, has remained in the U.S.A. ever since.

The book *Irish and English Freemasons and their Foreign Brothers*, published in 1878, throws considerable light on this phase of the conspiracy. Like all other books, which contain information which throws even a little light on the diabolical direction of the W.R.M., this book is practically unknown. There are, however, still copies in some of the remaining national archives. I am informed there was a copy in the Vatican Library as recently as 1946. Beginning on page 62 of the above named book we learn that the Highest Authority of the Grand Orient in Italy, i.e., Mazzini or Lemmi, issued "Permanent Instruction (or Practical Code of Rules) Guide for the Heads of the Highest Grades of Masonry."

One section of this document says "Our final aim is that of Voltaire, and of the French Revolution the complete annihilation of Catholicism, and ultimately Christianity. Were Christianity to survive, even upon the ruins of Rome, it would, a little later on revive and live. We must now consider how to reach our end with certainty, not by cheating ourselves with delusions, which would prolong indefinitely, and probably compromise the ultimate success of our cause .... The Pope, whoever he may be, will never enter into a secret society. It then becomes the duty of the secret society to make the first advance to the Church and to the Pope with the objective of conquering both. The work for which we gird ourselves is not the work of a day, nor a month, nor a year ... that which we should seek, that which we should await, as the Jews await a Messiah, is a Pope according to our wants....

"But when, and how the unknown cannot yet be seen. The Scriptures indicate and the greatest theologians confirm that despite the supernatural gifts of both angels who have fallen, and those which remain faithful to God, He (God) withheld from the angels the power of foreseeing the future. In other words, they can plan thousands of years in advance the Luciferian conspiracy, but they cannot be sure that their plans are going to mature as they expect. That is why their agents on earth are always trying to learn what the future holds. Thus the old saying "Man proposes, but God disposes." Nevertheless, as nothing should move us from our mapped out plan, we must labor at our newly commenced work as if tomorrow would bring us success."

The Supreme executive of the Lodges of the Grand Orient then issued instructions that the document was issued for the information of the rulers of the Supreme Vendita. They said, "the information is to be kept concealed from those simply initiated." The brethren were to be inculcated by means of "insegnamento" meaning "secret memoranda."

The plot cooked up by Weishaupt and Mazzini was for Italians and others posing as Roman Catholics to infiltrate into the Vatican and, as Weishaupt had previously stated, "bore from within until it remains nothing but an empty shell." What Mazzini was instructed to do in the Vatican by Weishaupt himself, he later instructed General Albert Pike to do at the top levels of Freemasonry; and what Adolphe Isaac Cremieux was selected to do in the higher controls of Orthodox Judaism.

The instructions given were the same. Those selected to put this phase of the plot into execution were to place agentur of the Illuminati in executive positions in all three organizations and get themselves recognized as "specialists," "experts," and "advisers." They were not to attempt to interfere in anyway with the established teachings and policies of the three religions, but they were to guard against the directors of the three world powers getting information which might make them suspicious that the Synagogue of Satan controlled ALL subversive movements AT THE TOP. They were by one means or another to enforce silence on any who grew suspicious.

The late Pope Pius XII must have suspected something was radically wrong within the Vatican because he couldn't possibly have remained ignorant that he was under continual surveillance. It is most significant that when this surveillance was relaxed, when it was thought he was at the moment of death in 1958 he sent for a trusted secretary and ordered him to ask the 500,000,000 members of the Roman Catholic Church to pray for the "Silent Church." A misinterpretation was put on the meaning of his words. It was published in the Catholic Press that His Holiness meant the Church behind the Iron and Bamboo Curtains. This is not so. He invariably said exactly what he meant. If he had wanted the Faithful to pray for the "Persecuted Church" he would have said so. He asked them to pray for the Church that was silent although free.

Then again the Pope said, and afterwards reiterated that he had seen and talked with Christ. But this was also hushed up. WHY?

Adolphe Isaac Cremieux (1796-1880) came from a so-called Jewish family, of the south of France. He was admitted to the bar at Nimes in 1817. He was typical of the lawyers Weishaupt had said were to be recruited into the Illuminati. Exactly as Pike was afterwards, Cremieux was infiltrated into Freemasonry. He was a member of the Lodge of Mizraim, the Scottish Rite, and subsequently was initiated into the Lodges of the Grand Orient.

Cremieux worked to unite the above named secret societies and became the Grand Master in France as did Pike in America, and Mazzini in Italy.

Cremieux's activities were financed by the Rothschilds and the Montifiores. He engaged in the most ruthless forms of political intrigue and chicanery. The whole resources of the S.O.S. were used to try and make him Chief Executive to Louis Napoleon so he could promote policies which would further the Luciferian conspiracy from behind the scenes of the British government about the same time. But his double crossing methods were discovered, and when Louis Napoleon pulled off his coup d'etat on December 2, 1851, making himself Emperor Napoleon III, he made General Cavaignac his Prime Minister and threw Cremieux into prison. He was confined in the prisons of Vuicennes and Mazas. Upon release, Cremieux was selected to help direct the activities of Karl Marx and other revolutionaries including Louis Blanc, Ledrun, Rollin, Pierre, and many others.

Cremieux put the S.O.S.'s plans for wars and revolutions into effect in France as Mazzini's other national directors did in Germany and other countries. Thus the overthrow of Napoleon was accomplished as was the defeat of France by Germany in the year 1871. At this point Cremieux again became openly engaged in politics and he was made president of the "Alliance Israelite Universelle" (A.L.U.). As far back as May 31,1864, Cremieux told the General Assembly of the A.L.U.: "The alliance is not limited to our cult, it voices its appeals to all cults and wants to penetrate in all the religions as it has penetrated into all countries. Let us endeavor boldly to bring about the union of all cults under one flag of Union and Progress. Such is the slogan of Humanity." (Internationalism)

We hear today the same old double talk in favor of a One World Government. John Leopold, when head of the anti-subversive section of the Royal Canadian Mounted Police, admitted to me in 1944 that the American

Jewish Committee is the outgrowth of the Alliance Israelite Universelle. Leopold was a real Jew (Hebrew). He told me the American and Canadian Jewish Committees controlled Jewish Communists AT THE TOP absolutely. He agreed the Alliance Israelite Universelle was organized and directed AT THE TOP by the Synagogue of Satan. He said the A.I.U. and A.J.C. were no more genuine Jewish associations than are the Illuminized Lodges of Grand Orient Masonry nor the Councils of the Palladian Rite, genuine Freemasonry as practiced in the Scottish Rite Lodges in Britain and America.

Chapter 11

GENERAL ALBERT PIKE AND THE CONSPIRACY

Fully cognizant with the fact that telling the truth will hurt many people, and anger those who serve the Devil's purpose, we still feel it is necessary to give the public proof that General Albert Pike lived a dual life. The fact that so little is known regarding his secret, private life isn't to be wondered at. The Synagogue of Satan are sons of the Father of lies (Lucifer); those who control and direct the Luciferian conspiracy on this earth are "Masters of Deceit."

For this reason, those who have constituted the S.O.S. down through the centuries have been represented to the masses as great patriots, great philanthropists, great Gentiles, great Jews. When history or research proves they had Jekyl and Hyde personalities, we call them "Idols with feet of clay." People the S.O.S. use to further their secret plans are built up as public personages so they can better influence the minds of "their public." The present practice of deification of everyone who is connected with Hollywood illustrates perfectly what I mean.

Actresses are given parts depicting them as being as promiscuous as the proverbial mink. This is Satanism in action. The purpose behind this is to break down the morals of the younger generation. If it is 'right' for their idols to live 'modern' and have sexual intercourse with every man who takes their fancy, the teenagers are led to believe there is no sin involved in living 'modern' also. Parents and ministers who say differently are branded silly and old-fashioned. Those who direct the W.R.M. AT THE TOP say, "The best revolutionary is a young person absolutely devoid of morals."

Hidden history proves that General Albert Pike is one of those men for whom the Holy Scriptures tells us to watch out. In Matt. 24:24, Mark 13:22, 14:56, etc., we are told false prophets and false Christs shall arise and shall show signs and wonders, to seduce (deceive), if it were possible, even the 'Elect.' Documentary evidence proves that Pike was not only a false Christ, he was, before he died, the High Priest of the Luciferian ideology on this earth, and as such, controlled the Synagogue of Satan.

His military blueprint called for three world wars, and three major revolutions, to bring Weishaupt's revised version of the age-old Luciferian conspiracy to its final stage. In the 1860's he is recorded as saying his military program might take one hundred years or a little longer to reach the day when those who direct the conspiracy AT THE TOP will crown their leader King-despot of the entire world, and impose a Luciferian totalitarian dictatorship upon what is left of the human race.

When Weishaupt organized the Illuminati 1776 to 1784, to put his revised and modernized version of the Luciferian Protocols into effect, he and his associates are recorded as discussing whether they should use Christianity, Judaism, Freemasonry, or atheism as a cloak under which to hide their secret plans and activities. This was much the same decision the Khazar leaders had to make when they set out to conquer Europe 300 A.D. Those who directed the Khazar invasion into south-eastern Europe decided to force Talmudism on those they led and conquered, in preference to Mohammedanism or Christianity. They therefore used anti-Mohammedanism and anti-Christianity as emotions to serve their evil purpose.

Weishaupt and his Illuminati decided to benefit by the lessons history had taught in this regard. They decided to use all four of these religions to cloak their evil purposes and further their own secret plans and diabolical ambitions.

Weishaupt decided that the Illuminati would infiltrate into Freemasonry because it was a secret society wherein members could be bound by oath not to divulge anything they might hear or learn. Even the apprentices, the very beginners are required to swear "In the Name of the Supreme Architect of all the World, I... name ... will never reveal the secrets, signs, touches, words, doctrines, or customs of the Free-masons, and will maintain above all an eternal silence concerning them. I promise, and I swear to God, not to reveal anything by pen, signs, words, or gestures, and never to have written, lithographed, printed, or published anything which has been confided to me up to now and may be confided henceforth. I bind myself and I submit to the subsequent punishment if I fail to keep my word; May they burn my lips with a red-hot iron - may they cut off my hand, and my neck, and snatch out my tongue, may my corpse be hanged in the Lodge during the admission of a new brother so that it may serve as a stigma of my infidelity, and an object of horror to the rest. May it be burned afterwards, and the ashes cast to the wind so that no trace remains of the memory of my treachery. Thus may God and His Holy Gospel help me. So be it." (Eckert Vol. I, pp. 33-34.)

We publish the oath only to prove that the lower degree Masons honestly and sincerely believe they are joining the secret society to further the cause of God and help their fellow men as God commanded. When initiated they unselfishly intend to fulfill this duty to the limit of their ability and resources. The vast majority of 32nd and 33rd degree Masons do not know, or even suspect, that AT THE VERY TOP, beyond the reach of all except those specially selected is the Synagogue of Satan, controlled by High Priests of the Luciferian Creed.

Weishaupt was quite implicit in his instructions that Masonic Lodges are only to be used as places in which the Illuminati could organize a secret society within a secret society. He made it perfectly clear that the purpose of infiltration was to place Illuminists in position so they could contact men of high social standing and proven ability in business, the arts, professions, and politics, etc. The Illuminati then use their power and influence to place their agentur in key positions in all levels of society and fields of human endeavor. The ordinary members were to be used only for promoting the idea of One World Government and One World Religion.

The Masters of Deceit wanted to use Masonic philanthropy simply to cover their diabolical purpose and to give their agents an air of respectability. The lesson to be learned is this: No Christian should swear to maintain secrecy unless he has full knowledge of what the oath of secrecy involves. To promote God's intentions, we must make them known. Those who promote Luciferianism keep their plans and objective secret.

The following is the frontispiece of a book written by Albert Pike.

MORALS AND DOGMA OF THE

ANCIENT AND ACCEPTED SCOTTISH RITE

of FREEMASONRY

Prepared for the Supreme Council of the Thirty-third Degree

for the

Southern Jurisdiction of the United States

And

Published by its Authority

On the back of the frontispiece is: "Entered according to Act of Congress, in the year 1871, by Albert Pike, in the Office of the Librarian of Congress, at Washington, D.C. Entered according to Act of Congress in the year 1905, by the Supreme Council of the Southern Jurisdiction. A.A.S.R, U.S.A., in the Office of the Librarian of Congress, at Washington, D.C."

We quote from Chapter XXX, Knight of Kadosh; page 819: "The Blue Degrees are but the outer court or portico of the Temple. Part of the symbols are displayed there to the initiate, but he is intentionally misled by false interpretations. It is not intended that he shall understand time; but it is intended that he shall imagine he understands them. Their true explication is reserved for the ADEPTS, the PRINCES OF MASONRY. The whole body of the Royal and Sacerdotal Art was hidden so carefully, centuries since, in the High Degrees, as that it is even yet impossible to solve many of the enigmas which they contain. It is well enough for the mass of those called Masons, to imagine that all is contained in the BLUE DEGREES: and whose attempts to undeceive them will labor in vain, and without any true reward violate his obligations as an Adept. Masonry is the veritable Sphinx, buried to the head in the sands heaped round by the ages."

The book this was obtained from bears this publisher's name: L.H. Jenkis, Inc., Richmond, Virginia, May, 1920.

The manner in which Illuminists infiltrated into the Lodges of the Scottish Rite located throughout the world is best illustrated by telling the life story of General Albert Pike. This story reveals how professors who are of the Illuminati, select exceptionally brilliant students and indoctrinate them into one form or another of internationalism. They then use them to serve those who direct the Luciferian conspiracy. Pike's life also illustrates how those who direct the World Revolutionary Movement AT THETOP obtain control of high ranking officers in the armed forces of their respective countries. I solemnly declare that until 1957, I knew only the side of Pike's life story which showed him to be a great scholar, a clever lawyer, a brave soldier, a fervent Christian, and all-in-all, a great American patriot. I did not even mention his name in connection with the World Revolutionary Movement in the first editions of *Pawns in the Game* or *The Red Fog Over America*. My belief regarding General Albert Pike prior to 1957 was that of literally millions of other people, particularly Freemasons, in every country of the world. But quite by accident, while studying what was behind the "Little Rock Incident" I picked up a clue that indicated Albert Pike had lived a double life. Investigations proved he was the greatest Dr. Jekyl and Mr. Hyde of the 19th Century. First I shall give my reader the picture I had of Albert Pike prior to 1957.

Albert Pike, American Patriot and Christian Gentleman

General Albert Pike was born in Boston, Mass., December 29, 1809. His parents moved to Newbury Mass., when Albert was four years old. It was here he grew up. He attended the 'common' schools, but because he showed exceptional mental ability, he was given a few terms in a private school, and then at the Academy in Framingham. His capacity to study and absorb knowledge was so great that he actually started teaching others at fifteen years of age. At sixteen he passed an examination which enabled him to enter Harvard University as a freshman.

Because his parents could not afford to pay his tuition fees, Pike taught school in Gloucester during the fall and winter seasons and paid his own way. He qualified for the junior class at Harvard, but because of trouble with the faculty, he left the university and returned home and educated himself. He told his parents and friends that he left Harvard because of a misunderstanding over tuition fees.

Upon his return home he taught school in Fairhaven and Newburyport. He became assistant to the principle.

Afterwards, for a short time, he became principal of Newburyport Grammar School. He was still in his early twenties. Next, he became headmaster of a private school, serving in this capacity until the end of the spring term of 1831.

In the early summer of 1831 he broke away completely from his successful teaching career and started for the west on foot. He traveled, explored, traded, and lived with the Indians. He learned their language and customs. His honesty when dealing with them, his straightforward approach when discussing a problem, or clearing away a misunderstanding, won for him the confidence of the Indians. He settled in Little Rock, Arkansas, in 1833.

He became editor of the Arkansas Gazette. He also wrote articles for other publications, including a series of poems for *Blackwoods Magazine* in Edinburgh, Scotland. These were published by John Wilson, the editor in 1838. Wilson eulogized Pike as "The coming poet in America, whose fine hymns entitle him to take his place in the highest order of his country's poets. His massive genius marks him to be the poet of the Titans." Pike used the money earned as the result of his literacy efforts to educate himself in law.

Pike volunteered and served the U.S.A. in the war with Mexico. He became a Captain of Cavalry and served with distinction while participating in the Battle of Buena Vista. He afterwards took forty-one men and rode from Saltillo to Chihuahua, a distance of five hundred miles, through country infested with bandits and fugitive soldiers from Santa Annas defeated armies. The city of Mapini surrendered to him while on his outward journey.

Pike built an impressive mansion in Little Rock in 1840, which contained thirteen rooms. He transferred his law practice to New Orleans in 1851, and practiced before the Supreme Court of the United States. He returned to Little Rock in 1857 and lived there until the outbreak of the Civil War. He was made a Brigadier General in the Confederate Army, and Commissioner for negotiating treaties with the Indians whose claims against the United States Government he prosecuted afterwards.

After the war he resided in Memphis, Tennessee for several years, moving to Washington about 1869, where he resided for the rest of his life. He died April 2, 1891.

Pike's advance in Freemasonry was truly extraordinary. According to his daughter, Mrs. Liliana Pike Broom, her father was initiated in the Western Star Lodge at Little Rock, Arkansas in 1850, when 41 years of age. He became Worshipful Master, July of the same year.

He was a charter member of Magnolia Lodge No. 60, Little Rock, and was Worshipful Master ad vitam of that Lodge in 1853. Prior to this he was "Exalted in Union Chapter No. 2 RZ.M., Little Rock, created Knight Templar No. 1 Lodge in Washington, 17.C. He was also elected Grand High Priest of the Grand Chapter of Arkansas in 1853.

In 1858 he received from Brother Theodore Satan. Parvin, of Connecticut, the 4th to 32nd degree inclusive in the Ancient and Accepted Scottish Rite, March 20, 1853. On April 25, 1857, he was coroneted Hon. Inspector General and crowned Active Member of the Supreme Council, Southern Jurisdiction, March 20, 1858 at Charleston, South Carolina. When Brother John Honour resigned as Grand/Commander, Albert Pike was elected M.P Sovereign Grand-Commander of the Supreme Council for the Southern Jurisdiction of the United States, January 2, 1859. He afterwards became Sovereign Pontiff of Universal

Freemasonry. This is Pike's public record, and one which justifies Americans looking up to him as an example of real Americanism.

But what of his secret record?

It was while investigating the Little Rock integration incident in 1957 that I first learned of Pike's rapid advance in Freemasonry, and knowing that Weishaupt, using Thomas Jefferson and Moses Holbrook, had infiltrated Illuminists into the Masonic Lodges of America, I decided I would find out if the fact that Pike's mansion in Little Rock had thirteen rooms had any significance. "Thirteen" figures prominently in Satanic, Luciferian and Cabalistic rituals, codes, and writings, etc.

My investigations produced documentary evidence to show that, because of Pike's exceptional mental ability, he came under the notice of professors in Harvard who were members of the Illuminati, who developed in his mind the idea that a One World Government, a One World Religion and a One World financial and economic system was the ONLY solution to the world's many and varied problems.

I next discovered that his departure from Harvard was not due to lack of finances or because of a misunderstanding with the faculty over tuition fees, but because of his 'radical' ideas and teachings.

When he returned home determined that he would 'fight' his way to the top despite all opposition, he was in a suitable frame of mind to be recruited as a 'Minerval' or 'apprentice' into the lower degrees of the Illuminati.

I found that those secretly directing the Luciferian conspiracy in America decided to use Pike's mental capacity, his qualities as a teacher, and his ability to master languages, to further their own secret plans. They tested his physical courage and resourcefulness by sending him among the Indians to earn his living by use of his brains while learning their language and customs. As those fomenting the American Civil War, they could use Pike and his connections with the Indians when they considered the time was ripe for the outbreak of hostilities.

Pike came out of this test with full marks and colors flying. He was next required to gain military experience by a period of active service. This is an unbroken principle, and must comply with by every man who wishes to advance to a position of leadership in the World Revolutionary Movement. Thousands of American citizens, thousands of British citizens, and over two thousand Canadians joined Major Attlee's International Brigade and fought in the Spanish Civil War, 1926-1929, in order to obtain military experience necessary for a Communist to qualify for leadership in the World Revolutionary Movement. The Mexican War provided Pike with just the opportunity he needed.

Having proven himself to be a man of exceptional ability, personal courage and leadership, in 1850 Pike was infiltrated into the Scottish Rites of Freemasonry. He again distinguished himself and won the confidence and respect of members.

The archives in Washington, D.C. throw some unexpected light on Pike's connections with the Indians during the Civil War. These records show that he at first commanded a regiment, and afterwards a brigade of Indian Troops, C.S.A. It also discloses the fact the Pike's Indian troops had been disbanded by order of President Jefferson Davis because of the atrocities they had committed under the excuse of conducting legitimate warfare.

Investigation into Pike's associates while in Harvard and while teaching private school, proved he had become acquainted with men who were members of the Illuminati, men who were connected with Moses Holbrook, Clinton Roosevelt, Danna, Greeley, etc. There is evidence to indicate that after 1840 Pike's thirteen room mansion was used as the secret headquarters of those who constituted the Synagogue of Satan, and that within those walls they practiced occultism, and performed Satanic rituals, based on the Cabalism, as used by Moses Mendelssohn when he conducted initiations into the higher degrees of Weishaupt's Illuminati in Frankfort, Germany prior to 1784.

Further light was thrown on this phase of Pike's secret life when research revealed that after Pike gave up living in his Little Rock mansion, it was occupied by John Gould Fletcher, who also practiced spiritualism and occultism. He won the Pulitzer Prize for his poem written about Pike's mansion entitled, "The Ghosts of an Old House." It may be assumed that there is a great deal more truth than poetry in those verses, because evidence was later dug up which proved Pike conducted séances in St. Louis and other places throughout the world.

It was next discovered that Pike had been intimately associated with Guiseppe Mazzini from 1834 onwards, and remained closely associated with him until he died in 1872. Mazzini had been sent to America to assist Thomas

Jefferson in laying the foundations for the part Weishaupt intended America should play in the semifinal stages of the conspiracy.

Research into the writings of Mazzini's associates in France and Italy proved that Pike climbed the rungs of the ladder of Illuminism as fast as he had advanced in Freemasonry.

Moses Holbrook was secret head of the Synagogue of Satan in America during the first half of the 19th Century. He used the Cabalistic Rites as taught by Moses Mendelssohn when initiating specially selected candidates into Satanism as practiced in the higher degrees of Grand Orient Masonry in France and Italy by Cremieux and Mazzini respectively. The Caballas talmudic teachings, i.e., Satanism, was substituted for the 'Books of Moses' during the time the 'Jews' (so-called) were captive in Babylon.

Because some of the Founding Fathers of America had been openly anti-Semitic, and because the manner in which Illuminism had been exposed as having infiltrated into American Masonry, and because those who directed the activities of the Illuminati were mostly men who called themselves Jews, even if they were not, and lied about the matter, Pike decided that he would 'pretend' to clean Jewry out of control in America as far as Freemasonry was concerned. We will prove later that we are justified in using the word 'pretend.' He also decided that because the Illuminati was becoming suspect as directing the W.R.M. he would reorganize Palladism, and establish councils throughout the world, to take the place of Lodges of the Grand Orient and the Illuminati. In other words, Pike decided to set up a different 'front' in order to give the Synagogue of Satan, which directs the W.R.M. AT THE TOP, a new face. He was determined to throw historians and research workers off the scent which stank to high heaven after Captain Morgan was murdered.

MOSES MENDELSSOHN'S RITUAL FOR THE HIGHER DEGREES OF GRAND ORIENT MASONS was known as "The Black Mass." Its words and ceremonies expressed bitter hatred of Christ and Christianity. Pike suggested to Moses Holbrook that it would be a good idea if they revised and modernized the ceremony of "The Black Mass" so that it didn't appear so Talmudic. Holbrook agreed, and worked with Pike on a new ritual. Holbrook died before the task was completed, and Pike completed the work alone. He called the new ceremonial "The Adonaicide Mass," which means "The Death of God." It was on Pike's doctrine that Nietzche in Germany based his ideas and theories calculated to bring about 'The Death of God,' so Lucifer can reign in peace and security. We know these theories as Nietzcheism.

We have referred to the writings of Domenico Margiotta on many occasions when dealing with the manner the Illuminati infiltrated into Freemasonry because Margiotta was a 33rd degree Mason before he seceded. He did not quit Masonry until AFTER he had been selected for initiation into the higher degrees of Grand Orient Masonry and/or the New and Reformed Palladian Rite. He gives as his reason for refusing to be initiated, that the study of the lives of those who wished to initiate him convinced him they were Satanists. We have Margiottas word for it that Grand Master Pike reestablished the supremacy of his supreme council, and succeeded gradually in becoming an important Masonic personage, and the real chief of the Scottish Rite.

As a 33rd degree Mason and Sovereign Pontiff of Universal Masonry, Pike traveled the world. Masonic libraries reveal he was Honorary Grand Commander of the Supreme Councils of Brazil, (United), Egypt, Tunis, France, Belgium, Italy, Spain, England, Wales, Ireland, Scotland, Greece, Hungary, Neuva Grande, Canada, Colon, Peru, Mexico, Uruguay, and Oceania. But what the Masonic libraries do not reveal is the fact that while pretending to be traveling on business concerning the Scottish Rite, Pike was actually establishing twenty-six councils of the New and Reformed Palladian Rite, which he superimposed on the Grand Orient Masonry. Grand Orient Masons worship Satan as Prince of this world. Satan is their God.

Palladism recognized Satan as 'Prince of this World.' But, according to the Luciferian doctrine as expounded by Pike, Lucifer is God, the equal of Adonay, and rules over all that part of the Universe not included in Adonay's part which we term Heaven. Pike stated that Satanism is to be tolerated among 'imperfect members.' Imperfect members are all members of Grand Orient Lodges and Councils of the New and Reformed Palladian Rite who haven't been initiated into the final degree and made acquainted with the FULL SECRET. Perfect members are exceedingly few in number. But Pike insisted that those selected for initiation into the FULL SECRET accept Lucifer as their God and worship him as the God of Goodness and the God of Light, from whom all knowledge and intelligence originates. Pike, himself, and the ritual of the Adonaicide Mass specifically condemn Lucifer's opponent as Adonay the God of ALL EVIL and the God of Darkness.

Dom Paul Benoit made a special study of Pike's New and Reformed Palladian Rite, and on page 456 of Vol. I of his book, *La France Maconnerie* he says, "In the reception of the Elect of the Reformed Palladian Rite, those who are to be initiated are taught to punish the traitor Jesus Christ and to kill Adonay (Adonai), the God of the Bible, (and Father of Jesus Christ), through the power of their own evil, done first by Master and then by initiate, piercing the Host with a dagger, in the midst of horrible blasphemies, after they have been assured that it (The Host) is a consecrated Host." Dom Benoit also says that in 1894, 800 consecrated hosts were stolen from a church in Paris to be used by the 'sectarians' for their abominable mysteries, and that the truth of this statement was verified.

I realize how difficult it is for the average decent person, regardless of race, color, or creed, to realize that Satanism is actually practiced, and that the Synagogue of Satan is controlled AT THE TOP by human beings who are the High Priests of the Luciferian Creed who plot to enslave what remains of the human race, after the final social cataclysm is ended. Therefore, I shall quote Pike's own words as recorded by Arthur Preuss on pages 157-158 of Vol. I *A Study in American Freemasonry.* While Pike was explaining WHY those directing the W.R.M. AT THE TOP intended to use international Communism as THEIR manual of destructive action, Preuss quotes him as saying:

"There is a merely informal atheism, which is the negation of God in terms, but not in reality. A man says, 'There is no God'- that is, there is no God WHO originates in himself, WHO ever was originated, but a God Who always was and has been, who is the cause of existence, who is the MIND and the PROVIDENCE of the Universe, and therefore, the ORDER, BEAUTY, and HARMONY of the world of matter and mind do not indicate any plan or intention of Divinity. But Nature that is powerful, wise, active and good; Nature originated within itself, or perhaps, it always was and has been, the cause of its own existence, the mind of the Universe and its own Providence. Clearly there is a plan and purpose from which proceed order, beauty, and harmony. But this is the plan and purpose of Nature. In such matters the absolute negation of God is only formal and not real. The qualities of God are recognized, and they affirm HIS existence; it is a mere change of name to call the possessor of these qualities Nature and not God."

The word Nature, as used by Pike, means "The sum total of existence," exactly as the word "Universe" means the totality of everything within and without space, including everything in and on this earth.

Pike is also recorded as saying that Atheistic Communism will be only '*A passing phase in the over-all revolution*,' and as is mentioned elsewhere Pike told Mazzini exactly how Communism and Christianity were to be made to destroy each other in an all-out war with each other, in order to usher the Luciferian conspiracy into its final stage.

It is only when we dig down deep, and look behind the curtain of Pike's life that we realize that when talking of God and/or Nature he was really meaning Lucifer.

We have said Thomas Jefferson became a member of Weishaupt's Illuminati. Regardless of what Americans have been taught to believe about Thomas Jefferson as a Christian and a Patriot, the fact remains that he did play a leading part in bringing about Weishaupt's plan which required that America be separated from the British Empire. Therefore he was a traitor to his Mother Country. He became a traitor because Illuminism had convinced him that ONLY a One World Government, managed by men of brains, could solve the world's problems and end wars and revolutions. He felt he was justified in helping destroy Britain and her Empire in the interests of world peace.

Exactly the same principles and feelings caused President F.D. Roosevelt to tell Winston Churchill, Britain's Prime Minister, when they met on an American battleship in Agentia Bay, Newfoundland, in the summer of 1942, to discuss the North Atlantic Treaty Organization (NATO.) "It is time the British Empire was dissolved in the interests of world peace." Very few people seem to realize that NATO was organized so that those who direct the W.R.M. AT THE TOP could 'contain' the terrible destructive force of Communism, which they had created in accordance with Pike's plan, until they wished to use it to usher in the final stage of the Luciferian conspiracy.

A slip of the tongue may go unnoticed by millions, but to a historian it may disclose a great deal. Early in World War Two Winston Churchill made one of his most famous speeches after he had dined well if not too wisely. There is an old saying, "When liquor is in the truth comes out." On this particular occasion Churchill said, "I will shake hands with the Devil himself if by so doing he will help me defeat that -- Hitler." Here we get a glimpse of the truth; if Churchill had been a God-loving and God-fearing person it would have been only natural that he would have spoken the name of God, and not that of Lucifer.

Exactly the same line of reasoning explains many of the political actions of Mackenzie King during the quarter century he was Prime Minister of Canada: He was indoctrinated into Internationalism while he was going to the University. His record as a young man is very similar to that of Pike. He was openly a radical, and a true descendant of his rebellious grandfather. He was so utterly ruthless and unscrupulous when in Toronto University that he was heartily disliked by the vast majority of his fellow students. But once he sold his soul to the Rockefellers he directed the Canadian government's policies so they fitted in with Luciferian plot to bring into being a One World Government. And the masses ... the Goyim ... are so thoroughly brainwashed by the Luciferian propaganda machine that the people of Canada kept reelecting him Prime Minister, although his treachery as far as Britain and the rest of her Commonwealth (Empire) was concerned, had been proven to the hilt in letters he wrote early in the first World War to prominent Americans who were friends of the Rockefellers, or obligated to them for financial favors, and asked them to use their influence with the American government so that financial and other aid would be withheld from Britain and France, "And so prolong the war and seriously weaken the British Empire." The control of the S.O.S. has, over the so-called FREE AND INDEPENDENT PRESS is such that even as a professional journalist and author of many books, I couldn't get the truth regarding Mackenzie King and his treachery and occultism over to the public until I published *Red Fog Over America* privately in 1955.

It was Thomas Jefferson who had the Illuminati's symbol secretly engraved on the reverse side of the Great Seal of America. It was his intention that its presence remains a secret until America should disintegrate due to internal trouble and strife, and fall into the hands of those who direct the W.R.M. AT THE TOP, like overripe fruit, and introduce the "New Order." We have explained that the words "New Order" are double-talk for 'Luciferian dictatorship,' and used to deceive the general public into accepting the 'IDEA' of a One World Government. F.D. Roosevelt was so sure he would introduce the "New Order" that he started his presidential reign by introducing his "New Deal," which was a version of dictatorship intended to be developed into totalitarianism as soon as the time was ripe. He (Roosevelt) was so sure he was going to be the first King-despot of the entire world that he brought the Illuminati's symbol, the Satanic coat of arms, out of mothballs and used it on the back of American dollar bills. He thus assured all those "in the know" that the Luciferian conspiracy was about to enter the final stage. The fact that Stalin double-crossed him after Yalta is the only thing that prevented his dreams from coming true. Instead of becoming the first King-despot, he went insane. The reason the public wasn't permitted to see his face before his body was buried was, I am informed by good authority, because there was no face to see. He is said to have ended his hate against Stalin, his disappointments and misery of mind and soul, with a shot gun.

When we revealed the truth that the symbol of the Illuminati was on the back of the United States one dollar bills, it caused consternation among those who direct the W.R.M. AT THE TOP they immediately commissioned some of Hollywood's best writers to interpret the symbols as being of great patriotic meaning. If this lame effort to "kill" the truth was correct then why was the fact that the symbol was on the reverse side of the Great Seal kept so secret from Jefferson's day to that of Roosevelt?

The power, the cunning, and the deceit of those who serve the S.O.S. can be better understood when we explain that according to Weishaupt's own interpretation of the symbol the pyramid represents the plot to bring about the destruction of Christendom. To deceive the enemies of the Roman Catholic Church into believing that they were not marked down for destruction also, the agentur of Weishaupt's organization made it appear their only hate was against Catholicism and not against Christ and Christianity in general. Such is the power and influence of the S.O.S. that they caused the priests who direct the youth departments of Catholic Action to publish the Hollywood writers' version of the meaning of the symbol and they published it far and wide and urged Catholics to accept 'Satan's' version as the version despite historical facts and documents which expose the Hollywood version as a deliberate lie. When the truth was explained to the priests responsible they could not do anything to correct their mistake because they had acted under orders of higher authority.

This indicates that the S.O.S. have their agentur within the hierarchy of Roman Catholicism just as they had Judas among Christ's own Apostles.

For many years I have known that men who have directed the W.R.M. AT THE VERY TOP, used the game of chess to symbolize their march of 'peaceful progress' towards ultimate world domination. In their chess game one player represents God, the other the Devil, Lucifer. Pawns represented the masses or Goyim. The Gods sacrifice as many of the pawns as is necessary to enable them to kill off the knights, bishops, and castles, and queens, and make one or the other King checkmate. It was because I knew that chess symbolized the struggle to bring about a One World Government under a totalitarian dictator, that I named one of my books, *Pawns in the Game*, and another one, dealing with Nazism, *Checkmate in the North*, (published by Macmillan in 1944). But it wasn't until November, 1958, while writing this chapter, of this book, that I learned by accident, or 'an Act of God,' that Albert Pike owned an extremely rare set of chessmen copied from the originals.

Part of the chessmen belonging to his set were taken from his home when a detachment of the Second Kansas Cavalry raided Little Rock in the summer of 1863. When the raiders distributed their loot, Pike's chessmen fell into the hands of Captain E.S. Stover, of Company 'B.' After the war, he moved to New Mexico and became Grand Master of the Grand Lodge of Scottish Rite Masons. In 1915, when Stover was over 80 years of age, he had Pike's chessmen placed with other relics of Pike, in the Library of the Supreme Council.

Then, from an entirely different source, I received a copy of Susan Lawrence Davis's *Authentic History of the Ku Klux Klan* (1865-1877), published by the American Library Service, New York, 1924. The author gives a detailed account of General Albert Pike, and as much of his activities as the general public is intended to know.

But the old, old saying, "Murder will out" applies to the Luciferian conspiracy (mass murder), as it does to individual homicide. Susan Davis just happens to mention that the chessmen which belonged to Pike were identical with a set with which she had played with General Forrest when she was a little girl. Susan Davis says she and General Forrest used to play a game he called, "Make Believe." These are the very words Weishaupt used when telling Illuminists how they should act.

This scrap of information wouldn't mean anything at all as far as the World Revolutionary Movement is concerned, if it weren't for the fact that General Forrest originated and organized the Klu Klux Klan, and, at a convention of the KKK held in Nashville, Tennessee, U.S.A., Forrest made Pike, who had organized the KKK in Arkansas, "Grand Dragon" of the "Realm." Pike was also appointed "Chief Judicial Officer of the Invisible Empire." It was Pike who advised the leaders of the KKK to memorize their secret ritual, and pass it down from leader to leader, so a copy would never fall into hostile hands. General Pike appointed Henry Fielding and Eppie Fielding of Fayetteville, Arkansas, to assist him in organizing 'Dens' in Arkansas. The Fieldings had been original members of the Athens, Alabama Klan until they moved to Arkansas in 1867.

History, as generally taught in American schools and colleges, doesn't put much importance on the fact that the political, religious, and racial strife now rife in Arkansas and other southern states, is only a repetition of what went on in Arkansas during the dark days of reconstruction following the Civil War. General Albert Pike was "The Secret Power" who directed what was going on from behind the scenes in Arkansas, as is proven by what is published on page 277 of the *Authentic History of the Klu Klux Klan.*

Few people with whom I have discussed this matter seem aware of the fact that Arkansas had TWO governments in 1872, and that great excitement prevailed. Public opinion was so much against what Washington was doing that civil war threatened; until Albert Pike called a mass meeting. With dramatic effect Pike unfurled the Stars and Stripes, and with great eloquence, he appealed to the people gathered in the Capitol building to be patient, "And follow this flag until the Klu Klux Klan can redeem the state." He promised that he would go personally to Washington and intercede on their behalf. This promise he kept.

In view of the events of history since 1872, Pike did what he did because he knew the time for the final social cataclysm wouldn't be ripe for nearly a hundred years. This statement and warning was written into the lectures delivered to members of the councils of his Palladian Rite between 1885 and 1901. I have had the "pleasure" of meeting present day leaders of the KKK. I even had the "privilege" of addressing some of them, and they gave me an attentive hearing while I explained how those who directed the World Revolutionary Movement planned to cause the U.S.A. to disintegrate in the final stages of the conspiracy as the result of civil war, combined with a Communist revolution. I told them how it was planned to line up Jews against Gentiles, colored folk against white, atheists against Christians, etc., quoting from the letter Pike addressed to Mazzini August 15,1871, to prove that what I told them was the truth, explaining that laws regarding integration were passed to help bring this division about. I pointed out how, in every state south of the Mason-Dixon Line, men and women had appeared from nowhere in particular and immediately worked their way into position from which they could exert great influence in opposing groups. I pointed out that this parvenu always seemed to have unlimited sums of money at their disposal, and how they could always arrange a deal to procure arms and ammunition. I told them bluntly that these agents were agentur of the Illuminati, and that their purpose was to cause the tensions to develop into strife and bloodshed.

The night I addressed one group of leaders the tension was taut as a piano wire, due to the fact that federal government officials had announced that a new building project in a white section of the community, was to be integrated. My audience had announced that they would prevent integration by armed force, if necessary. They asked me point blank, "What do you expect us to do-accept integration without a struggle?"

I replied with another question. I asked, "How many white and colored people are there in this community who really want to slit each other's throats and commit atrocities?" There was silence. I pointed out that those who controlled the armed forces of the U.S.A. had paratroops in strategic locations throughout the country, and planes ready to take them wherever required. It was the middle of the night, and I could hear the tick of an old-fashioned clock. As kindly as I could, I said, "I doubt if there are five white or colored men who actually want to involve the whole community in the horrors of civil war. The hour is late-literally, in more ways than one.

Why don't you leaders of the white section of the population go at once and see the leaders of the colored folk. Tell them you don't want war and bloodshed any more than they do. Ask them, for the sake of all concerned, to tell the few colored folk, whom the conspirators intend to use as pawns in this experiment, that if they allow themselves to be used thus, the Negroes who don't want trouble with the whites will knock the living daylights out of those who do. Tell them not to allow Negroes to move into the segregated areas."

At daybreak, the white leaders met with the Negro leaders. They agreed to do as I requested. No colored people moved into the segregated section. No trouble broke out. Two nights later, I met some of the leaders and told them to watch carefully for those who disagreed with the action they had taken, because those would be the provocateurs of the Illuminati.

The agentur of the Illuminati don't lie timidly or for a while only. They lie boldly and continuously, like the Devil. They know that if they can deceive the masses into putting them into office, they can do that direct opposite of all promises afterwards. As Voltaire said, "That is of no consequence."

So we have Jefferson carrying the ball for the Illuminati politically for 1786, while Moses Holbrook looked after the dogmatic end of the Luciferian conspiracy in the Americas towards the end of the 18th and the beginning of the 19th Centuries.

Since then presidential candidates have been selected and elected by those who direct the conspiracy AT THE TOP. The masses have been made to think they elect the men of their own choice, but, in reality, as Weishaupt intended, they are given "Hobson's choice." Could anything illustrate this truth more clearly than the last few presidential elections, and the last election fight between Harriman and Rockefeller for the governorship of New York? If a president or other top level politician slips into office unexpectedly, he or she is silenced one way or another. Presidents not amenable to control by the agentur of the Illuminati are assassinated. Senators who are uncooperative are blackmailed, smeared, or liquidated. There are hundreds of cases on record to illustrate exactly what I mean. Lincoln, Kennedy, Forrestal, and McCarthy are just typical examples in America. Lord Kitchener, Chamberlain, and Admiral Sir Barry Domvile were typical examples in England. The recent murders in Iraq were all part of the same ruthless and diabolical conspiracy to destroy ALL governments and religions, and to bring about a One World Government, the powers of which the High Priests of the Luciferian ideology intend to usurp.

Chapter 12

THE PROTOCOLS OF
THE SYNAGOGUE OF SATAN

For many years I have contended that while the information contained in the so-called Protocols of the Learned Elders of Zion does contain verification of the existence of a conspiracy to destroy ALL remaining governments and religions (as exposed by Professor John Robison in 1797), gives an account of how the plan has progressed since, and tells what remains to be done to enable those who direct the conspiracy AT THE TOP to reach their final objective, which is absolute world domination, I still maintain that the Protocols (original plans) are not those of the Learned Elders of Zion. I know that 'sticking to my guns,' in regard to this matter, is going to provide a double-edged sword that the enemies of God will use to discredit what I have written. One edge of that sword will be used by anti-Semites, who will accuse me of having Communist sympathies, the other edge will be used by Satanists to try to convince those who would wish to read my works that I am Semitic. So be it. I am going to tell the truth as I see it.

To you, my readers, I will explain how I reached the opinion that the protocols' are not, I repeat, are not, those of the Elders of Zion, but those of the Synagogue of Satan, which is a very different matter. One or more of the Elders of Zion can be Satanists-they probably are-but that does not prove the Protocols are a Jewish plot designed to win world domination. The fact that Judas was a traitor does not prove that all Jews are traitors. The further fact that certain Jews have, and still do belong to the Synagogue of Satan, and to revolutionary and subversive movements, doesn't make them a race apart. The Synagogue of Satan always has, since Judaism started, contained so-called (Khazar) Jews, as well as Gentiles.

Since September 1914, I have enjoyed the friendship of a man who is one of Britain's greatest scholars and intelligence officers. He is one of the world's finest linguists. He has done post-graduate and research work concerning geo-political science, economics, comparative religions, etc., in most of the old universities throughout the world. He has been decorated by the British government, and by most of her allies, including the U.S.A. in both world wars, for special services efficiently rendered. When World War Two broke out, all

141

these honors proved rather embarrassing, because when he and I resumed to naval service in 1939, he had to 'usurp' from his uniform the ribbons of medals given him by nations with whom we were allied in the First World War. Several of them were now our enemies.

Special service has taken my friend all over the world, and involved him in political intrigue. He made a thorough study of the 'Protocols' shortly after Nilus first published them as "The Jewish Peril," in Russia in 1905.

Serving in Russia as an intelligence officer both before World War One and during the Russian Revolution, the Menshevics, and afterwards, the Bolsheviks, offered a higher reward for his capture, dead or alive, than for any other foreign agent during the years 1916 to 1918. My wife and I spent our delayed honeymoon with my friend and his wife, a Russian lady he married and helped to escape from Russia early in 1918. His ability to translate so many languages provided me with a great deal of information I could not possibly have obtained if it had not been for our close association over the years.

Having had access to his private papers, I am under promise that I will not reveal his identity or write his biography till after his death. The officer to whom I refer knows more about the origin of the Protocols, and how they fell into the hands of Professor Nilus, than any other living man. He knew Nilus when he lived in Russia. He knew Marsden and his wife when they lived in Russia before, and during the revolution. I share that knowledge with him.

Also, at my request, the son of a high ranking Russian officer, who was one of the greatest leaders of the WHITE RUSSIAN MOVEMENT, checked the information and conclusions I have published regarding the Protocols since 1930, and he agrees with my writings.

Serving in British submarines in 1916 to 1919 as navigating officer, I knew Commander E.N. Cromie, who died in 1917 holding back the revolutionary mob which tried to break into the British Consulate in St. Petersburg, (now Petrograd). The leaders of the mob wanted to get secret and confidential documents they knew my friend had placed in the consulate. Cromie held the mob back with small arms until his associates had burned the documents. He was repeatedly wounded, and so severely that he died on the steps of the embassy. I know what information the leaders of the Menshevics wished to obtain so badly.

My friend's wife is godmother to one of my children, and I have discussed many times with her Russia and Russian affairs. She read my manuscripts dealing with this phase of the W.R.M. before they were published, as did her husband.

Victor Marsden translated Nilus' book, *The Jewish Peril* into English, and - published it under the misleading title, *The Protocols of the Learned Elders of Zion*. I met him in 1927 when he was touring the world as public relations officer with the then Prince of Wales, now the Duke of Windsor.

Victor Marsden lived in Russia before the revolution as a correspondent for the *London Morning Post*. He married a Russian lady. When the revolution started the Mensheviks threw Marsden into prison on suspicion that he was a spy. While he was in St. Peter and Paul Prison he was treated brutally, so much so that his heart became filled with hatred for the Mensheviks, most of whom were Jews.

Victor Marsden was physically ill and mentally disturbed when he translated the copy of Professor Nilus' *Jewish Peril* into English. The copy from which he worked was in the British Museum, having been received by the librarian there in August, 1906. Marsden was in such poor health when he did this work in 1920 that he couldn't work more than an hour without taking a rest. He rarely worked more than two hours a day. But in 1921 he published his translation of Nilus' book in English under the title, *The Protocols of the Learned Elders of Zion*.

Because of his experiences in prison, it seemed impossible to convince him that those who directed the World Revolutionary Movement AT THE VERY TOP were using Jews to serve their own diabolical purposes, as 'Whipping-boys,' upon whose shoulders they placed the blame for their sins against God and their crimes against humanity.

My friend told both Professor Nilus and Victor Marsden the TRUE story of the Protocols as he told it to me. I have published the story in *Pawns in the Game*. A brief outline will place readers who haven't read the other books, in a better position to understand what I am going to say about this much-discussed publication.

When Pike established councils of his "New and Reformed Palladian Rite" in the principle cities throughout the world, he gave definite instructions that the members of those councils were to organize Women's Auxiliaries, to be known as Lodges or Councils of Adoption. These women were carefully chosen from the higher levels of society in their respective countries. They are still active. In England in World War One high society women, belonging to the London Council of Adoption of the Palladian Rite, acted as hostesses to officers on leave from various theatres of war, at the Glass Club. They included wives and daughters of Britain's nobility and members of Britain's government. These women entertained the officers invited to the club while they were on leave. During this period they remained masked, so the officer they entertained would not recognize them. Most of their photos appeared frequently in society publications. The information they picked up was all passed to the supervising directorate of the Palladian propaganda and intelligence service.

In 1885, or thereabouts, a series of lectures was prepared for delivery to the members of the Grand Orient Lodges and Councils of the Palladian Rite. Those who prepared these lectures did so in a manner that allowed the hearer to know just as much as was necessary to permit him to contribute his share towards furthering the W.R.M., intelligently, without letting him penetrate the full secret that it is the intention of the High Priests of the Luciferian Creed to usurp world power in the final stage of the revolution. If Pike did not prepare these lectures personally, he most certainly inspired them.

The limiting of knowledge to adepts in the lower degrees, deceiving them into believing their objectives are other than is really intended, and by keeping the identity of those who belong to the higher degrees absolutely secret from those even one degree lower than they, is the principle on which the heads of the Synagogue of Satan base their 'SECURITY.' It is this policy which enabled them to withhold their secret even from men like Mazzini and Lemmi, leaders of the W.R.M., until the High Priest decides they might be initiated into the FULL SECRET.

In studying the lectures we must also remember that those who prepared them were literally members of the S.O.S. We must therefore look for words with double meaning, and phrases which are intended to deceive.

Word by word, sentence by sentence, study of this horrible document reveals many double meaning words and deceptive phrases.

Those who prepared the lectures knew it was almost impossible to prevent copies falling into hands other than those intended. This they knew from experience in 1784-1786; so extraordinary precautions were taken to make sure that if the contents of these lectures became known, people other than themselves and the Palladian Rite, would be blamed.

I have explained these things to the Briton's Publishing Society, which has published the English edition of the Protocols since Marsden's death. I pointed out that, according to Pike's own written instruction, the word 'God' was to be used when the word 'Lucifer' was intended.

When the Synagogue of Satan plotted Christ's death, and accomplished that foul purpose, they stayed in the background and worked from the dark. They hired Judas to carry out the betrayal, and then made the Jews assume the blame for their sin against God and their crime against humanity. It is the adepts of the Grand Orient and the Palladian Rite who glory in the celebration of the Adonaicide Mass, and, as we shall prove by study of the lectures, those who prepared them for delivery don't care if they sacrifice two-thirds of the world's population in order to reach their final objective and impose a Luciferian totalitarian dictatorship upon what is left of the human race. Those who prepared the lectures served the 'Father of Lies.' They were 'Masters of Deceit.' Knowing this, we must be alert if we wish to penetrate through to the truth.

Contrary to popular belief, Nilus was not the first person to publish the contents of these lectures. I pointed this out to the publishers many years ago. Now the eighty-first impression of the so-called Protocols of the Learned Elders of Zion has been given the much more realistic title "World Conquest through World Government." I also notice that the publisher admits, in this new edition, that Nilus wasn't the first to publish the documents.

As mentioned in another chapter, the series of lectures had first been published in the winter of 1902-1903 in Russian in a newspaper named *Moskowskija Wiedomosti*, and again in the same language, in August and September of 1903 in a newspaper called *Snamja*.

These publications didn't have the desired effect, failing to cause a rise in anti-Semitism, as the directors of the W.R.M. expected would happen in Russia. The S.O.S. wanted to use anti-Semitism to enable them to foment the revolutions which would lead to the overthrow of the power of the Tsars as required by Pike's military blueprint of wars and revolutions.

Professor Nilus was a priest of the Russian Orthodox Church. My friend thought him honest and sincere in his belief that the World Revolutionary Movement was a Jewish plot. There can be no gainsaying the fact that Khazar Jews headed the revolutionary movements in Russia; they filled the ranks of the revolutionary underground armies. Lesser Jews had been taught from childhood to hate their Gentile rulers, and to believe that they were being persecuted because of their religion. This was a lie. The fact remains that Nilus knew of Weishaupt, the Illuminati, and Pike and his Palladian Rite. Only Nilus, and his Maker, know whether he was one of those priests who are wolves dressed in sheep's clothing.

When Nilus published the lectures as part of his book, *The Great and the Little* in 1905, and said it exposed "The Jewish Peril," he set the world on fire. Intentionally or otherwise, he gave birth to anti-Semitism as the S.O.S. intended, so they could use it to foment World Wars One and Two and bring about the Russian revolution, as required to further their plot.

My information about Nilus' part in the publication of the "Protocols" was published in 1955 in *Pawns in the Game*. Since then, I have learned considerably more about this remarkable man. He told three different stories to three different people, when asked to explain HOW the lectures first came into his possession. That is not characteristic of an honest man. As an ordained priest he was supposed to have been working to serve God's purpose. As such, he would tell the TRUTH.

The TRUTH regarding the "Protocols" is as follows: There is evidence to indicate that the lectures were being delivered to Grand Orient Masons and Members of Pike's Palladian Rite all over the world from 1885 onwards. When first published in Russia in 1902, they were said to be "Minutes of a meeting held by the Elders of Zion." That was so obviously a lie, to anyone who took the trouble to read the material carefully. Nilus covered up this up by saying, "The material is a report with parts apparently missing, made by some powerful person." My friend says, and I agree, that the series of lectures were inspired or written by Pike. The wording and phraseology are almost, if not absolutely identical with his other writings. They were delivered over a period of three or more days and nights. The first of the series explains Weishaupt's revision and modernization of the Protocols of the Luciferian conspiracy. The second of the series describes the progress which the conspiracy had made since 1776. The third and final series of the lectures tell what remains to be done, and how Pike intended it should be accomplished, to reach the final goal of a One World Government during the 20th Century.

Professor Nilus is on record as saying: "Apparently there is a lecture, or part of a lecture missing." The part that is missing is the final lecture, reserved for those being initiated into the FULL secret that the high priests of the Luciferian

Creed intend to usurp the powers of the first world government, regardless of how, or by whom, it is established.

It would be interesting to know what Professor Nilus would have answered if he had been asked, "How do you know that a part of a lecture is missing?" It is things like this that alert research workers to the true facts. We ask ourselves: "If Nilus lied regarding how he came into possession of the documents, and if he claims there is a part missing, it is reasonable to suppose he was an adept of the Palladian Rite, and knew the FULL SECRET. If he wasn't, it isn't likely he would know that some is missing."

Nilus admitted that it was impossible for him to produce written or oral proof of the authenticity of the document. On the other hand, when all the loose ends are tied together, we get a clear picture of the continuing Luciferian conspiracy, how it is directed by the S.O.S.-not the Jews, and its ultimate purpose. We see that the W.R.M. is direct AT THE VERY TOP by the S.O.S., which in turn is controlled by the High Priests of the Luciferian Creed.

When Kerensky formed Russia's first provisional government, he ordered all copies of Nilus' book to be destroyed. This made it appear more than ever that the Jews were trying to cover up his exposure. After Lenin usurped power and put Kerensky out of business, the Cheka imprisoned Nilus. He was exiled and died in Vladimir January 13, 1929.

According to one story Nilus told, and the one of the three which appears nearest to the truth, the documents he received, translated and published, were stolen by a woman of easy virtue from a High Degree Mason who spent a night with her after completing his engagement as 'Lecturer' to the members of the higher degrees of the Grand Orient Masonry in Paris, France.

This sounds like a plausible explanation. But let us examine it in detail. What Mason who has been tested and tried, until judged suitable for initiation into the highest degree of Grand Orient Masonry, and/or the New and Reformed Palladian Rite would be so careless as to take top secret and incriminating documents with him into the apartment of a woman of easy virtue? That he would do so just doesn't make sense. Had the documents been stolen the Illuminati would have used their wealth, power and influence, and the millions of pairs of eyes they control, to get them back.

Investigating every angle of the mystery of the missing documents, my friend reached the conclusion that they were given to a lady high in French society who also happened to be a member of "The Lodge of Adoption" attached to the Paris Council of the Palladian Rite. Evidence indicated that the man who gave the documents to this lady was one of the highest and most influential Grand Orient Masons in France, and was undoubtedly a member of Pike's New and Reformed Palladian Rite.

The lady in question was undoubtedly instructed to whom she should entrust the documents so they would get into the hands of those who directed the anti-Semitic movement in Russia. By telling this Russian nobleman that the documents had been stolen from a Jew who was a high degree Mason, it was thought to deceive him into believing the woman's motives were 'pure' and that no intrigue and deceit were involved.

These deductions explain also how the documents first were given to one newspaper and then to another. It was not until after publication had failed to produce the anti-Semitic reaction that the original or another copy was placed in the hands of Professor Satan. Nilus and produced the desired result. I know for a positive fact copies of Nilus' *Jewish Peril* were placed in the possession of every prominent Russian who was attached to the Imperial household and employed by the Tsar in any kind of executive capacity. Copies were placed on the bureaus of Ladies-in-waiting in their rooms within the Imperial Palace.

Revolutionary activities had divided Russian society into two groups: those who were loyal to the Tsar, and those who were not. Publication, and wide-spread circulation, of the documents under the title *The Jewish Peril* undoubtedly enabled those who directed the Russian revolutionary movement, from behind the scenes, to develop their plot and further their secret plans. One of them was the international banker, Jacob Schiff of New York, U.S.A., whose revolutionary leader was, Trotsky.

Working with Schiff to bring about the subjugation of Russia was the Warburg family of Hamburg, Germany. The members of this banking house were closely connected with, and on exceptionally friendly terms with Gerson Blechroeder, who was director of Pike's supervisory Council of the Palladian Rite in Berlin. The secret headquarters of those fomenting the Russian revolution in Germany was the big building on Valentinskamp Strasse where Armand Levi had established the "Secret (Jewish) Federation," which became known as "The Sovereign Patriarchal Council," backed by the Rothschild's millions.

Strange as it may seem but as additional proof that the S.O.S. does not consist of orthodox Jews, but of them who say they are Jews, and are not, and thus lie, we find that Lenin was being coached to take over leadership of the revolutionary war in Russia by none other than Lemmi who had succeeded Mazzini as Pike's director of political action. Lemmi had set up his headquarters near Geneva, Switzerland.

Thus we see how the lectures inspired by Pike, were made to appear to be a conspiracy of Jews to win world domination. This charge the real Jews bitterly resented. But when we clear away all confusing aspects of the case the TRUTH stands out clear and unmistakable. The version of the lectures placed in the hands of Professor Nilus was used to help those who direct the W.R.M. AT THE TOP to foment the Russian revolutions of 1905 and 1917, and thus put Pike's plans into effect EXACTLY as he intended.

Marsden explains the meaning of the word 'Goyim' to be 'Gentiles or non-Jews.' With this I cannot agree.

The word 'Goyim' meant originally, "The masses of/or the common people." But as the word was used by Weishaupt, its meaning changed to 'Lesser Beings-the mob.' Pike used the word to mean 'human cattle.' The whole of humanity, whom he said was to be integrated into a mass of mongrelized humanity, and enslaved body, mind and soul.

The word 'agentur' is also used frequently in the lectures. Marsden says the word means, "The whole body of agents and agencies made use of by the Elders (of Zion), whether members of the 'tribe' or their Gentile 'tools.' With this explanation I must disagree also. The word 'Agentur' as used in the Protocols, means, 'every member of society the Synagogue of Satan control and use to put the Luciferian conspiracy into effect, and keep it progressing towards its ultimate goal, regardless of race, color or creed.'

The words 'The Political' are said by Marsden to mean not exactly the 'body politic,' but the entire machinery of politics. With this definition I do agree.

It must be clearly understood that I believe the PROTOCOLS are those of the Synagogue of Satan. The copy given Nilus was altered slightly to make believe they are those of the Elders of Zion, so that those who direct the conspiracy AT THE TOP could use both Zionism and anti-Semitism to further their own secret plans to cause revolution in Russia.

PROTOCOL #1 is nothing more or less than a reiteration of Weishaupt's principles.

A. That in the beginnings of the structure of society mankind was subjected to brutal and blind force, afterwards to law, which is exactly the same force disguised. This being so, the principle of 'The Law of Nature' is that 'Right' lies in force, or, to put it in other words, 'Might is Right.' Pike secretly endorsed this principle.

B. Political freedom is an 'Idea,' not a fact. But those plotting to obtain absolute control of the masses must use this idea as a 'bait' to attract the masses to one of their parties (organizations) so they can be used for crushing those at present in authority, and thus remove obstacles which stand between the S.O.S. and ultimate world domination.

C. So-called 'Liberalism' is to be used to soften up rulers so that for the sake of the 'idea' of freedom and 'liberalism' they will yield some of their power. The lecturer then remarks, "It is precisely here that the triumph of theory appears." He explains that those who plot to subjugate the rest must gather up the slacked reins of government into their own hands, "because the blind might of any nation cannot for one single day exist without guidance, and thus the new usurped authority will fit into the place of the old."

What happened in France before the lectures were given, and what has happened in Russia, Germany, China, and is happening in England today, typically illustrates how this phase of the conspiracy has been put into effect.

D. First, the Emperors, crowned Kings and Sovereign Rulers must be disposed of by assassination, revolution or other means. Then the natural, or genealogical aristocracy shall be destroyed in a revolutionary reign of terror. The lecturer explains how the conspirators will replace the power of the rulers they destroy with the 'power of gold,' and replace the genealogical aristocracy with people of wealth whose fortunes the conspirators control. In other words, those who create the 'new' aristocracy of 'wealth' can make those they wish to use wealthy, and they can just as easily break those who refuse to do their bidding.

It is interesting to note that most of those who now form the aristocracy of wealth got their start promoting rackets of one kind or another, which separated gullible people from their hard-earned money. The Rothschild's got their feet on the lower rungs of the Ladder of Fortune by providing the British government with Hessian soldiers at so much a head. Thus they were well paid for providing troops to fight Britain's colonial wars, which they, the Rothschild family, had fomented.

The Morgan fortune was founded on the sale of arms and ammunition to the Confederate army, which arms and ammunition had previously been condemned by the Federal authorities. The Rockefeller fortune was founded upon medical quackery and the sale of 'patent' medicines. The 'Newly Rich' we find in the luxury resorts of southern Florida and the Caribbean are mostly ex-racketeers, while a goodly number have not as yet qualified to have the 'Ex' put before the word racketeer. Bootleggers and professional gamblers now form the crust of modern society. This illustrates how Weishaupt's and Pike's plans have replaced the genealogical aristocracy with an aristocracy of wealth (gold), whom the S.O.S. control body, mind, and soul through control of their bank books.

E.   The lecture goes on to point out that when states become exhausted by involvement in external wars or revolutions, the conspirators use the despotism of capitalism which is entirely in the hands of those directing the conspiracy. He says the exhausted states must accept the financial help and advice of those who plotted to destroy them, or go under completely. This explains how the national debts have been foisted upon the remaining nations and how republics have been financed since Weishaupt's day.

F.   The lecture then says the word 'Right' is an abstract thought and proved by nothing. The word means, 'Give me what I want that thereby I may prove that I am stronger than you.' He explains that the POWER of those who direct the conspiracy will become more invincible as they develop the tottering conditions of rulers and governments because their existence will remain invisible. He then informs his hearers that out of the temporary evil and chaos which they are 'compelled' to commit, will emerge 'Good' government in the form of an absolute dictatorship because "without an absolute despotism there can be no existence for civilization which is carried on not by the masses, (democracy), but by their guide." May I point out that the word 'democracy' as applied to republics and limited monarchies, was introduced by those who direct the conspiracy at the instigation of Voltaire, in order to deceive the masses into believing that they ruled their countries after the overthrow of their monarchs and aristocracy. The masses have elected those whom the directors of the WRM. selected to run for office: but the agentur of the S.O.S., using Illuminists and agentur, have governed from behind the scenes always since absolute monarchs ceased to exist. The biggest lie the S.O.S. ever foisted on the public is the belief that Communism is a workers' movement designed to destroy capitalism in order to introduce socialist governments which can then be formed into an international of Soviet (workingmen's) republics and a classless world. The lie must be apparent to any reasonable person who stops to think. As has been proved by documentary evidence and historical data in *Pawns in the Game, Red Fog Over America* and this book, capitalists have organized, financed, directed, and then had their agents take over the powers of government in EVERY country subjugated to date. It costs up to hundreds of millions of dollars to finance revolutions such as took place in Russia and China. The preparation period in both countries extended over more than fifty years. We ask the workers where they think the money comes from to pay the cost of reconstruction necessary to repair and replace the ravages of war and build up the economies of the so-called republics? (National debts, repaid through taxation is one source of the wealth of the S.O.S.)

It is time we took the blinders from our eyes so we can see clearly. The truth is that those who direct the W.R.M. AT THE TOP, call them the S.O.S. or the Illuminati, or what you wish, control GOLD, and GOLD controls every aspect of the World Revolutionary Movement. It is the men who control GOLD, the men we commonly refer to as capitalists, who finance, direct, and control all revolutionary efforts in order that they may lead the masses (Goyim) out of their present oppressions, into new and complete subjection-a totalitarian dictatorship.

The reader will do well to remember that God is an absolute God. He requires that absolute obedience be given willingly and voluntarily. Lucifer also will rule as an absolute King for all eternity. The word 'democracy' actually means mob rule, and because it does, the lecturer proceeds to inform his fellow conspirators that the idea of freedom is impossible of realization, because no one knows how to use it with moderation. He said "it is enough to hand over a people to self-government for a short time for them to turn themselves into a disorganized mob." Internal strife than reduces them to a heap of ashes. This is what is intended to happen in the remaining so-called FREE nations.

Considering the fact that these words were uttered half a century ago, they have proved exceptionally true. They prove the devilish cunning and diabolical knowledge the S.O.S. have regarding the weaknesses of human nature. The lecturer then tells his audience, "The mob is a savage, and displays its savagery at every opportunity. The moment the mob seizes freedom in its hands, it quickly turns to anarchy, which is the highest degree of savagery."

G. The lecturer than explains how, since Cromwell's day, the Goyim (masses of the people-human cattle) are being reduced to one common level. My friend, AK Chesterton, editor of *Candour*, doesn't agree with me that since Weishaupt and Pike took over, the word 'Goyim' means 'human cattle;' but the fact remains that Chapter 1, Par. 22 of Marsden's translation of the Protocols says, "Behold the alcoholized animals, bemused with drink, the 'right' to the immoderate use of which comes along with freedom. It is not for us and ours to walk that road. The people of the Goyim are bemused with alcoholic liquors (supplied by our agents); their youth have grown stupid on classicism and from early immorality, into which it has been inducted by our special agents-by tutors, lackeys, governesses in the houses of the wealthy, by clerks and by others, by our women in the places of dissipation frequented by the Goyim. In the number of these last I count the so-called society ladies, voluntarily followers of the others in corruption and luxury." Does this not prove we are being reduced to the level of 'human cattle'?

Can any reasonable person deny that society as a whole is being reduced to one common level of iniquity? This is really what class war means. God's plan enables His creatures to progress by personal application to the highest levels of spiritual attainment. It is possible for a human soul to reach the Seventh Heaven, and, according to some theologians, even fill the seats left vacant by Lucifer and his defecting angels. The Luciferian ideology requires that all human beings be dragged down to one common level in sin, corruption, vice, and misery.

H.   The lectures then explained that the Illuminati and Palladians must play a game of "Force and Make Believe." Force must be used to obtain political control, and make-believe, to obtain control of governments which do not want to lay down their crowns at the feet of some new power. The lecturer says, "This evil is the one and only means to attain our end, which is good therefore we must not stop at briber's deceit or treachery when they can be used to serve our purpose. In politics one must know how to seize the property of others without hesitation if by it we secure submission and sovereignty."

What has the creation and pyramiding of the national debts done since the 1700's? What are income and corporation tax and so-called luxury and other taxes doing today? How much of our earnings is left for our own use after those who direct the financial policy of the Palladian Rite get through with us? By controlling the policy of our governments they are taxing us into economic slavery. By giving "Lend Lease" in the name of 'Charity,' the S.O.S. uses our money to control Communism until they foment the final social cataclysm.

I.   The first lecture ends with an explanation of how the Illuminated ones have deceived the Goyim into delivering themselves into their hands. The lecturer says, "Far back in ancient times we were the first to cry among the masses (Goyim) the words, 'Liberty, Equality, Fraternity,' words repeated many times since those days by human parrots who from all sides flew down upon these baits and with them carried away the well-being of the world, true freedom of the individual, formerly so well guarded against pressure of the mob."

The lecturer then gloats over the fact that even the wisest men among the Goyim, even those who consider themselves intellectuals, could not make anything out of the uttered words in their abstractness, and did not note the contradiction of their meaning and interrelation. He points out that in 'Nature' there is no equality and there can be no freedom, because nature has established inequality of minds and characters and capacities, just as immutably as Nature has established subordination to her laws. He then explains how from the very beginning those who direct the conspiracy AT THE TOP have contravened God's Law of Dynastic Rule under which a father passed on to his son knowledge of the course of political affairs in such wise that none could know it but the dynasty, and none could betray it to the governed. The lecturer then points out that as time went on the meaning of dynastic transference of the TRUE position of affairs in the political was lost, and this loss aided the success of their cause. (See Pike's dogma re 'Nature' elsewhere in this book.)

Thus the lecturer proved that what I said about the conspiracy in the previous chapters is true. What he said proves that the Protocols were not drawn up by the Learned Elders of Zion for the information of those who attended the Zionist Congress at Basle, Switzerland in August, 1903, as has been claimed by those selected to lead the anti-Semitic phase of the Luciferian conspiracy, but that the conspiracy ante-dates Weishaupt. The Synagogue of Satan, which Christ exposed, goes back further than the days of Solomon. It goes back to the time when Satan first caused our first parents to defect from God for the purpose of preventing our putting His plan for the rule of the Universe into operation on this earth. Thus the S.O.S., by directing the Luciferian conspiracy on this earth, prevents our doing God's will here as it is done in Heaven.

The lecturer winds up his initial address with a boast: He says, "The deceptive slogan of 'Liberty, Equality and Fraternity' brought to our ranks whole legions who bore our banners with enthusiasm, while, all the time, those very words were a canker-worm boring into the well-being of the Goyim, putting an end to peace, quiet, solidarity, and destroying the very foundations of our Goya states.

He then lets his hearers into the FIRST SECRET. He tells them the triumph of the conspiracy to achieve world domination to date (between 1885 and 1901), was due to the fact that when they came across a person they wished to control and use to serve their purpose, they always worked upon "The most sensitive chords of his or her mind, upon the cash account, upon their cupidity, upon their insatiability for material needs and each one of their human weaknesses which, even when taken alone, is sufficient to paralyze initiative, because it hands over the will of men to the disposal of those who buy their activities."

Thus we see how the conspirators, working through their agentur, have been able to convince the 'mob' that their government is nothing but the steward of the people, who are the owners of the country, and that the steward may be replaced by the people like a worn-out glove. Don't feel badly. I myself was fooled into that belief. It was 1950 before I began to suspect the TRUTH, that, as the lecturer put it, "It is his possibility of replacing the representatives of the people frequently which has enabled those who direct the conspiracy AT THE TOP to gradually obtain control of ALL candidates for political office." Nothing has impressed this truth upon my mind more than the more recent general (federal) elections in Britain, Canada, and the U.S.A. Today the people really have "Hobson's Choice."

Chapter 13

HOW THE CONSPIRACY WAS DEVELOPED IN AMERICA

Professor John Robison has been smeared and his books have been burnt by agentur of the Synagogue of Satan because he proved himself to be incorruptible. He refused to help Weishaupt and his Luciferians infiltrate Illuminism into Freemasonry. History proves, however, that what he did write and publish regarding a conspiracy to destroy all governments and religions has turned out to be true. Robison tells us that before 1786, when the Bavarian government exposed Weishaupt and his gang, several Masonic Lodges in America had been Illuminized. He also points out the similarities of the American and succeeding French Revolutions.

We have been ridiculed by some influential people for quoting Professor Robison, evidently to shake the confidence of our readers. In support of our statements we give the following documentary evidence, most of which can be confirmed by simply referring to the National Archives in Washington, D.C.

In 1798, David A. Tappan was president of Harvard University. On July 19th of that year he addressed a graduating class in the chapel at Harvard College. He warned America's future leaders of the dangers of Illuminism, which he said had infiltrated into America. He told them of the influence of the Illuminati used to bring about the French Revolution.

That same year (1798), Timothy Dwight was president of Yale. He gave Americans much the same warning in a paper entitled, "The Duty of Americans in the Present Crisis."

By the time Pike entered the University as a student, Harvard was being brought under the control of the Illuminati.[25]

Also, in 1798 Jedediah Morse preached his Thanksgiving Day sermon on "The Illuminati and their Masonic Affiliations." Still in the same year, John Wood exposed the Clintonian faction of the Society of Colombian Illuminati.

25 Harvard has remained under the influence of "Internationalist minded men" ever since, as explained in *Red Fog Over America*, by WG. Carr

In 1799, John Cosens Ogden wrote an article, "A View of New England Illuminati," who are indefatigably engaged in destroying religion and government in the United States under feigned regard for their safety."

There were, as recently as 1957, in the Rittenhouse Square Library in Philadelphia, three letters written by John Quincy Adams, the 6th President of the United States, to Col. Wm. Lucifer Stone, a Knight Templar and editor of *The New York Advertiser*. These letters were very critical of Thomas Jefferson and the manner in which he had subverted Freemasonry in the New England states. Adams knew of what he was writing, because he had been mainly responsible for organizing the Lodges into which Jefferson infiltrated his Illuminati. Adams gives as his reason for running against Jefferson for the presidency, Jefferson's subversiveness. The letters he wrote Col. Stone are credited with defeating Jefferson.

Adams listed five main objections to Illuminism as being proselyted by Jefferson and his fellow Illuminists:

1.   Their teachings are contrary to the law of the land.

2.   They are in violation of the precepts of Jesus Christ.

3.   They require members to take a pledge to keep undefined secrets, the nature of which is unknown to the man taking the oath.

4.   They require a member to express his willingness to suffer death should he violate his oath.

5.   They require a member to say he will accept a mode of death which is unusual, inhuman, and so cruel that the details are unfit for utterance from human lips.

Then, in 1826, an incident happened which should prove to Freemasons themselves that only members who have been carefully selected are permitted to know anything of what goes on in the secret society which Illuminists organize within their own secret society. It is therefore as reasonable to condemn as inhuman and diabolical a person suffering from cancer, as it is to blame the rank and file of secret societies, orders, and organizations and groups for the sins against God and crimes against humanity committed by the Synagogue of Satan who infiltrate their agentur into the secret societies. It would be better for the world if there were no secret societies, because those who direct the W.R.M. AT THE TOP would then be unable to practice their parasitic policy, and place the blame for their devilish actions upon shoulders other than their own.

The incident we refer to concerns Captain Wm. Morgan, who was accused of breaking his oath. The Illuminist influence within Masonry's top executive insisted that Morgan be given the "death," the manner of which Adams had been so disgusted and critical.

A Mason named Richard Howard was selected as 'executioner.' Morgan got warning of his pending fate. He tried to escape to Canada, but got only as far as Niagara Falls, where Howard murdered him.

According to Col. Stone, the Knight Templar to whom Adams had written the letters referred to above, Howard resumed to New York and reported to a meeting of the Knights Templars at St. John's Hall, New York, how he had 'executed' Morgan. Stone says he was then supplied with money and put aboard a ship bound for Liverpool, England. Stone's statements are published in his "Letters on Masonry and anti-Masonry." What Stone exposed regarding Morgan is confirmed in an affidavit taken by Avery Allyn when he seceded from the Knights Templar of New Haven, Connecticut. He swore that Richard Howard had confessed himself to have been the 'executioner' of Morgan.

Masonic records prove that when these repulsive facts became known in Masonic circles, a terrific reaction set in approximately 1,500 lodges in the United States surrendered their charters. It is estimated that of the 50,000 Masons belonging to these lodges, 45,000 seceded from the secret society. Thus it was that Freemasonry nearly died a natural death in America.

But such is the power and influence of the Synagogue of Satan that today hardly a Mason with whom I have discussed this phase of their history, knows anything about it. I have copies of the minutes taken at the meetings which led up to this mass withdrawal from Masonry in America. These TRUTHS are not published to hurt Freemasons, but to prove conclusively that out of a possible 50,000 Masons, at least 45,000 didn't know or even suspect what goes on behind the scenes under the direction of Satanists who hide like worms in the bowels of their and other secret societies.

Those who served the S.O.S. decided a native-born must succeed Moses Holbrook, who at the time these events happened headed Masonry in America, so General Albert Pike was approached. He measured up to the requirements because his rise from an initiate in 1850, to Grand Commander of the Supreme

Council for the Southern Jurisdiction of Freemasonry in the U.S.A. in 1859 was phenomenal.

Pike's task was to rejuvenate Freemasonry in the U.S.A., so that the influence, wealth and power of its members could be, used again by the Illuminati to place their agentur in key positions in all fields of human endeavor, including politics and religion. Today, as in 1826, the vast majority of Freemasons don't know about the secret life of Albert Pike. They have been lied to and deceived by Satan's agents into believing Pike to be the greatest Mason that ever lived, and one of Americas greatest patriots. But they are wrong, as we prove Pike was literally a devil incarnate.

Because the Illuminati had been proved to have corrupted Freemasonry in America, Pike decided to organize the Palladian Rite, to be above even Grand Orient Masonry and the Illuminati. Palladism wasn't exactly a new secret society, so Pike called his organization, "The New and Reformed Palladian Rite," (N.R.P.R.)

Guiseppe Mazzini had been selected by the Illuminati in 1834, to be their Director of Political Action (Director of the W.R.M.). In a letter Mazzini sent to Pike January 22, 1870, he wrote, "We must allow all the federation (of different Masonic orders) to continue just as they are, with their systems, their central authorities and their diverse modes of correspondence between high grades of the same rite, organized as they are at present, but we must create a supreme rite, which will remain unknown, to which we will call those Masons of high degree whom we shall select. With regard to their brothers in Masonry, these men must be pledged to the strictest secrecy. Through this supreme rite we will govern all Freemasonry, which will become the one international centre, the more powerful because its directions (directors) will be unknown."

This letter proves that not even Mazzini, at the time he wrote the letter, knew the High Priests of the Luciferian Creed controlled the Synagogue of Satan, of which he was a member, AT THE TOP. But after working a while longer with Pike, he began to suspect there was some "Secret Power" above or beyond the highest degrees of Grand Orient Masonry, of which he was a member, which controlled them AT THE TOP. He expressed these suspicions in the letter he wrote Dr. Breidenstein, already quoted.

Pike and Mazzini signed the decree for the constitution of a Central High Masonry, September 20, 1870. This was the day the Grand Orient Mason, General Cadorna, entered Rome to end the temporal power of the Pope.

Pike assumed the title of Sovereign Pontiff of Universal Freemasonry. Mazzini assumed the title Sovereign Chief of Political Action, i.e., Head of the World Revolutionary Movement, (W.R.M.).

Pike immediately proceeded to complete the work on the new ritual he had started with Moses Holbrook, and he called it "The Adonaicide Mass" (The Death of God").

Margiotta, a 33rd degree Mason, who wrote Masonic history, and the biography of Adriano Lemmi, (who in 1873 succeeded Mazzini as Director of the W.R.M.), has this to say regarding Pike and Mazzini: "It was agreed that the existence of this rite would be kept strictly secret, and that no mention of it would ever be made in the assemblies and inner shrines of other rites, even when by accident the meeting might happen to be composed exclusively of brothers having the perfect initiation, for the secret of the new institution was only to be divulged with the greatest caution to a chosen few belonging to the ordinary high grades."

This explains why even 32nd and 33rd degree Freemasons know so little about what goes on AT THE VERY TOP.

Margiotta also states that 33rd degree members of the Scottish Rite are carefully selected for initiation into the Palladian Rite because of their extensive international ramifications: Thirty-third degree Masons are specially privileged to visit and take part in the rituals of other Masonic Lodges throughout the world. Those who become members of Palladism recruit others. That is why the Supreme Rite created its triangles (the name given Palladian Councils) by degrees. These are established on a firm basis. The lowest of the initiates are brothers long tested in ordinary Masonry, and proved to have defected from God and Christianity.

Margiotta adds: "One will better understand these precautions knowing that Palladism is essentially a Luciferian rite. Its religion is Manichean neo-gnosticism, teaching that the divinity is dual, and that Lucifer is the equal of Adonay, with Lucifer the God of Light and Goodness struggling for humanity against Adonay the God of Darkness and Evil.[26]

As Lucifer's Sovereign Pontiff on earth, Pike was the president of the Supreme Dogmatic Directory, assisted by ten Ancients of the Supreme Council of the Grand Orient. Pike's Supreme Grand College of Emeritus Masons (Palladian Rite), accepted the Adonaicide Mass, sometimes referred to as "The Black Mass," as the ritual for the New and Reformed Palladian Rite. Mazzini was sent a copy of the ritual. He was high in his praise of Pike, as his articles published in *La Roma del Popolo* prove.

With these preliminaries completed, Pike and his assistants organized with a Supervisory Triangle, or Council, in Rome, Italy, to direct the W.R.M. in all its many phases. He placed Mazzini in charge. After Mazzini's death, he made Lemmi Supreme Director.

Pike organized another supervisory council in Berlin. He called it, "The Supreme Dogmatic Directory." It was kept functioning by means of a constantly renewed committee of seven, selected from the Supreme Council, Grand Encampments, Grand Orients, and Grand Lodges of the world. Two delegates looked after propaganda and finance. The director of propaganda was also director of intelligence, keeping the other two supervisory directors and the Sovereign Pontiff fully informed regarding important news and events gathered into this central clearing house, from the 'millions of pairs of eyes' which their agentur control throughout the world. They boast that not even a minor piece of legislation can be put through any parliament without them having full knowledge of it, and giving approval.

The financial agent draws up a general balance sheet of all rites, in all countries, working with an accountant as a sworn expert under his orders.

Under the Sovereign Directory in Charleston, South Carolina, and the Executive of Political Action in Rome, and the Administrative Dogmatic Council in Berlin come the 23 Grand Central Directories which are bureaus or Councils established in Europe, Asia/Africa, Oceania, and North and South America.

---

26 We wonder what the Rt. Hon. John Deifenbaker, Prime Minister of Canada, and the Hon. Leslie Frost, Premier of Ontario, Canada's largest and richest province, have to say about this. In our monthly newsletter, N.B.N., Oct. Issue, 1958, we published the fact that they both were initiated into the 33rd degree of the Scottish Rite in Windsor, Ontario, September 9, 1958.

And above all these, the Synagogue of Satan-the High Priests of the Luciferian Creed rule-invisible, unidentified, and supreme. When the League of Nations was first organized (1919), Pike's organization was slightly revised, and the supervisory, executive, and administrative branches were established in Switzerland and New York. But it doesn't matter where the BRAINS are located, they have perfect communication systems, and they control and direct ALL other subversive organizations and activities. That control and direction are the same today as in Pike's lifetime and at the time the League of Nations was formed. The same conspirators who formed and developed those, also developed the U.N.O.

Please don't take my word for it. St. Paul, in II Corinthians 11:13 told us, "For such false apostles, deceitful workers, transforming themselves into the Apostles of Christ. And no marvel; for Satan himself is transformed into an angel of Light. Therefore, it is no great thing (not to be wondered at) if his ministers also be transformed as the ministers of righteousness whose ends shall be according to their works."

Let us pull aside the veil with which Pike enshrouded himself, still further. I am aware that Dr. Bataille, author of *Le Diable au XIXe seicle*, has been accused of publishing misstatement as facts on various occasions, but that does not mean he was always lying and publishing untruths. What he has to say regarding Pike and his "occultism" on page 360 of the above publication is confirmed in "Occult Theocracy" on page 223, written by Lady Queensborough. Further confirmation is to be found in the Masonic Library in Charleston, South Carolina.

That Pike believed in occultism is proved by the fact that there is on record a report of the speech he made before the Supreme Council of the Grand Orient, Charleston, South Carolina, October 20, 1884, at which time he said: "At St. Louis, we operated the Grand Rites, and through Sister Ingersoll, who is a first class medium, received astonishing revelations during a solemn Palladian session at which I presided, assisted by Brother Friedman and Sister Warhnburn. Without putting Sister Ingersoll to sleep, we saturated her with the spirit of Ariel himself. But Ariel took possession of her with 329 more spirits of fire, and the séance from then on was marvelous.

"Sister Ingersoll, lifted into space, floated over the assembly, and her garments were suddenly devoured by a flame which enfolded her without burning her. We saw her thus in a state of nudity for over ten minutes. Flitting above our heads as though borne by an invisible cloud, or upheld by a beneficent spirit, she answered all questions put to her. We thus had the latest news of our very illustrious brother Adriano Lemmi then Astaroth, in person, revealed himself, flying beside our medium, and holding her hand. He breathed upon her, and her clothes, returning from nowhere, clothed her again. Finally,

Astaroth vanished, and our sister fell gently on to a chair, where, with her head thrown back, she gave up Ariel and the 329 spirits who had accompanied him. We counted 330 exhalations in all at the end of this experience."

Pike's claim that he was able to talk with Lemmi, his Director of Political Action located in Italy during a séance held in St. Louis, caused me to do some further digging. I knew that those conducting séances often resorted to fakery to deceive those in attendance, into believing they had supernatural powers. This research produced documentary evidence which strongly indicated that scientists belonging to Pike's Palladian Rite had supplied him with wireless sets (radio) long before Marconi made it available for commercial purposes.

I had always wondered WHY Marconi was given such strong opposition when he tried to make his discovery available to the general public. Investigation indicates that the opposition originated with men who had been closely associated with Pike prior to his death in 1891. In the background of the opposition was Gallatin Mackay, who succeeded Pike as head of Universal Masonry and Palladism.

Documentary evidence exists which records Pike's ability to contact and speak with the heads of his supervisory councils, regardless of where they happened to be located. He always used a code. He referred to the box he used while conducting these conversations as Arcula Mystica (The Magic Box). Obviously he and the heads of his 26 councils were connected together by wireless (radio), long before Marconi made his discoveries. There is evidence to prove that Pike's set did pass to Gallatin Mackay after he died. Therefore it is likely Pike used wireless telegraphy during the séances he directed in St. Louis.

Pike and his supervisory directors of the W.R.M. (Palladian councils) all used code names, as had Weishaupt and his head Illuminists before him. Pike and his supreme council in Charleston was known as "Ignis," the code word for "Sacred Fire," or "Divine Endeavour." The code word for the supervisory council in Rome was "Ratio," meaning "Reason shall triumph over superstition." In Berlin the supervisory council's code name was "Labour."

It is interesting to note that the head of the Berlin Council, and the one in control of the Palladian treasury during Pike's time, was Gerson Bleichroeder, a man who has been proven to be one of the highest and most trusted agents of the House of Rothschild. It is obvious that while Pike was High Priest of the Luciferian ideology, and thus controlled the activities of the Synagogue of

Satan, the Rothschilds, through Bleichroeder, controlled the purse strings of the Palladian Rite. Thus, they, indirectly controlled Pike's activities as they had those of Weishaupt a hundred years before.

This information proves that the present Rothschilds believe in the advice passed down to them by one of their ancestors: "Give me control of a country's money, and I care not who makes its laws." Another interesting fact is that both the Rothschilds and the Bleichroeders are, as Christ put it, "Them who say they are Jews, and are not, and do lie." They are Khazars; their veins contain no more real Jewish blood than do mine. Research proves that Bleichroeder belonged to the highest degrees of the Palladian Rite and of Grand Orient Masonry, and must therefore have been a Satanist.

During Pike's reign as "Prince of this world" under Satan's inspiration, his directors in England were Lord Palmerston and Disraeli, who told his readers that the masses (Goyim) don't realize that the real 'power' which governs them and their country remains invisible and directs from behind the visible governments.

Although Pike is credited with having ended Jewish control of Freemasonry in America, research proves that on September 12, 1874 he signed an agreement with Armand Levi, who represented the Jewish B'nai B'rith of America, Germany, England and other countries. Under this agreement Pike gave Levi authority to organize the Jewish Freemasons in those countries into a "Secret Federation," to be known as "The Sovereign Patriarchal Council." Its international headquarters were setup in a big building on Valentinskamp Strasse, Hamburg, Germany. There is documentary evidence to show that the head of this "Secret Federation" collected in fees approximately $250,000 a year, which money was used mostly for payment of propaganda favorable to secularism: It is safe to say that the "Lesser Jew" doesn't know any more about what is going on behind the scenes among those who control Judaism AT THE TOP, than do Masons up to the 33rd degree, or the vast majority of the Goyim. It is obvious, therefore, that in the final stage of the conspiracy all lesser beings will find themselves in the devil's stewpot. We are all intended to be simmered down in the devil's brew.[27]

If the present revolutionary movement didn't extend into the celestial world, and eternity, but was confined to this world only, there would be no sense in risking exposure, imprisonment and even premature death. If everything ends with death, as atheists would have us believe, then why put ourselves out furthering a plot or plan we will not live to see accomplished?

Pike's military blueprint, as given to Mazzini and passed on to Lemmi, was as simple as it proved effective.

Using the 26 Triangles, or councils of the Palladian Rite, those who direct the W.R.M. AT THE VERY TOP were to foment three world wars and three major revolutions. These were to be so directed that all remaining governments would be reduced to such a state of weakness and economic ruin, that the people would clamor for a world government as the only solution to their many and varied problems.

After three global wars and two major revolutions, the United States would remain the only world power, but, during the third revolution which Pike said would be the greatest social cataclysm the world has ever known, the United States was to be disintegrated by internal treachery, and fall into the hands of the Luciferian conspirators "like over-ripe fruit."

Pike set forth quite clearly that World War One was to enable the directors of the W.R.M. to subjugate Russia and turn that Empire into the stronghold of atheistic-communism. This was accomplished with the first major revolution in

27 In the hope of bringing order out of chaos, and united humanity in the service of God against Lucifer, I wish to point out once more that the struggle going on in this world is for the eternal possession of the souls of men. God wants us to   prove that we wish to love Him and desire to serve Him voluntarily for all eternity. Lucifer is determined that his agents on this earth will take away from us our God given gifts of an intellect and freewill, so we will be unable to make this decision. Lucifer, by use of Satanism, is determined to capture out immortal souls; not because he doesn't know that he was wrong, and that his totalitarian ideology will end in turmoil and chaos, but because he just can't stand to see other souls happy. He is determined that as many as possible will share his eternal misery.

1917. Communism and Nazism were to be used, together with anti-Semitism, to enable the directors of the W.R.M. to foment World War Two. This was to end with the destruction of Nazism as a world power, because it would, by then, have served its purpose.

The Sovereign State of Israel was to result from World War Two, as was also the United Nations. Political Zionism was to be used to enable the directors of the W.R.M. to foment World War Three, by playing up the real and supposed differences between Israel and the Arab states. World War Two was to end with communism taking over control of most of the Far East. Sufficient territory was to be kept free so that communism in Russia and China could be kept in check, or 'contained' until the Synagogue of Satan were ready to use it in the final stage of the Luciferian conspiracy. Communism was to be organized and also kept in check in all the remaining nations until the directors of the W.R.M. decided it was time to throw ALL communists and ALL non-communist at each other's throats. Pike explained all this to Mazzini in his letter dated August 15, 1871.

This program has been carried out EXACTLY as Pike intended; he simply applied his military genius to put Adam Weishaupt's plans into effect. Thus the people on this planet are involved in the semifinal phase of the Luciferian conspiracy.

After Pike died, Mackay took over. He, as did Lemmi, considered that ALL the executive members of the Grand Orient Lodges and the Councils of the New and Reformed Palladian Rite should be given special instructions in regard to the W.R.M. They were told in a series of lectures

1. What Weishaupt's revised plans called for.

2. How the World Revolutionary Movement had progressed since 1776.

3. The purpose of political intrigue going on at the time, i.e., 1889 to 1903.

4. What was intended should happen to bring the conspiracy to its successful conclusion, a One World Government the powers of which they would usurp.

The lectures were prepared by Pike or writers who had been inspired by Pike's revolutionary ardor. These lectures were delivered by high degree members of the Palladian Rite, over a period of days, (or nights), to gatherings of selected adepts who met in the Lodges of the Grand Orient or New Palladian Rite throughout the world. It was a copy of these lectures, slightly altered to give them a Zionist touch, which 'fell' into the hands of Professor Satan Nilus, and which he published as *The Jewish Peril*.

There is plenty of evidence available to prove these lectures were being delivered as early as 1885. As invariably happens, despite the greatest security precautions, information regarding the delivery of these lectures, and their purpose, to develop the conspiracy to the final social cataclysm, leaked out.

The plot to develop the World Revolutionary Movement to its final state, as explained by Pike to Mazzini in his letter dated August 15, 1871, was discussed by several publications, two of which were, *Le Palladisme*, by Margiotta, p. 186, published in 1895, and in *Le Diable Au XIXe Siede*, published in 1896. The lectures in their entirety were published by the Russian newspaper *Moskowskija Wiedomosti* during the winter of 1902/1903, and again by the Russian newspaper *Snamja* in August of 1903.

The point I am trying to make in this: the first meeting of the Learned Elders of Zion to discuss Political Zionism, as we know it today, took place in Basle, Switzerland, in 1897. The origin of the Luciferian conspiracy dates back to before Zionism was even mentioned in the Bible. The first series of lectures are in no way different from Weishaupt's revised version of the plot as exposed in 1786. How the plot was developed from Lucifer is concerned only with capturing souls. He doesn't care if they be the souls of Jews or Gentiles, colored folk or white folk. The Fable of the Messianic Age is just as much of a deception to enlist Jews to serve the cause of Lucifer as is the dream of One Worlders that they will form the government when the first world government is established. Roosevelt honestly believed he was going to be the first King-despot. He was disillusioned when Stalin double-crossed him after Yalta. How he got fooled. To get our sights on the real target we have to elevate the barrels of our rifles above the materialistic images which, like a mirage, reflect something beyond the range of our naked eyes. Let Christians believe what Christ and the Scriptures tell us-Luciferianism is the root of all evil. Satanism is the name by which most people know Luciferianism on this earth.

1786 to 1886 is told in the second series of lectures, and in no way differs from lectures delivered by Pike and his top officials between 1870 and 1886.

Chapter 14

THE LAST CHAPTER OF A BOOK
AND ALSO OF A LIFE

What you have read up to this point is the last work, cut short by death, of the author, Commander W.J.C. Carr, R.C.N.R. I, his oldest son, have tried to finish the work in order that it might be published to fulfill my father's last wish. I could not do so, and in all honesty, I do not believe it possible for any man, at this time, to do so either.

The life work of one man can seldom be picked up and completed by another, particularly when the work covers the field dealt with in this book and in the books previously published by Commander Carr. I believe that he was a man gifted, or perhaps cursed, with the ability to see things that the rest of us cannot see or even conceive to be possible in our wildest imaginings.

This ability to see clearly the workings and machinations that go on behind the scenes in all governments and many international organizations, and the ability to follow clearly the often dimly marked trail of evil that has crawled and slimed its way through the history of mankind, is given to few men. I believe that my father had this ability and that it died with him.

For most of my early life I watched him doggedly tracing one lead after another to find the ultimate answer to the problem of evil in the affairs of men. At that time I was not really aware of what he sought or understood the terrible strain under which he worked. His searches were never easy on him or on those close to him, for he had all the human traits, both good and bad, that bless and plague the rest of us. He asked me several times, particularly after my discharge from the Canadian Army in August, 1945, if I would work with him and eventually carry on the fight he felt was so important. I could not do so then and I cannot do so now for the reasons given above. At his death, he bequeathed to me his library, his manuscripts, and all his notes. He did not specify that I must try to carry on his work in order to qualify for this inheritance. I must confess that I rather spurned the idea of doing anything to further his efforts and even felt in a vague way that he was way off the beam in his writings.

This manuscript was left in storage for about six years before I started to think of some of the things of which he had written and how accurately he seemed to be able to pinpoint certain future events in the affairs of men and of the world in which we live. I think it was particularly true at the time of the assassination of President Kennedy in 1963. If the author is anywhere near correct in his charges that the S.O.S. pretty well controls all governments, it would be impossible for anyone to learn of the truth behind that murder. And I still cannot believe that the assassin's murder by Jack Ruby was not part of a prearranged plan to keep all details and information from the public view. I could be wrong. The author had an uncanny ability to pinpoint such events and even his own death. If you will reread Chapter 3, page 41, he says that he seriously doubts that he will write any more books and at that time he was not any more seriously ill than at other times, and was only 62 years of age. With these thoughts, I reread the manuscript and became convinced that I had to do whatever I could to publish the information, incomplete though it was.

How much you actually believe of what you read in this book is really of little importance. It would be too much to expect anyone to be able to assimilate such material in one bite. The exposure of such monstrous and inhuman plots verges on the impossible and yet, down deep inside me, I know that such plots are in existence. The more I think about these matters, the more convinced I become and this in spite of a natural disinclination to believe at all. This latter feeling I think will be a common one for the majority of readers.

Even though this knowledge of the existence of a supernatural plot to destroy mankind has come to me, I do not particularly fear the plot in itself. I have always believed, in a general way, of the existence of evil and what evil tried to do with me and by me. But, by the grace of God, I also know that good exists and that by trying with all my strength to follow that good, automatically I relegate evil to its proper place on the fringe of my existence, in much the same way that cold is displaced by heat and mist burned away by a hot sun.

I do believe now that evil exists and has been fostered and organized by men directed by the Devil. But as the same time I believe even more strongly that God IS and that Christ, as our closest and best example of good, also exists actively in the affairs of men. To me, the study of evil and its effect in the world, is rather a negative approach to finding solution to the problems that have existed, do exist and will always exist, for all men, until the end of earthly time. Undoubtedly the knowledge of my father's work and the reading of his many works have influenced my life greatly. Several years ago, when our children were self-supporting and no longer needed our direct help, my wife and I decided to dedicate several or all of our years to full time work in the foreign mission field. I think this decision was taken, and is being followed, not so much to be 'do-gooders' as for our own peace of mind and well-being; a long time ago I discovered that human happiness can best be found by giving of oneself in the service of others as long as the motive for that giving rests in the love of the God who created me.

I think that the answer to the evil, as exposed and defined by my father, is for every man and woman of goodwill, to dedicate himself or herself to some phase of the human scene in such a way that the scene is improved by the effort expended. It really doesn't matter very much if the effect achieved is visible or measurable by the person or by his contemporaries, but rather that each man gives of his best to try and succeed.

At this moment, the famous quotation of the late President Kennedy comes to mind: "Ask not what your country can do for you, but rather what you can do for your country." Substitute the words God, neighbors, religion, community, or whatever, for country, and we all have a working blueprint for our future efforts.

To comment further on this work or on any particular phase of the Luciferian plot or the intrigues of the S.O.S. would be to labor the point.

To those who knew my father personally or became interested in him through the reading of his books, perhaps a few words about his personal philosophies on life and living might prove of interest and give a clearer insight into the mind of this remarkable man.

From my earliest recollections of him, certain salient points of his character stand out boldly. He often told me that no man had the right to ask another to do or give what the asker was not willing to do or give first. I have talked to quite a number of naval men who served with or under Commander Carr in both World Wars and they, to a man, confirmed that Dad had followed this thought to the point where he was known as 'The Iron Man' in the sections in which he served in the Canadian Navy during the 2nd World War.

Another point he stressed was that: 'A man should work like Hell while alive in order that he didn't wind up in Hell when dead.' This book you have just finished reading is proof that he followed this dictate of conscience also because he worked up to the limit of his strength and even beyond it into his final illness.

171

During the hungry days of the 'Dirty Thirties,' we lived in a small town just outside of Toronto, Ontario. Our house was on the main north-south highway of that time, and literally scores of hungry men begged for food at our door.

Even though we were a large family and money was always scarce (or non-existent), he never permitted a hungry man to be turned away without adequate food. His point was that: "If I refuse a hungry man some food, or cannot see in him some mark of Christ which makes him my brother, then I deny my own humanity."

In the same way, no one hurt or in distress ever appealed for help from Dad and was turned away without a sincere effort to give the help needed. Many the widow and distressed ex-serviceman who came to him for help and as a result, he gave uncounted days of work to win pensions or other relief for these unfortunates either through the Canadian Legion or by himself working through the hundreds of contacts he made in high places as he went along with his work.

No amount of money or proffered honors could win his support for a cause or an organization in which he did not believe fully or which could not withstand his close scrutiny as to its reason for being. Because of his strong attitude in this respect, I know that he gave up many lucrative opportunities in order that he could, as he put it, "Shave myself in front of my own mirror." He was self-educated, self-confident, and self-opinionated. When the going got toughest, he refused to go to others for help until he had literally exhausted himself economically, physically, or mentally. He had a hair-trigger temper that threw him into terrible rages ... and a soft heart that prevented him from holding that rage for more than a few minutes or a grudge against even his worst enemy ... and he made plenty of them as he went along.

He could and did walk and talk with Kings and those who occupy the High and Mighty places of the earth ... and he could and did sit in hovels and be completely at home in that setting. With those who opposed him, he was a hard, fair, and tough fighter and he neither asked nor gave quarter. With the weak and the helpless, he had the tenderness of a good woman and a heart as soft and as sweet as melted butter.

With his family and with himself, he was a hard and driving taskmaster. With others weaker than himself, he had an infinite capacity for pity and patience. For the last fifteen years of his life he suffered many illnesses and incapacities, not the least of which was a telescoped spine which necessitated him wearing a cumbersome steel and leather brace to keep him from becoming badly deformed. I do not think that he ever considered these health problems anything more than a nuisance that handicapped his ability to follow the path of work which he had chosen for himself... always his motto was: "Carry On."

If ever an epitaph be written for him, let it be as follows:

He lived the hard life of a truly Christian man.

And died the easy death reserved for such a one.

If anything he ever wrote has helped even one person to find a purpose in life or helped any individual to better understand the purpose and meaning of life or helped one soul to regain its place in the divine scheme of things, then I am certain that his noble soul rests in peace within the love and protection of the God he tried so hard to serve while he lived his few years on earth.

Other books by William Guy Carr

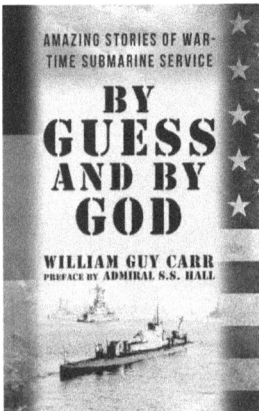

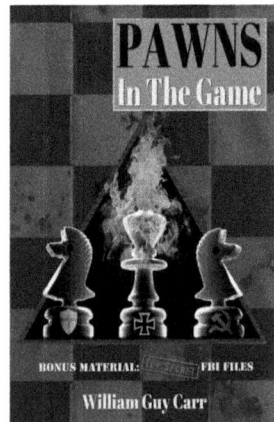

HELL'S
ANGELS
OF THE
DEEP

WILLIAM GUY CARR

AMAZING STORIES OF WAR-
TIME SUBMARINE SERVICE

BY
GUESS
AND BY
GOD

WILLIAM GUY CARR
PREFACE BY ADMIRAL S.S. HALL

PAWNS
In The Game

BONUS MATERIAL: FBI FILES

William Guy Carr

www.ingramcontent.com/pod-product-compliance
Lightning Source LLC
Chambersburg PA
CBHW052044090426

42739CB00010B/2041